PARTIES AND DEMOCRACY IN BRITAIN AND AMERICA

AMERICAN POLITICAL PARTIES AND ELECTIONS

General editor: Gerald M. Pomper

Copublished
with the Eagleton Institute of Politics,
Rutgers University

PARTIES AND DEMOCRACY IN BRITAIN AND AMERICA

EDITED BY

Vernon Bogdanor

PRAEGER SPECIAL STUDIES • PRAEGER SCIENTIFIC

New York • Philadelphia • Eastbourne, UK
Toronto • Hong Kong • Tokyo • Sydney

Library of Congress Cataloging in Publication Data

Main entry under title:
Parties and democracy in Britain and America.

(American political parties and elections)
Includes index.
1. Political parties—United States—Addresses, essays,
lectures. 2. Political parties—Great Britain—Addresses,
essays, lectures. I. Bogdanor, Vernon, 1943–
II. Series.
JK2265.P33 1984   324.273   83-24794
ISBN 0-03-062599-8 (alk. paper)

Published in 1984 by Praeger Publishers
CBS Educational and Professional Publishing
a Division of CBS Inc.
521 Fifth Avenue, New York, NY 10175 USA

456789 052 987654321

Printed in the United States of America
on acid-free paper

Contents

Preface

The purpose of this book is to analyze recent trends in party politics in Britain and the United States. Among the developments discussed are the pressures of popular participation, the alleged "decline of party," the growth of voter volatility, and the effects of changing methods of finance and campaign technology upon the parties. Most of the chapters were completed before the end of 1982, and they do not in general take account of developments since then.

The idea for the book arose from a conference held in May 1981 at Ditchley Park, Oxfordshire, on The Role of Political Parties in Britain and America at which some of the chapters were first presented. The conference was organized jointly by the Hansard Society for Parliamentary Government and the American Enterprise Institute for Public Policy Research and co-sponsored by J. Sainsbury Ltd. The contributors would like to thank the organizers both for arranging such a stimulating conference and for allowing papers first produced for the conference to be published in this book. Of course, neither the Hansard Society, the American Enterprise Institute, nor J. Sainsbury Ltd. bear any responsibility for what follows.

The editor would like to thank Professor Gerald Pomper, editor of the series in which this book appears, and Mrs. Maxine Vlieland of the Hansard Society for their helpful advice and encouragement.

Introduction

Vernon Bogdanor

Political parties are an indispensable part of the democratic process. In almost every modern democracy, government by the people turns out to be government by party; and democratic elections are choices between competing parties or party nominees who offer themselves as candidates for office. Since mass suffrage began, parties have been the central instruments of representation in democracies; they have been, to adapt Bagehot, the hyphen joining the electorate to government,[1] the main transmission belt through which the demands of the people are conveyed to those who aspire to rule the state. It is because they are so fundamental to popular government that the changing fortunes of political parties can be said to mirror the health of democracy itself. The purpose of *Parties and Democracy in Britain and America* is to analyse these changing fortunes in the light of the social and political trends that have so affected the role of parties in the world's two leading democracies.

Since the time of Bagehot, Britain and the United States have been seen as the exemplars of two contrasting models of government. The two countries have sought, with considerable success, to safeguard the same liberal values—representative and responsible government, the rule of law, the protection of minorities—through very different institutional arrangements. It is for this reason that the structure of government in Britain and the United States, their party systems and the electoral behaviour of their citizens have been such frequent objects of juxtaposition and contrast.

Parties, Max Weber declared, live in a house of power. Since the shape of the house—the constitutional and political environment within which they operate—is so different in Britain and the United States, the relationship between parties and power is also quite dissimilar in the two countries. Parties in Britain exist to take control of government, and they operate in a highly concentrated political system within which party leaders enjoy considerable authority over both their parliamentary followers and their extraparliamentary supporters. On the other side of the Atlantic, by contrast, the fragmentation of American institutions prevents parties from asserting themselves in government. Government in the United States is not party government, but rather the laborious construction of legislative coalitions of an essentially fluid and ad hoc kind; and these coalitions are frequently bipartisan.

There is, moreover, a sense in which the very meaning of "party" can be quite different to politicians and electors in Britain and the United States. In Britain, "party" connotes a closely knit parliamentary grouping, a strong centralized bureaucracy and a regularized dues-paying membership. But American politics is deeply marked by a widespread distrust of parties and by the urge to maximize popular participation, attitudes less fundamental to British political experience. As a result, American parties are more porous than their British counterparts and without the clearcut membership arrangements characteristic of parties on the other side of the Atlantic.

Perhaps the greatest single cause of the comparative indiscipline of American parties is the primary, that instrument of Progressivism whose effects have been so different from those imagined by its originators. American primaries are unique in that participation in them is not confined to dues-paying party members but is open to all registered supporters—a far wider constituency. The direct primary is a specifically American contribution to democratic practice, and its adoption has rendered the American party system, in contradistinction to the party systems of Britain and the Continent, essentially candidate-based. Indeed, the American party system approaches more closely than any other to the loosely organized, individualistic structures favoured by such nineteenth-century liberals as John Stuart Mill and Ostrogorski; although, as many of the essays in this volume will show, the consequences of this individualism have been rather far from those which would have been predicted by its advocates.

But the differences between British and American parties have not only been structural. For, in the past, their attitudes to the electorate have been quite dissimilar. This was obscured because Britain and the United States were so often cited as exemplars of a "two-party system," a description that served to hide rather than to illuminate the central features of each polity.

Until quite recently at least, American parties were paradigm examples of "catch-all" parties in the sense that, disdaining ideology, they sought to maximize their vote somewhat in the fashion of a commercial organization, developing, as Kirchheimer put it, "many features of an interest-market."[2] British parties, on the other hand, cannot be understood without appreciating how their conceptions not only of the ideal society, but even of democracy itself, are embodied, as Samuel Beer has shown, in their organizational structures, which differ sharply from each other.[3] It is, indeed, precisely because the two main British parties—the Conservatives and Labour—are not catch-all parties that they have been so much more suscepti-ble than their American counterparts to an erosion of support by "third forces": Liberals and Social Democrats, as well as nationalists in Scotland and Wales. However, the resurgence of ideology in both countries has led to some convergence—the Conservatives and the Republicans are more alike in their political approach than was the case even a decade ago, while both Republicans and Democrats are probably more cohesive on policy issues than they have ever been.

These fundamental differences between the constitutional and political structures of Britain and the United States and the contrast-ing approaches of British and American parties towards their elector-ates make it unlikely that comparative analysis will be very fruitful if confined to a straightforward comparison of particular institutions. Where comparative analysis can prove illuminating, however, is in examining the reaction of two quite dissimilar party systems to cur-rent social trends. For the same social forces—increasing social mobili-ty, the expansion of higher education, the growing impact of the mass media, and, above all, the pressures of popular participation—have affected the parties of both countries. These forces have altered the relationships between the electorate and the parties on both sides of the Atlantic, so that party identification has come to be eroded by a more pragmatic awareness of governmental performance and of the credibility of party policy proposals. The electoral environment with-in which parties must operate has changed drastically since the 1950s, and they have been compelled to come to terms with the reality of a more volatile and disenchanted electorate. How has the process of social and electoral change altered the role of party in Britain and the United States, and how have British and American parties reacted to the social forces that press upon them? These are the central questions that the essays in *Parties and Democracy in Britain and America* seek to answer.

* * *

The decline of party has been a familiar theme in recent writing on British and American politics. Yet, as both S. E. Finer and Philip Williams show, the thesis of party decline cannot be properly evalua-ted unless the different components of party are kept firmly in mind. Political parties are complex organisms operating at three different levels: government, the legislature and the electorate. Further, "the decline of party" has meant something different to observers in the two countries. In Britain, it has been used to denote decreasing con-fidence in and lessening support for the two main parties and the growth of challengers to the two-party system; in the United States, "the decline of party" thesis has also emphasized the growing independence of candidates from their party organizations, a phenomenon that has been encouraged by the extension of primaries and, according to some, by the new campaign finance laws.

In both countries, pressures for participation have posed fundamental problems for political parties. They have not necessarily led to the "decline of party"; what they have done is to offer a challenge. Can the parties meet pressures that are perhaps inevitable in a modern democratic society without sacrificing their role as effective agents of government and organs of representation? It is this conflict between participation and effectiveness which constitutes the deepest theme of the essays in the present volume: for the conflict is one that is fundamental to the whole future of representative government in the West.

The forces of populism have left none of the parties unscathed. Paradoxically, both in Britain and in the United States, it is the parties of the Right—Conservatives and Republicans—rather than those of the Left, which have been able to adapt more easily to the facts of social change. Both Republicans and Conservatives—as David Adamany and I attempt to show—have taken more advantage of developments in campaign technology than their rivals; and they have used modern techniques of fund-raising in an attempt to develop a financial structure based upon small contributors, rather than relying, as in the past, upon a few donations from large corporations and wealthy individuals. In policy-making, also, parties of the Right seem to have been able to accommodate the pressures of populism without sacrificing their effectiveness in government.

Parties of the Left, by contrast, have encountered greater difficulties in reconciling their conceptions of the good society with the real aspirations of the electorate. The Liberal/Social Democratic Party (SDP) Alliance made a conscious decision not to become a populist political grouping; and, indeed, its leaders were too closely connected to existing networks of power and influence to have made such an option at all credible. The Democrats have been too divided and uncertain of their role to have been able to profit from the new issue-oriented politics in the United States; like European parties of the Left, they find themselves ill at ease when faced with populist claims and suspicious of instruments such as the referendum and initiative which undermine the need for mediating institutions between politicians and people.

It is, however, the British Labour Party that has provided the main arena within which conflicting conceptions of participation have contended for supremacy. In the long debate over whether authority should lie within the Parliamentary Party or outside it, the arguments of both sides have, as Leon Epstein shows, been peppered with (often quite misleading) allusions from American experience. The new method of electing the party's leader and deputy leader agreed by the special Conference of January 1981 have fundamentally altered the locus of power within the party. There are some who would claim that it has also destroyed the capacity of the party ever again to be an effective instrument of government.

* * *

Ivor Crewe and William Schneider analyse changing relationships between parties and the electorate in Britain and the United States. In both countries, parties have to face the problem of recruiting support from an electorate amongst whom party identification is weakening. Electoral support must be painfully won by parties and candidates; it can no longer be taken for granted, for the faithful constituencies of the past—whether New Deal or Labour—are visibly crumbling. In both Britain and the United States it has been suggested that existing party alignments no longer reflect popular opinion; realignment, it is argued, would enable the political system to respond more effectively to the facts of social change. Yet the case for party realignment sits uneasily with the "decline of party" thesis. For if parties are no longer able to perform their traditional functions of structuring the vote and setting the political agenda, how can they provide the foundation of a stable, realigned party system?

Crewe and Schneider provide the evidence upon which conclusions about realignment must be based. What is clear is that, in both Britain and the United States, there has been a decline in confidence in parties and in other political institutions since the 1960s, and an increase in the number of unattached voters. This phenomenon is only partially to be explained by citing the facts of social change; equal importance in the process of disenchantment must surely be assigned to the long succession of policy failures in the two countries and the reaction to the excessive expectations generated by Kennedy and Harold Wilson.

Neither in Britain nor in the United States has disenchantment led to extremism; anti-democratic movements in both countries remain inconspicuous and ineffectual. Instead, the electorate seems to have acquired a greater degree of wariness and scepticism in the face of the blandishments of politicians. Realignment has not yet

xiii

occurred in either country; and indeed dealignment seems a more likely outcome, both in Britain and in the United States.

For, whatever the outcome of the 1984 presidential election, it would be a mistake to assume that there has been a fundamental realignment in American politics. Indeed, even Kevin Phillips, the originator of the slogan "the emerging Republican majority," has conceded in his recent book, *Post-Conservative America*, that the uneasy coalition of Northern Catholics, Southern Protestants, Orthodox Jews, Midwestern wheat farmers and Western populists, which helped elect Reagan in 1980, cannot be dignified with the title of "Republican majority." For there are clearly serious strains amongst the component parts of the coalition, and, in particular, between its populist and conservative wings.[4] Moreover, the elections of 1980, with their low turnout indicating lack of voter interest, the split Congress, together with the fact that Reagan secured the lowest share of the vote of any Republican President in this century except for Richard Nixon in 1968 and gained only 2% more of the vote than Gerald Ford in 1976, are hardly the materials from which party realignment is made. The truth is that socio-economic patterns may no longer be sufficiently stable—or party allegiances sufficiently deep—for the kind of realignment that occurred in 1896 or 1932 to recur in the 1980s.

Parallel conclusions, as Crewe demonstrates, can be drawn from British experience. In spite of the policy failures of successive governments and dissatisfaction with the major parties, the Liberal/SDP Alliance has not yet been able to transform generalized discontents into a positive and stable basis of support. The Alliance confronts the same problem that the Liberal Party has so long faced: how to convert protesters into committed partisans. Support for the Alliance seems no different in kind—although it is greater in magnitude—than the highly fragile and volatile allegiance which is all that the Liberals have been able to attract in the past.[5]

In both Britain and the United States, therefore, simplistic predictions of party realignment are likely to be confuted by experience. Instead, party strategists will have to face the problem of how transient and issue-orientated support can be transformed into more permanent political allegiances. The consequences of the decline in strength and depth of party identification could prove serious and far-reaching for parties in Britain and the United States. For it can be argued that the very centrality of party in the institutional structure of Western democracies rests upon the assumption of a loyal and fundamentally stable electorate. But, as public opinion comes gradually to be detached from party, so the parties may lose their crucial role in the formation of the political agenda, while their pedagogic function comes increasingly to be undertaken by the mass media, which can communicate a more balanced picture to the electorate than the political parties have been able to do. In addition, the resurgence of populism as a political force puts great strains upon those institutions that attempt to mediate between the voter and government. The parties could easily come to find themselves victims of those very processes of social change that they have attempted to guide.

* * *

The last group of essays in *Parties and Democracy in Britain and America* deals with changing patterns of political finance, campaign technology and mass media influence. All have helped to shape the changing party systems of Britain and the United States.

David Adamany and Larry Sabato present conflicting views on the significance of American campaign finance laws—the Federal Election Campaign Act of 1971 (FECA), and subsequent amendments to it. To what extent has this legislation contributed to a weakening of American parties? The evidence is not easy to interpret, but certainly some of the arguments of those who link FECA with party decline implicitly posit a "golden age" of American politics when parties provided the bulk of their candidates' finance and effectively insulated them from outside pressures. But such a golden age has never existed.

Whether or not they have contributed to the "decline of party," the campaign finance laws have certainly offered considerable advantages to a party sufficiently united and far-sighted to exploit the possibilities opened up by the new campaign technology. FECA puts a premium upon party unity and may well have played some part in making the Republicans a more cohesive party of the Right. Indeed, the gradual demise of the liberal Republicans of the north-eastern seaboard, together with the movement of Southern conservatives into the Republican Party, may be helping to polarize American politics around an ideological fault-line: the liberal/conservative axis.

The provisions by which presidential candidates in the United States can benefit from the public funding of their campaigns make it easier for Democrats and Republicans than for candidates from minor parties or independents to avail themselves of funds. In the United States, therefore, the new campaign finance laws have helped to entrench the two-party system. In Britain, also, the pattern of political finance helps the Conservatives and Labour who can secure institutional finance from companies and trade unions more easily than their competitors. Eugene McCarthy would find a number of supporters within the Liberal/SDP Alliance for his argument that the regulation of political finance serves the interests of the dominant parties in the political system. Indeed, the provisions regulating political finance in Britain may well have been even more fundamental in shaping party alignments than FECA in the United States, in that they have so underwritten the dominance of the Conservatives and Labour.

This has important consequences for the British political system. It enables the trade unions to exert a massive influence upon the policy processes of the Labour Party; and, it has been suggested, it has helped to entrench class politics at a time when class ties are visibly weakening in Britain as in other industrial countries. The pattern of party finance acts—critics would claim—like the first-past-the-post electoral system, as a life-support mechanism for the major parties.

Political finance has become a subject of controversy in Britain and the United States for quite opposite reasons. In the United States, the debate concerns itself with whether the campaign finance laws of the 1970s have been responsible for the "decline of party." In Britain, on the other hand, the pattern of political finance has been criticized for buttressing the two-party system and helping artificially to preserve it. Perhaps neither country has yet succeeded in balancing voluntariness—a basic desideratum of party finance in a liberal democracy—with the needs of strong and coherent party government. American legislation has tended to emphasize the former element, while British practice has stressed the latter.

* * *

Like the American campaign finance laws, the mass media have been accused of responsibility for a multitude of political evils. In both Britain and the United States, the focus of much of the political debate on the role of the media has, unfortunately, concentrated upon the question of party bias. But this, as Butler and Ranney convincingly demonstrate, is hardly the central issue to be confronted. Rather, attention should be directed to the question of whether the media are responsible for "structural bias," whether they have fundamentally affected the way in which the electorates of the two countries perceive their political systems. This is a fascinating area all too little explored. To what extent have the mass media helped to end deference in politics, instilling a sceptical attitude towards political leaders, and so encouraging a loss of confidence in political institutions? Can it be a coincidence that the increasing influence of television over the last 30 years has coincided with the progressive weakening of party influences in both countries? These are the questions to which Butler and Ranney direct attention, and they are, surely, fundamental to any analysis of what is happening to parties in Britain and the United States.

Political parties are, to a considerable degree, dependent variables. Their power to influence the direction of social change and of electoral loyalties is, under modern conditions, severely limited. To survive as effective political institutions, therefore, parties must adapt to social and electoral change. Many of the party reforms in the United States have been undertaken to satisfy the participatory demands of a modern electorate. Despite widespread criticism of the effects of these reforms, it may be that American parties have made greater efforts to accommodate themselves to the society within which they live than their British counterparts. For, in Britain, attempts at party reform have foundered upon ideological divisions within the Labour Party and the ethos of the Conservatives with its emphasis upon the authority of the party leader.

Since the time of Woodrow Wilson, many Americans have looked with longing at the British party system and sought to recreate its virtues in the United States. It is for this reason that the model of "responsible party government" has retained its allure, even though its inapplicability to American conditions should have been quite obvious. What is so remarkable, however, is that the "responsible party government" model finds itself under such critical scrutiny in Britain, the country that gave it birth. In seeking to adapt the British party system to modern conditions, British reformers can derive both inspiration and warning from the fate of party reform in the United States.

In both countries, party reform is bound to threaten the position of existing elites who will, therefore, have a vested interest in opposing change and may also suffer from the tendency of idealizing the status quo; while reformers will be tempted to make light of the intractability of human institutions which have a tendency to resist changes threatening the fundamental principles according to which they operate. It is, perhaps, for this reason that the institutional reforms of the 1960s and 1970s have not done more to alter the relationships between parties, government and the electorate. They have had the character of shifts in the institutional furniture rather than radical attempts to reconstitute the very principles upon which government is based. Britain remains a system of Cabinet government whose contours would be easily recognizable by Bagehot and Morley; while the structure of American government still approximates more closely the principles laid down by the Founding Fathers than it does any of the more recent models that reformers have sketched.

In both Britain and the United States, therefore, a rapidly changing political culture is confronted by an unchanging and indeed deeply resistant political structure. It is hardly surprising if the result has been electoral disenchantment. For, even if parties and party leaders are able to control the machinery of government, they cannot similarly dominate the environment within which they have their being. The influence exerted by parties over the rules of the political game is ensured only so long as there is some congruence between their own preoccupations and the aspirations of the electorate. Where this congruence no longer exists, where the parties find themselves unable to adapt to the processes of social change, their role is bound to come under challenge. It is to a consideration of the fascinating interplay between political parties and social change in two very different democracies that the present volume is devoted.

NOTES

1. Walter Bagehot in *The English Constitution: The Collected Works of Walter Bagehot* (The Economist, London, 1974) Vol. 5, p. 212, referred to the Cabinet as "a *hyphen* which joins, a *buckle* which fastens, the legislative part of the state to the executive part of the state."
2. Otto Kirchheimer, *Politics, Law and Social Change* (Columbia University Press, 1969) p. 272.
3. Samuel Beer, *Modern British Politics* (Faber, 1965).
4. Kevin P. Phillips, *Post-Conservative America: People, Politics and Ideology in a Time of Crisis* (Random House, 1982).
5. See John Curtice, Liberal Voters and the Alliance: Realignment or Protest, in Vernon Bogdanor (Ed.), *Liberal Party Politics* (Oxford University Press, 1983).

PARTIES AND DEMOCRACY
IN BRITAIN AND AMERICA

1

THE DECLINE OF PARTY?

S. E. Finer

As long as representative government endures, parties will continue to perform certain roles that may be described as primordial. They will be the central—if not indeed the unique—organs, first, for generating candidates; next, for fighting the elections that will put them into office; and, finally, as a consequence of this, for determining the character of a country's governing body. However, if in this immediate context we mean by "party" not that fraction of it which enjoys executive-legislative functions when in office, but its entire body of members considered as a kind of corporation, then, as a consequence of the three primordial functions, the party has historically enjoyed a privileged status compared with all other social and political organizations.

This privileged status expressed itself in four different ways: In the first place, parties have enjoyed a relatively privileged position with respect to the policies pursued by their leaders when these are in office. Next—and by the same token—they have enjoyed some control over the executive branch. Thirdly, they have enjoyed patronage. Finally, and above all, they have been able to gain prompt access to government.

The maximal status of parties with respect to all four of these modes has been expressed in the concept of the *Parteienstaat*. This is an "ideal type." In a *Parteienstaat*, the executive government, its policies, the leadership of ministries right down to the middle levels, all types of patronage, as well as all pressure groups, are mediated exclusively by the party. All policies must be effected *via* the party;

correspondingly, there are very few autonomous nonpoliticized groups in society. The nearest we approach to this ideal type in actual practice—and it is only a mere approximation—is, perhaps, found in Israel. There, all important pressure groups—for example, the Zionist Organization, the Histradut [labor unions], the health service [Kupat Holim], and the like, are run by representatives of the political parties according to the strictest proportional representation. Again, the coalition partners in a government have a "key," giving them entitlement to the patronage of the top echelons in the ministries that they control. The parties themselves are communitarian, with youth movements, housing associations, kibbutzim, party newspapers, party banks and suchlike enabling a member, if he so wishes, to spend all his life from cradle to grave inside the party environment.

It seems to me that everywhere in Western Europe and America (which I shall hereafter abbreviate to Euro-America) we can discern today a marginalization of party in all four of the modes mentioned above. While the three primordial functions remain, the other privileged positions entailed by them have been eroded. Without doubt, parties are much stronger today than they were a hundred years ago. I would surmise they are stronger than they were at the turn of the century. But I suggest that with respect to the four-fold privilege mentioned earlier, the party today is less strong, less central, and, indeed, less important than it was at the close of the Second World War. This is demonstrable in two major areas: First, the party leaderships increasingly bypass the party-members; secondly, the public, or publics, increasingly by-pass the party as such; they tend to deal directly with the government of the day. Furthermore, when they do deal with government, they do so as with an executive organ, not as with a party one. Consequently, what I have to say falls under three headings: The first comprises two extended comments on the marginalization of mass membership; the second concerns the political marginalization of the parties as such by other mass groupings and elements in society; the third concerns what, to coin an ugly word, I must call the departifying of public policy.

The marginalization of the mass membership manifests itself in two great trends. The first can be summarized simply by saying that today Weber's leader–follower model is more appropriate than the participatory one. The assumption that parties are effectively republics of likeminded people who have come together to formulate policy, press it on their leaders, and make them implement it can hardly be sustained. In the world of today the participatory model is more prescriptive than descriptive. The notion of a leader-follower relationship, à la Weber, corresponds much better to what happens in the real world. In Weber's phrase, "A relatively small number of men are primarily interested in power. They provide themselves with a following through free recruitment, present themselves or their protégés as candidates for election, collect the financial means and go out vote-grabbing."

There is a vital implication to this view of party. It is that when folk attach themselves to parties, these are already going concerns; people adhere to them and their already formulated policies according to how closely these approximate their perceptions and interests. Such adherents are indeed "represented" by the party; but the representation is "virtual" (as Burke would have it), not contractual.

Before passing on to describing marginalization proper, there are, however, three caveats to be made: First, neither the leader-follower model nor the participatory model is very applicable to the Congressional elections of the United States; these have been denatured by the populism of the primary system. By contrast, in the Presidential elections the model is unquestionably the leader-follower one. The second caveat concerns the relationship between these two models and the two categorizations of parties that have enjoyed some vogue, namely, the distinction between the "mass parties" (like the old social-democratic parties) and so-called "catch-all" parties (like the British Conservative party and, indeed, the two great American parties). The catch-all model is consistent with the leader-follower model but hardly so with the participatory one. The reason is obvious: Members in the participatory-democracy party tend to be exclusive and sectarian—that is, the very reverse of a "catch-all party". The final caveat has a significance going beyond Britain and the United States; the so-called "mass parties" have in the past been communitarian and integralist, either on the left, like the early social-democratic parties on the eve of the First World War or the Communist parties after it, or to the right, like the few remaining Fascist parties and—more toward the centre-right—like the Christian Democrat parties of Europe today. All over Europe all such parties, Left and Right, are being either eroded or deserted. In Italy, slowly but inexorably, the rival sectarianisms of the Italian Communist Party (PCI) and the Christian Democratic Party (DC) are being eroded by the general secularization of attitudes. That is also true if we look at the relationship in Germany between religious practice and membership of the Social Democratic Party (SPD) on the one hand and the Christian Democratic Party (CDU) on the other. While such parties are being eroded, others are simply being deserted, like the French Communists, the Italian M.S.I., or the Spanish and Portuguese fascist party formations. Similarly, the Christian parties of Holland took 52% of the vote just after the Second World War, while now their percentage is down to a mere 32%.

In the parties of Euro-America (more so in Europe than in North America), it is the leaderships rather than the rank-and-file who, increasingly, formulate party policy. Policy is simply put to the rank-and-file to be endorsed, possibly with some minor amendments, by them. Furthermore, this policy is increasingly prompted, not so much by the ideology or outlook of the mass membership, but by what opinion polls—often chartered by the party leadership—tell of what mass public (and not narrow party) opinion demands. Naturally, a nexus exists between the sentiments of the mass membership and what the leaders propound to it, for the leaders have to maintain their followings; but thereupon what comes into play is the well-known law of anticipated reaction.

A second aspect of this marginalization of the mass membership is that the leadership is less and less dependent upon it for winning and keeping power. What is true in respect of the British parties applies throughout most of Euro-America; that is to say, the power of the local "machine" has declined. Parties can and do reach the electorate via the media, not necessarily or exclusively via the local party activists. Since the party can test the views of the general public via opinion polls, it does not have to rely exclusively on what the local party activists tell it about popular sentiment. And, finally, in many countries an institutional innovation has occurred by which the public can express its views directly to the government of the day without any mediation of the parties at all, via popular vetoes, popular initiatives, and popular referenda. It is true that the United States and the Federal Republic of Germany still know nothing of such devices at national level (there are, of course, provisions for referenda and initiatives in most of the American states); but in Europe referenda are common and have begun to obtrude even on the political system of Britain. To the extent that these devices multiply, so they bypass the formerly unique channel of communication—the party.

The marginalization of the mass membership, the first trend to which this paper draws attention, has proceeded at different rates in different countries; but if we compare the situation today with that immediately after the war, the trend is distinct and indubitable.

The second trend is the way in which other institutions and processes in society have bypassed or supplanted the political party. Nowadays parties are no longer—if indeed they ever were—the unique or even the most highly privileged highways to influencing government policy, to patronage, or even to access. One reason lies in the increased political autonomy of the mass media. The day of the party newspaper has gone. As to television, although in some countries, such as the Netherlands or the Federal Republic of Germany and to some extent France, party-controlled television is still the rule, in many other countries the medium has emancipated itself from party influence. The United States enjoys a plethora of stations, and the criteria of government regulation have nothing to do with party. The British rely on a public service system in which, moreover, programmes have to be governed by the principle of "balance," and party broadcasts and telecasts are allocated by a formula freely worked out between the respective political parties. In Italy, although RAI is controlled by representatives of the political parties, it is effectively attenuated by the abundance of alternative independent channels.

A second way in which the parties are being bypassed lies in the increasing tendency of corporations and major pressure groups to address government directly rather than going to them via the political party. Most pressure groups do not use the party to mediate their efforts. In Italy there are feminist groups who call themselves the "autonomi" precisely because they are independent of the political parties, which they distrust as being unsympathetic to their demands. There are, again, pressure groups, such as the British Campaign for Nuclear Disarmament (CND), which aspire to a mass basis and deliberately hold aloof from parties because they feel that to be allied with any one would lose them support from the adherents of all the others. And above all there are so-called "voice parties" such as the "Greens" or the ecologists, which remain outside the major political formations. All such groups are bypassing what was formerly the primary means of communication with and access to the government.

Thirdly and finally, the parties have, on the whole, lost much of their former grip on patronage; but here, it must be noted, there has been an important backlash. In recent years there has grown up, outside the regular government departments, a host of inter-mediate bodies, neither quite public nor quite private, which escape the rigid recruitment rules of the civil service. These are the bodies known in Britain as the Quasi-Autonomous Non-Governmental Organizations, or Quangos for short. In Italy these rejoice in the more picturesque name of "sottogoverno." Immune from the merit-system rules, these bodies present to the government (as patron) and the mass members (as beneficiaries) what Edmund Burke in his day richly described as a "ripening hotbed of influence." To the extent that party government dishes out jobs for the boys and bears its own partisans in mind when doing so, the development of the Quango certainly runs counter to the tendency for parties to lose their grip on patronage. But now, consider the civil services proper: In these establishments, grossly swollen in comparison to their size at the turn of the century and in the years immediately before the First World War, the parties have been almost entirely excluded from what have in effect become self-governing, syndicalist organizations—organizations that themselves determine their rules of recruitment, criteria for promotion, and rules of discipline. In the United States only a few thousand jobs out of millions remain at the disposal of the party patrons; in Germany and Italy only a few; more in Belgium than is common elsewhere; in Britain, virtually none.

The third and final trend, therefore, is the departifying of public policy. This is so obvious as to require little elaboration. It is clear that even the most ideologically committed of governments today—and how many are very ideologically committed?—are the prisoners of forces beyond their control. Some of these forces represent external factors: all governments are constrained by the world economy, most of them have entered into associations with other states that curtail their economic independence or their foreign policies. But they are also prisoners of their own *folie de grandeur*, as they preside over vast bureaucratic systems. The day has long since gone when a minister or a president could exert direct control and acquire first-hand information. This is no longer possible and never will be as long as governments operate on such a massive scale. The only sure way of ensuring tighter political control of public management is by having less of it. But nowadays the commitment is virtually limitless. Governments thus find themselves trapped between the pressure of organized interests with whom they arrange package deals and the inertia of governmental policies which, by reason of their bulk, they cannot cast off overnight. Add what has already been said about the ineluctable constraint of external forces, and the extent to which governments are prone to be "blown off course"—the course that the mass membership expects it to steer—becomes manifest.

To conclude: at different paces in different countries—with the United States perhaps at one end of the scale and France at the other—what we are witnessing is the slow, uneven, but ineluctable erosion of the once central and dominant position assigned to the political parties and, equally, to the aspiration to collective participation of huge masses who saw in the party their chosen vehicle for transmitting their hopes and demands upwards, to be imposed, imperatively, upon the government formed out of this chosen instrument—their political party.

2

POWER AND THE PARTIES: THE UNITED STATES

Philip M. Williams

PARTIES AND PARTY SYSTEMS: UNITED STATES AND UNITED KINGDOM

There is something baffling to the European (particularly perhaps to the British) observer in the current laments about the loss of power of political parties in the United States. Qualified writers disagree somewhat about the extent of their decline and the prospects of reversing it, but with virtual unanimity they accept the fact and regret it. Yet from across the Atlantic it seems hard to understand the disappearance of a phenomenon that had no discernible existence in the first place. From Roosevelt's single-vote majority for conscription in 1939, to Truman's resort to bipartisanship to pass Marshall Aid and the Atlantic Pact through Congress, to Eisenhower's reliance upon the Democratic leaders to save him from his own Republican fellow-partisans, to Kennedy's inability to get his tax cut even discussed in Congress for eighteen months, to Nixon's inability to stop the War Powers Act and Carter's humiliating failure over SALT II and almost equally humiliating success over Panama, Presidents have repeatedly found it impossible to rely on their parties even in the foreign and defence field, where they are supposed to have most influence.

There is another surprising feature of the debate. Sixty years ago, party allegiance in the United States seemed so totally detached from political outlook that, whatever the functions that parties were supposed to perform nationally, support for any specific policy orientation could never conceivably be among them. Republicans were mostly conservatives who believed the business of the United States to be business, yet the midwestern agrarians in their ranks were the most radical politicians in the country. Franklin Roosevelt made the Democrats a progressive big-government party, relying on the support of trade unionists, northern blacks, and working-class Catholics in the big cities—yet also of a solid South dominated by an elite committed to white supremacy, suspicious of Catholics and organised labour, and increasingly conservative in its general outlook. But in the subsequent years a very considerable reshuffle of groups and attitudes took place. In so huge and diverse a country it would be too much to expect two united and homogeneous coalitions, which even the much smaller nation-states of Europe have been unable to generate (although Britain came nearest, once Southern Ireland was detached). But the extremes have vanished, with no radical Republicans left and precious few really reactionary Democrats; the incongruent wings have shrunk, leaving the conservative Democrats a dwindling band and the liberal Republicans a pathetic and isolated rump. Their old homes find increasing difficulty in accommodating either, and in all parts of the country, at almost every election, the Democratic candidate is more liberal or at least more moderate than his Republican opponent. Yet we constantly read that the parties were more powerful in earlier days when they were almost meaningless, and are becoming less powerful as they grow more meaningful.[1] It is a strange paradox.

The explanation is simple. When U.S. writers and British readers consider the power of the parties and the distribution of power within them, they have quite different considerations in their minds because they conceptualise parties quite differently. To Britons the essential feature of a political party is understood (not always rightly) to be the common outlook binding its members together and translating, however imperfectly, that outlook into political practice through the control of government. To Americans historically, parties have rarely had even the most rudimentary common outlook, or any recognised membership, or even a government over which they could reasonably hope to exercise real control. Britons have seen their parties (in realistic not legal terms) as units linked, more or less effectively, from the top to the bottom of a hierarchical structure subject to more or less complete central direction; even though independent power centres could often maintain their distinct existence, they rarely attained sufficient influence to challenge the established leadership. No such established leadership existed at all in the United States unless the party held the Presidency, and even then it was temporary, contingent, and contested at every turn by the numerous independent baronies that were the only permanent power centres in the system.

This was in part the consequence of federalism and the dispersal of authority to fragmented geographical units. Occasionally a state party (Ohio Republicans or Virginia Democrats) would exercise a continuous power in its own area, which the national party never tried to match on its bigger scale. Far more often the state party, like the national one, would depend for coherent leadership on having its candidate in the chief executive post, relapsing into warring factions whenever the Governor came from the other side. Local parties were more likely to be durable, being dominated in the great cities by bosses without public office, or by strong mayors; more recently where machines still survived, the mayor was usually the boss. Their perspectives and objectives were overwhelmingly local; elderly Chicago Democrats would go to Congress to retire, or promising young ones to learn their trade before returning to serious politics as city aldermen. Progressives saw the parties—with some reason— as obstacles to change, not instruments for achieving it, and that tradition still exerts a powerful influence; those who wish to promote reforming policies often seek to tear down existing organisations, rather than use them to mobilise support and clarify priorities.[2] Where the parties were weakened by these efforts, or declined for other reasons, they have become unable to control the nomination of candidates. Instead, the direct primary, in its manifold forms, enabled the party's regular supporters or its prospective supporters or even its opponents (according to the state law) to choose its standard-bearer—who, having won on his own, was unlikely docilely to accept advice, still less discipline, from any organ of the party.

Fragmentation was not merely geographical, for the separation of powers was designed to achieve the same result at the centre. The two houses of the legislature, elected in different units and at different times, each had their internal power structures in which, for two-thirds of a century (1910 to the mid-1970s), the committee chairmen who controlled the flow of business, and usually the terms of legislation, held their posts by seniority within the majority party, whether or not they shared the views of its congressional leadership or rank-and-file members, still less of its Presidents. When the Democrats controlled Congress, as they did for all but four years from 1930 to 1980, that nominal control was primarily exercised through these baronial chairmen who, being mostly conservative southerners, were increasingly out of touch with the majority of their party.

Before the New Deal the national parties were coalitions held together above all by the need, once every four years, to keep their rivals out of the most important office of all, the Presidency. Under a parliamentary and cabinet system with a collegial executive, a multi-party system might well have arisen; with a single chief executive, the barons were obliged to make their alliances before not after the election.[3] The territorial barons played the main but not the only role; their legislative counterparts were rarely serious rivals in this arena, but other groups could sometimes exercise great influence, notably the labor unions in the Democratic party in and after Roosevelt's day. Major parties are really coalitions not only in the United States, but in all two-party systems including the British. But during the Atlantic crossing the notion of coalition undergoes a subtle change. British national parties have their internal differences, which are sometimes sharp, but they turn—or have turned in the past, for the unity is visibly fraying—on tactical disputes about the pace of desirable change or the prudence of and degree of resistance to it. There have been clear and open differences between the aims of the two coalitions, exaggerated rather than minimised by the accepted rhetoric even if, in government, the two parties shared more common ground than either liked to admit. In the United States, however, it was thought politically unprofitable and divisive to emphasise ideological differences, and the two coalition-parties preferred to appear no more distinct than Tweedledum and Tweedledee: bottles with different labels, both empty. Appearing only every four years to elect a president, they did not enunciate a party policy but proclaimed support for his—a claim in no way binding on the party's spokesmen either in the national legislature or in the states.

Americans do not, therefore, write about their political parties as units with interlocking parts, which are supposed to mesh but inevitably clash from time to time. Instead, they write separately about segments of parties, operating independently at the different levels of government; the party-in-the-electorate (who supports it, and how reliably?); the party organisation (who runs it, and how much influence do they wield?); the party-in-the-legislature (how much notice, if any, do the members take of their leaders, and in what circumstances?); and, last and decidedly least, the party-in-government (when, if ever, does it exist?). In looking at party power, their standpoint is just the opposite of that of the British observer. He starts from the party-in-government and asks "How could it lose power when it never had any?" Just because the party-in-government hardly ever had any in the United States, Americans naturally assume that the question refers to something else.

These very different two-party systems have both been preserved until recently to some extent by artificial institutional constraints, while the societies that were supposed to find political expression through them have been changing rapidly. In Britain, the political conflict has been structured on ostensibly ideological lines, yet because both parties have until recently kept firmly to a moderate course for fear of offending the uncommitted voter, it has hitherto been difficult for any rival party to establish an identity; for minority support spread across the country, even when it reached a fifth of the national vote, produced only a derisory number of parliamentary seats under the first-past-the-post electoral system. The United States uses the same electoral system, and it is reinforced by other institutional barriers to the multi-party system that American society might otherwise generate. The duopoly of the historic parties is protected in many states by laws designed to keep their rivals off the ballot.[4] The organisation and importance of the presidential election make local third parties, which do sometimes arise, irrelevant to the principal political battle and tend to drive them back into one of the established coalition-parties. Individual dissenters within their parties need not leave them but can press their personal claims and political choices through the primaries. Until the 1960s, the incongruous wings of the two parties—liberal Republicans and conservative southern Democrats—each had an incentive to remain there because of the opportunities they enjoyed owing to the so-called "Double Gerrymander". The electoral college system, with states voting as units, gave disproportionate weight to the big states, which happened to be industrial and marginal, with the outcome decided by the turnout in the big cities; Republicans could win the presidency or governorship only if they were liberals. On the other hand, the failure to revise the boundaries of congressional and especially state legislative districts left the rural areas grotesquely over-represented and helped to keep the conservative southerners secure in their positions of power within Congress.

BREAKING THE BARONIES:
CUI BONO?

Those institutional barriers have broken down, and drastic changes have taken place in the composition and organisation of the parties at all levels; the rest of this chapter analyses the consequences of these changes. Their immediate impact, as most commentators have stressed, has been to weaken the already limited importance of party—in the legislature, among the voters, and to its elected office-holders. Everywhere the old baronies have crumbled. It has been less widely remarked that those baronies were as much obstacles to coherent party action as they were instruments of it, for the wielders of baronial power did not necessarily share and indeed often thoroughly detested the views of the majority of their party. Shifts of population, blacks voting in the south and the growth of a new breed of political activists interested in new issues have contributed to a redistribution of electoral preferences and a great simplification of the old hopelessly confused relationship between policy views and party allegiance. While that confusion prevailed, party coherence on policy was inconceivable; it still remains inhibited by many factors, both short- and long-term. But in a more congenial political climate it can now be conceived of, and some of the institutional changes of recent years could be well adapted to encourage it. These include the new if little-used powers of the Democratic party leadership in Congress, the spectacular growth of the national organisation of the Republican party, and a number of Democratic reforms that have either survived the storms of the last ten years and opened up party channels to its active supporters or have been introduced more recently to restore some influence to the office-holders and spokesmen who have a long-term stake in the party and in its successful performance on the national stage.

Sweeping social and institutional changes have affected the established party systems in both Britain and the United States, though without destroying in either the predominance of the two main parties. In Britain, suffering from economic stagnation and international decline, voters discontented with the party in office no longer turn automatically to its rival (despite the two-party system with its pressure not to waste a vote on hopeless candidates). Apart from nationalist successes on the Celtic fringe, this mood has spread in England too. Both the main parties have contributed to it, by flouting the old conventional assumption that only a moderate course can win the uncommitted voter. The Conservative Members of Parliament in 1975 chose an intransigent leader who, as Prime Minister, has installed her own supporters in the positions of power. In the Labour ranks party democracy, promoted by patient organisation from below, has been defined and limited by a strictly factional objective, to make the parliamentary leadership acceptable and responsive, not to the Labour voters, but to the activist left-wing minority; some of those opposed to this course have left to form a new party, while others remain in the old one, torn until 1983 by the most vitriolic factional strife. Americans unhappy with recent changes put the blame less on "snakes in the grass roots" and more on "tumbleweeds," blowing in on a sudden impulse and out equally suddenly and acquiring no lasting attachment to the party.

Their activities form only one side of a complicated picture. Institutional changes in the United States have had contradictory effects, weakening party structures in some respects, yet strengthening them in others. Traditionally, American party organisations had been held together by patronage. But in the more affluent post-1945 world, ill-paid spoils-system posts were much less attractive. A more prosperous and educated society generated a new type of political activist, more committed to particular policies or candidates and less to organisational maintenance and loyalty for their own sakes; many writers on American parties draw a sharp distinction between the "purists" with their ideological priorities, and the "professionals" anxious to maintain a strong organised party able both to win elections and to govern. (Yet Gary Orren persuasively argued that this distinction is too simple, confusing two quite separate attitudes— holding strong views and wanting strong parties.[5] In 1952 Senator Taft, and in 1980 Senator Kennedy, were *both* more "purist" *and* more "professional" than their successful rivals for the nominations, General Eisenhower and President Carter. This comes as no surprise to British observers, since their type of coalition-party could almost be defined by the tension between its hard-core following and its uncommitted supporters, and between the rival politicians who gave priority to appealing to one or the other.) Among Democrats, the reform activists first appeared in Adlai Stevenson's campaign in 1952, and in a number of state parties, notably New York, California, and Illinois. Their conservative equivalents in the Republican party emerged a little later, to overthrow the dominant eastern establishment wing and nominate Barry Goldwater in 1964. Similar tensions, latent among the Democrats, developed over civil rights and then erupted during the Vietnam war in furious protest against the measures by which the old guard preserved its control at the 1968 convention.[6] The consequent moves to reform party procedures began with widespread support. The established baronial powers were a target for all reformers who, however, while all aiming to democratise the party, disagreed on their priorities.

Most of them sympathised in differing degrees with four principal aims. Parties should not merely be vehicles for winning power, they should be committed to agreed policies. They should be effective in carrying out those policies. They should not be managed by established powers (whether or not holding elective office) but subject to democratic control from below, which implies a thoroughly decentralised structure open to participation at the local level. The members participating should be representative of the whole population, not confined to the social groups most accustomed to these activities, and those groups hitherto disadvantaged (by colour, age or sex) should be helped to secure their full share.

Unfortunately many of the reformers were inexperienced, and few were willing to recognise that these aims were incompatible.[7] A party could not be an effective instrument for implementing policy without organisation and discipline; if these were demolished by "tumbleweeds" in the name of openness and decentralisation, it would have no way of ensuring that its democratically agreed policies would be applied by its spokesmen in public office. If democratic choice by the local membership was paramount, representation for minorities could not be guaranteed. If the party represented all interests in the society, with all groups having their due weight, it was unlikely to develop a distinctive outlook and ideology separating it from its rival, offering different policies and so giving the voters a real choice. Instead, two catch-all parties were likely to emerge, each straddling every issue for fear of offending a section of its clientele, restoring the old Tweedledum and Tweedledee combination rather than the committed programmatic parties sought by so many reformers.

Even in Congress, where the reform decisions were made on more limited issues by practising politicians, there was a somewhat similar confusion of objectives.[8] By the mid-1970s a broad coalition was ready to strip the committee barons of their overweening power and security of tenure. But it was broad only because its members' aims were diverse. The Democratic Study Group (DSG) organised Democrats, many of them approaching senior rank themselves, who had long resented the frustrations of holding nominal control of the House or Senate but entrusting it to senior southern conservatives determined to block the very measures most Democrats favoured; they wanted to weaken the chairmen and make them more responsive to the caucus, in order to strengthen the hand of the party leadership. Junior liberals might feel the same, but they had a higher priority: to obtain more influence and more interesting activity than the stifling seniority system allowed them. That aim was fully shared by junior conservatives and by most Republicans, whose party was in the minority and excluded from influence in the committees. The DSG needed the juniors' votes, and its middle-ranking members were in line to chair new subcommittees at once. All these groups thus had a common interest in limiting the powers of the baronial chairmen, and all carried their preferred remedies. But the changes that disperse power have been much more fully implemented in practice than those that concentrate it.

Senior members can now be denied chairmanships, and even the unlikely possibility of this encourages them to behave responsively rather than autocratically. Subcommittees have proliferated, giving opportunities for influence and activity to quite junior members. Committee specialisation is less effective and committee prestige less recognised, so that their decisions are much more frequently challenged and even overturned on the floor. The legislative process is more fragmented than ever, and it becomes increasingly difficult to obtain timely decisions on any controversial or divisive subject; so that junior members feel no more satisfaction in congressional life, while seniors retire in frustration much more often and earlier than their predecessors.

The changes promoted by the DSG leaders have attracted less attention, yet they are of great potential importance for congressional party structure. The Speaker has regained many of the powers he had lost in 1910. He appoints the Rules Committee, for years the principal fortress of the conservatives in the House, and he has much discretion in referring bills to committee. The Democratic caucus meets monthly, instead of every two years at the start of each congress. It has exercised less influence than optimists hoped, partly because members cherish their independence and the will to reach an agreed party compromise has been weak, but also because a caucus of nearly 300 members is a quite unsuitable forum for doing so; and if it tries to impose majority decisions on the minority, they can easily frustrate it by staying away and denying a quorum. Nevertheless the Speaker and the caucus can impose ideological and loyalty conditions for membership or leadership of committees in a way that had not been possible for 70 years.[9] Moreover, should the political climate become more congenial to centripetal forces within the party, there is now a viable alternative for hammering out party policy: the Steering and Policy Committee of 24, composed half of members elected by the Democratic congressmen (in regional groups) and half of party leaders or spokesmen for other categories (blacks, freshmen, etc.). Chaired by the Speaker and largely selected by him, representing all sectors within the Democratic ranks, it offers an instrument with more potential for acceptable party leadership than ever before.[10]

OLD LOYALTIES IN ECLIPSE

A somewhat similar contrast exists beyond Capitol Hill, in the country at large. Here attention has fastened on changes taking place at the level of individual voting decisions, on often decrepit local organisations, and on presidential nominating procedures; less importance has been attached to the changing relationship between Democratic state and national parties or the growing importance of the national Republican organisation. The former developments have contributed to the widely-lamented weakening of party influence, while the latter have been quietly making it possible, for the first time, to envisage the development of fairly coherent national American parties, recognisable as such to a European observer.

The party-weakening changes are real enough. Among individual voters, particularly the young, the party label no longer attracts automatic loyalty. For highly visible offices—governor, U.S. senator, above all President—most people, whatever their nominal party identification, now insist that they evaluate the individual candidates on their personal merits (even if many nevertheless end up always choosing the same side). Whenever two or three of these offices are at stake simultaneously, large numbers of voters split their tickets and pick candidates from different parties to fill them. For less visible offices such as that of congressman, the challenger is usually less known and the advantage of the incumbent much greater. Either way, party affiliation does little to elect or defeat the member, who must organise, finance and publicise his own campaign and consequently feels little gratitude to his party for past services and has no expectation of future favours. There is not much electoral incentive for party loyalty when it brings no reward for observance and no penalty for breach.

Developments in the technique of electioneering reinforce these tendencies. The media, especially television, are indispensable to the projection of a candidate's message. Sophisticated technology and professional advice enable him to direct the message to receptive audiences and to make profitable use of his resources, which have to be substantial because every element in the process is expensive. Huge sums are spent to support or defeat an individual politician loved or hated by a well-financed single-issue group (promoting environmentalism, for instance, or opposing abortion or gun control) or by a political action committee seeking to ensure access to a congressional committee member dealing with its industry. Party discipline and the party ticket no longer cushion the politician against such pressures, and he has a strong incentive to avoid making himself a conspicuous target for a strong challenger financed by an interest-group seeking his electoral demise.[11]

In electioneering as in the national legislature, the reformers' efforts to destroy the power of the organised baronies have thus had unintended consequences. Committee chairmen in Congress have lost their old dominance and obstructive capacity, leaving an unstructured mass incapable of using effectively the freedom its individual members have supposedly acquired. Similarly, the city machines and the rural courthouse rings no longer exercise anything like their former power. Parties were once thought to be more solidly based on the state and local than on the national level, because they were so much less heterogeneous in composition. But now, even in the few states where they flourished, powerful state parties—Republicans in Ohio or upstate New York, Democrats in Virginia or Michigan or Connecticut—can no longer control the choice of candidates. Their influence has been shattered by the voters' reluctance to follow their advice. But those voters, proud of their independence, sink into an atomised mass without intellectual anchorage, vulnerable to the empty appeals professionally packaged on behalf of narrow, concealed sectional interests, or to the distorted propaganda of the New Right's "nattering nabobs of negativism" (to borrow Vice-President Agnew's phrase about the other side).[12]

The destruction of the baronies has been most evident in the most visible political arena of all, that of presidential nominating politics. Before the last decade or so, the chief examples of concentrated and irresponsible power influencing that process occurred in the Democratic party, where reformers were consequently most active. (The Republicans needed to make fewer and less sweeping changes but were still affected by some of the same pressures or indeed obliged to conform to similar rules under new legislation in particular states.)[13] The grip of the southern segregationist Democrats had been gradually loosened. They lost their absolute veto when the requirement of a two-thirds majority for the party's presidential nomination was dropped in 1936. Their habit of repudiating any obligation to the party while enjoying the advantages of continued membership was discouraged by the requirement of loyalty to its candidates by state parties in 1956 and the denial of seniority to the Goldwater Democrats in Congress in 1965. Their hold on their own state parties was broken when Mississippi's segregationist delegation was unseated at the 1968 Convention.[14]

Hubert Humphrey's nomination provoked the frustrated anti-Vietnam-war wing of the party into attacking all the devices by which the professional politicians, disturbed by the newly-active, middle-class enthusiasts, had manipulated the rules to their detriment. Caucuses had been held without notice, at the whim of the organisation, long (sometimes over a year) before the election was due or the non-professionals were paying attention; henceforward they had to take place after adequate publicity and within the calendar year of the contest. There was a ban on the unit rule (in British terms, the block vote) by which lower-level (county or state) conventions voted as a whole at the next higher level, enabling Texas, with its bitterly divided state party manipulated by powerful elites, to annex and cast the vote of the minority wing in addition to that of the majority.[15] Local politicians in the states, anxious to preserve their domination over the local elections that were their main concern, sought to separate these from the presidential process with its tiresome new rules. That preoccupation coincided with the liking of reformers for the system of primaries, which aimed at crippling the parties by removing their power to nominate candidates and giving it to those voters who pledged their support of the party's candidates—or, in some states, to voters without even that qualification. Introduced early in the century, presidential primaries had spread in the Progressive period but had later receded slightly. In 1968 they were used in only 17 states and chose only some two-fifths of the convention delegates. The new wave went much further. By 1980 primaries had been adopted in 37 states and territories, were binding in all but a handful, and selected about three-quarters of the delegates. The rules were tightened in other ways too, particularly by the Democrats, who allocated 91% of the seats settled in primaries in strict proportion to votes cast. Here the Republicans did not follow, and only 31% of their primary delegates were chosen by proportional representation.[16]

Often the results were far from those intended. Active politicians, hitherto almost guaranteed a seat at the convention, now found themselves obliged to fight for it in a primary; apart from reluctance to risk public humiliation, they often had no wish at all to commit themselves prematurely—as the rules required—by standing on behalf of any one presidential candidate. The new rules gave a marked advantage to groups with leisure or control over their use of time— students, some housewives and many professional people—and to the causes that attracted them, to the detriment of trade unionists and working-class grievances. The pressure to choose more female, young and coloured delegates inevitably operated to reduce the number of mature white males and hence in practice to cut down on working-class representation. This was not just the result of the exceptional excitement of the strife-ridden years between 1968 to 1972; in the latter year, 39% of delegates held post-graduate degrees (as against 4% of the population), but in 1976, when there was far less excitement and a moderate was nominated, the proportion had risen to 50%.[17]

The Convention, as we shall see, became an assembly not to choose the party's nominee but to ratify the earlier choice of the primaries. This did not deprive it of all its political importance, for pressure-groups within the party could exploit the new machinery for their own specific, limited purposes. The labor unions, the strongest single interest in the post-New Deal Democratic party, lost influence and, when they tried to reverse some of the rule changes, were thoroughly defeated by the feminists and the blacks. The National Education Association, lobbying first for the establishment of a new Department of Education and then to secure control of it, played a major part in President Carter's coalition in both 1976 and 1980 (when it had over 300 delegates at the Convention, more than any state except California).[18] In 1980 the National Organization of Women induced the Convention to forbid any financial aid to Democrats who opposed the Equal Rights Amendment. Opponents of the Amendment, and of abortion, used the Republican Convention's Platform Committee to equally good effect. The Conventions, which had once provided the quadrennial opportunity for the two vast and disparate national coalitions to work out terms for temporarily sinking their internal differences, had thus been transformed. Losing their nominating function, they offered instead an opportunity for activist minorities to impose sectional priorities even to the detriment of the coalition's electoral prospects: another factor that made for party disintegration.[19]

The changes had equally unintended and unexpected effects on the presidential nominating process itself. Hitherto primary voting had given the party regulars a useful indication of the relative popularity of the contenders, which the professionals could choose to accept or (as the Democrats did in 1952) disregard; they knew primary electorates to be unrepresentative and saw them as only one of many indicators of a candidate's strength or weakness. The candidates selected the primaries in which to compete, which were not necessarily their strongest: in 1960 John Kennedy needed to win in West Virginia to show that he could attract Protestant votes. Early success (particularly in New Hampshire, the highly unrepresentative little state that polls first) always conferred a disproportionate advantage, but it was limited when the primaries were only one factor among many. Even after they spread, victory in an important late primary such as that of California could offset early failures, as it did with Barry Goldwater in 1964; apart from its effect on morale, the winner there took all the delegates from what is now the largest state. With the growth in the number and relative importance of primaries, media attention concentrated on them more and more, and early successes (as interpreted above all by the television commentators) attracted the money and support that early failures forfeited. The candidates were increasingly obliged to compete in every primary, or else see the delegates swell the ranks of their rivals who did so. Momentum achieved in the early days could soon become irreversible, since under proportional representation the front-runner kept some delegates even where he lost. In 1976, Carter amassed a lead against divided opposition which could not be overtaken, despite his weaknesses in the later primaries when he faced only a single rival. In 1980 he was far enough ahead to be confident of nomination before even one primary had been held west of the Mississippi (an area where he was to win only a single state in the general election).[20]

As a means of choosing the party's strongest standard-bearer, primaries are deeply flawed. Those who vote do not represent the party's electorate; accidents (the order in which they are held and the number and identity of the competitors in specific states) play a large part; the media does too much to decide where essential resources will flow or be withheld. In 1981 the chairman of the reform commission which had provoked their proliferation ten years before declared "Presidential primaries denigrate a party's responsibility for selecting its own candidate."[21] But presidential candidatures are increasingly detached from party, and voters—inundated with information on this contest above all—make up their minds about the nominees as individuals, not as party spokesmen. The aim is to assess their character and ability, or decide according to their personal views on issues, rather than between the interests and attitudes embodied in their prospective governing coalitions. Indeed, some commentators believe that Independent candidates have a better chance nowadays, since partisanship matters less than ever before, and television can focus on the individual's performance.[22] Even the legal restrictions, introduced to keep minor candidates off the ballot, have been frowned on by the Supreme Court and successfully overcome in recent years by George Wallace in 1968 and John Anderson in 1980—both of whom were on the ballot in all 50 states.

The prospect of a President of the United States with no formal ties to any party does not seem imminent. But it would only mark the culmination of a trend that seemed irresistible until 1980: the disappearance of the links between the chief executive and the other holders of political power.[23] Nominated through their own efforts, elected with little or no appeal to party, surrounded by personal courtiers wholly dependent on them for political survival, recent presidents have had fewer and fewer obligations to their fellow partisans and less and less claim on their support. In 1972 Richard Nixon was reelected overwhelmingly after a campaign completely detached from the Republican party, which reaped no advantage from his triumph. In 1976 Jimmy Carter trailed behind the vast majority of Democratic congressmen and senators, who felt they owed him nothing. The President's power in his party waned so far that he could not count even on winning renomination uncontested. In 1948 Harry Truman was renominated at the nadir of his popularity. But in 1976 Ronald Reagan's challenge to President Ford came close to success at the Convention, in 1980 Senator Kennedy embarrassed President Carter in the later stages after having faltered earlier, and both insurgent leaders were able to use the platform debates to demonstrate that they, not the incumbent Presidents, had the stronger appeal to the party's core supporters.[24] Elected on their own, with few ties to the party organisation or its office-holders in Congress or the states, Presidents who preceded Ronald Reagan have contrived to isolate themselves from the very allies and associates whose support they needed if they were to govern the country effectively.

LESS HETEROGENEOUS COALITIONS?

Yet the internal disagreements, which once made parties so recalcitrant to any effort to seek unity or impose discipline over policy questions, are nowhere near as fundamental as they used to be. The United States is becoming far more of a single nation, though a very big one; and while its various regions have conflicting interests and distinct outlooks, they no longer cherish cultures and ways of life so mutually opposed as to make them see other Americans as dangerous enemies. Instead, the New Deal began and the civil rights movement has continued a gradual shift of allegiances, which means that, while political attitudes differ greatly in different parts of the country, virtually everywhere the locally most conservative elements overwhelmingly belong to the Republican party, and the relative liberals are Democrats.[25] Supporters of either party still disagree with one another on many issues, as their British counterparts always have. But the growth of a loose party consensus, defined in opposition

Table 2.1

Party and ideology in Congress (average ADA scores)[1]

States	United States 50	North-east 9	Mid-west 11	Pacific 5	Border 6	Moun-tain 8	South 11
Senate							
D. av. 1965–76	58	83	81	72	64	59	21
R. av. 1965–76	27	55	17	42	32	7	5
D. min. any year	43	74	59	59	52	39	9
R. max. any year	38	66	27	59	41	13	11
House							
D. av. 1975–76	56	77	75	78	49	57	21
R. av. 1975–76	17	31	15	13	19	9	4
D. min. any year	49	71	69	70	40	44	13
R. max. any year	23	44	22	23	25	19	8

[1] ADA scores measure the votes of members of Congress on key issues, and run from 0 (most conservative) to 100 (most liberal). Party differences narrowed slightly in 1977–78, except in the south, where Democrats were becoming more moderate. (The "D. min." and "R. max." years were the same in only two of the 14 cases.)

Source: Tables in W. R. Shaffer, *Party and Ideology in the U.S. Congress* (University Press of America, 1980).

to the loose consensus on the other side, has in the last 20 years become possible for the first time.

An artificial barrier to such a development disappeared in the later 1960s when the "double gerrymander" broke down. As population shifted out of the central cities and into the suburbs, it carried away an axiom of American politics. Liberals able to mobilise the big-city vote were no longer essential to carry the big marginal states for senator, governor or president, as Nixon and Reagan showed. Liberal Republicans were not, therefore, indispensable to their party after all, and its keen supporters could at least afford to express their old mistrust for those ideological misfits and indulge in their real preferences. In New York alone they were able in 1970 to replace Senator Goodell by a Conservative, James Buckley, in 1980 to defeat Senator Javits in a primary and elect the right-wing Senator D'Amato, and even in New York City to deny Mayor Lindsay the Republican nomination (he won re-election as a Liberal and subsequently switched to the Democrats). On the other side of the party divide, the conservative southern Democrats also found their opportunities restricted as they lost the protection of the other half of the double gerrymander. In the south, it was the cities that offered the best hope of Republican penetration, while the rural areas, as long as they could keep the modern world from intruding and the blacks from voting, remained solid bastions of traditionalism—grossly over-represented as their people left, but their representation nevertheless remained intact. But the Supreme Court imposed equal electoral districts, and the Voting Rights Act of 1965 belatedly but effectively enfranchised the blacks, substantially reinforcing the Democrats' more liberal wing and enabling moderate politicians to assert their views. Senators in the south became vulnerable to both Republican and even liberal challenges. The symbol of the old order, Senator Harry F. Byrd Jr. of Virginia, fought and held his seat in 1970 and 1976 as an Independent because he could not win the Democratic primary. Four years earlier Howard W. Smith, the southern conservative leader in the House and chairman of the Rules Committee, their procedural bastion, had been ousted in the primary by a liberal Democrat (who then lost the seat to the Republicans). Smith's committee ally and equally reactionary successor, William Colmer, retained his seat in Mississippi until 1972; when he retired at 82 his administrative assistant, Trent Lott, won it with his blessing and still retains it—as a Republican. Thus conservative Democrats are no longer secure electorally; and their tenure of positions of committee power is threatened both by their northern colleagues reaching the top of the seniority ladder, and by the caucus penalising those who defy the party's majority wishes too outrageously.

In addition to these changes in the working of institutions, a gradual reshuffling between the parties was accomplished by the voters and by the politicians themselves.[26] Younger voters entering the electorate chose the party that—irrespective of its history—they currently found more congenial to their views; and so they helped gradually to push the Democrats still further towards liberal positions on the issues, and the Republicans towards conservative ones.[27] Even without the drastic new developments transforming the south, northern politicians from the minority wings of their parties increasingly found their positions untenable, since the same views that helped them win the uncommitted voter at general elections offended their own partisans. In 1968, primary defeats removed Senator Kuchel of California, the minority whip, in a state where liberal Republicans had ruled almost without serious challenge until ten years before, and also Senator Lausche of Ohio, the last thoroughly conservative Democrat from a northern state. Above all, the parties became less and less congenial to those of their members who found themselves out of sympathy with the prevailing view and who have consequently switched their allegiance in large numbers. In the south, the prominent former Democrats turned Republican include Senators Helms and Thurmond of North and South Carolina and ex-Secretary of the Treasury Connally of Texas; in the north, President Reagan and Senator Hayakawa of California, Senator Hatch of Utah, and ex-Attorney General Mitchell of New York. In return, the northern Democrats recruited Senator Riegle of Michigan, ex-Senator Haskell of Colorado, ex-Mayor Lindsay of New York, Representatives Panetta of California, Foglietta of Pennsylvania and Peyser of New York. All these men headed the long lists of conservative Democrats or liberal Republicans who switched, while to count those who did so from the majority wings of either party, the fingers of one hand would need to be painfully amputated. Before the days of the New Deal such changes would have been thought unseemly as well as unnecessary, and so they were often delayed by a generation or two: Attorney General La Follette of Wisconsin is the Democratic heir of the state's great dynasty of progressive Republican congressmen; the leading Rockefeller in politics today is the Democratic governor of West Virginia; the grandfather of ex-Senator Brock of Tennessee, the architect of the 1980 Republican revival, was a conservative Democratic senator from the same state; the grandson of Speaker Garner of Texas, F. D. Roosevelt's conservative vice-president, was a Republican candidate for Congress in the state of Washington.

This long-term process of ideological sorting-out has made internal party divisions much less acute than they were, and some effort to centralise power might have seemed possible. But it ran contrary to the American political tradition, and the organisational framework was in decay. Other obstacles have appeared. No single group of political issues dominates today's agenda as economic and welfare questions did in the days of the New Deal and Great Society, and liberal Democrats are no longer so confident, so united or so sure of majority approval even on those matters. The cultural divisions and conflicts that have always played a major part in American political life have been revived again over questions of racial discrimination, moral standards and the extent to which they should be legally imposed, and in the field of foreign and defence policy into which these domestic disputes are sometimes projected. (In recent years they have plagued the Democrats most, but the Republicans' turn may be coming if the New Right behave as they have threatened to do.) The decline of the old industrial regions, the growth of new industries in the "sunbelt," and the crisis over energy that sets producing against consuming areas, have exacerbated sectional differences. These have arisen also over the distribution of the enormously increased sums spent by the federal government in aid to states or localities, or placing defence-related establishments in one area rather than another.

Short-term electoral considerations have played a part too. After Nixon's disgrace in 1974, many normally Republican districts fell to the Democrats. These freshmen, the "Watergate babies," sought very successfully to entrench themselves by devoted attention to constituency services, and sometimes by adjusting their voting record to suit their conservative districts.[28] Again, after 1980, with a popular Republican President and a much exaggerated impression that the electorate was swinging towards conservatism, a good many southerners preferred to follow his leadership and the wishes of their local business supporters rather than that of their party leaders in the House. These "Boll Weevils" were led from Texas, the southern state with fewest blacks (proportionately) and a Democratic party whose conservative wing is based on economic rather than racial attitudes. In the three critical votes supporting Reagan's budget, they only once attracted a majority of the 78 southern Democratic Congressmen (46, 26 and 36 votes respectively) and never more than a few from northern states (9, 0 and 8), in strong contrast to the preceding decades when the "conservative coalition" of most southerners and most Republicans could frequently control Congress. But with the nominal Democratic majority reduced to fifty, smaller defections were enough to carry the President's programme.

They were sufficient, however, only because of the unexpected and unprecedented unity among Republicans, whose majority in the Senate held together to give Reagan better support (84%) than any of his predecessors had enjoyed since these scores were first compiled in 1949. In the House, Republican rebels on the three key votes numbered 0, 2 and 1. In both chambers they "exhibited more party discipline in support of their president's legislative program in the 1981 session than occurred at any time since the early 1930s";[29] and that, rather than the familiar but now limited indiscipline of a minority of southerners, was the real news of 1981. The liberal Republican minority, the "Gypsy Moths," were already showing signs of unhappiness and did not remain loyal in 1982, when the end of the presidential honeymoon thinned the rebel ranks among Democrats while swelling those among Republicans. Nevertheless, the 1980 election, far from marking another stage in the collapse of the congressional parties, might even begin to reverse that process and supply at last the deficiency underlined by Gerald Pomper three years earlier: "the national parties are more organisationally coherent and better able to enforce a measure of internal discipline. What the parties increasingly lack is a palpable reason for coherence and discipline."[30]

BUILDING NATIONAL PARTIES?

The Republicans began the process of developing a coherent national organisation. Their national chairman, Bill Brock, set out to rebuild the party that Richard Nixon had so neglected and damaged--and to do so from the ground up. He made a major nation-wide effort to recruit strong candidates both at the lowest level, for the state legislatures, and also from within those nurseries of American political talent, to select able people to run for Congress and for statewide office; by 1979 a prominent Democratic political commentator, Michael Barone, was remarking that ten years earlier there had been far more attractive and capable Democratic candidates than Republicans, but in the next few contests the situation would be vastly changed and perhaps entirely reversed.[31] Brock also skillfully exploited the ability of the Republican party to raise much more money than its rival; although its more numerous wealthy supporters were now restricted by campaign finance legislation, they were also supplemented by successful efforts to raise large amounts through small direct-mail contributions, a source the Democrats quite failed to tap. (They raised less from them than John Anderson did.)

Brock used these resources to excellent purpose. The Republicans have always given their National Committee more attention than their rivals; the party's staff has almost invariably been bigger, and in 1977 the disparity had already reached a peak (220 as against 40).[32] Brock used it to provide centrally, with resulting economies of scale, the elaborate technical assistance and services that have become necessary as campaign methods have grown so immensely sophisticated and expensive in recent years. Developing a practice begun under his predecessor, he identified winnable contests and directed money to them at the time it was most useful—early in the campaigning season when it helped challengers to make themselves known, show a respectable prospect of success, and so raise more money from other sources. "For the first time in many years, the largest single contribution almost every Republican candidate received came from—the Republican party."[33] Nor was the effort confined to the more visible offices; again for the first time, even the humble state legislative hopefuls were assisted substantially, with $2 million in 1978 and $3 million in 1980. Amendments to the campaign finance law allowed national parties to contribute directly to state parties and to House and Senate candidates; with more money and effective control of it, the Republicans made the best use of this provision. Local Republican organisations were revived, with the help of 57 professional field organisers,[34] and began appearing in towns across the south where the party had never existed before, although its presidential candidates had been making substantial electoral inroads for two decades or more. There was no such corresponding effort on the Democratic side. What little money that party had was absorbed by the President's campaign; candidates for Congress or for governorships received very little if anything, and those for state legislatures none at all.

Brock did not attempt to use his resources to impose discipline in any crude way: on the contrary, he tried to extend the Republicans' appeal more widely, even into the black community where it was weakest, and he tried to protect liberal Republican senators like Ed Brooke of Massachusetts, whom the ideological conservatives fought in a primary in 1978. (Brooke won, but lost the election to a Democrat.) In 1980 the Republicans as a party ran a major nationwide advertising campaign on television, costing $9 million and modelled on the Conservatives' effort in Britain the year before.

Ronald Reagan was nominated by the right wing of the party but, in sharp contrast to Barry Goldwater 16 years earlier, he promptly set out to reconcile the losers, using the Convention to bring his followers together: all his main rivals were deployed on the podium, he spoke at a rally to raise funds to pay their campaign debts, his own acceptance speech was carefully conciliatory, and he won endorsements from leading liberals such as Senator Javits. In September, in a spectacular demonstration of party unity, he and his running-mate George Bush appeared with nearly 300 congressional candidates on the steps of the Capitol to pledge to work together for a common party programme. The whole tone was unprecedented, and after his victory it was seen to pay political dividends: Republican members of Congress were not merely aware of the President's personal popularity among the voters, but also conscious that their party had helped them to electoral success at the moment when they needed help, and that it could do so again in the future.[35]

The passionate ideological purists, who had seized control of the party in 1964 in the name of principle, had evolved into pragmatic politicians willing for the sake of victory to make compromises that often shocked a younger generation of conservative ideologues; without that evolution Ronald Reagan would have lost, as Barry Goldwater did. On the Democratic side too, the bitter strife between regulars and rebels had led to a victory for the latter, which turned into a joint disaster for both; again the lesson had been learned and the two wings had become reconciled. "Liberal and conservative activists have become 'regulars' in their respective parties. The situation is far different from 1964 [for the Republicans] . . . or 1968 [for the Democrats]."[36] Gary Orren is increasingly justified in contending that the purist/professional distinction is frequently overdrawn, and that—within reasonable limits—the two roles can be reconciled, and often are.

That change has not yet led to any strengthening of the Democratic organisation to match the Republican. Until 1980 it was blocked by President Carter, who treated the National Committee as his exclusive domain. No congressional Democrats owed him anything, for in 1976 he ran behind them everywhere; and four years later they were all too well aware of his unpopularity and anxious to distance themselves from him. The party organisation did nothing at all to assist them. Yet the election results clearly demonstrated, in most unfamiliar fashion, that the voters were to a great extent making a choice between parties. The Democrats lost the White House, half of the Senate seats and a third of the governorships they were defending, and 33 seats in the House of Representatives—a record number for any party losing the Presidency since 1932. (Members have become increasingly secure recently, and the few heavy losses have come only in off-years late in the life of an Administration.) It was, however, the character rather than the magnitude of the losses that was striking. The explanation was not ideological; despite early and superficial reports, liberal Democrats as such fared no worse than moderates or conservatives. Nor was it electoral marginality; on the contrary, long-standing members in supposedly safe seats suffered more than apparently vulnerable juniors. Those who were rejected were the most prominent. In the House, the Democratic whip and the chairmen of four committees and 14 sub-committees were defeated, so that almost two-thirds of the losers had belonged to the party leadership (in the previous six general elections, no chairmen had lost). Three Senate committee chairmen were beaten, and the losers in Democratic seats included 60% of the senior incumbents—those who had served three terms or more—but only 27% of the candidates with less or no service.[37] The Democratic party had controlled both chambers and the White House for four years, and the Republican effort to stigmatise the nominally governing party as directly responsible for failure appeared to have been successful.[38]

The voters' wrath was directed not against a party with a clear yet unpopular policy, but against one in total disarray, for President Carter's own course was far from consistent or coherent, and he had neglected party wishes and advice even more than his predecessors had. There was no Democratic effort organisationally to match the Republicans; they had neither the money nor the impulse, since the President was determined to keep the national committee under his own control in order to avoid any policy embarrassments from his critics or any diversion of its limited resources to any election campaigns but his own. Nevertheless, the Democrats did make drastic changes of a different kind, both before and during Carter's term of office. These changes began with the factional battles of 1968 and 1972, which had led first to defeat and then to disaster. During the subsequent decade serious efforts were made to arrive at a lasting settlement acceptable to the party's rival wings, retaining the reforms that ensured wider access while modifying those that tilted the balance too far against the party's regular supporters and elected spokesmen.

A party charter established a written party constitution for the first time in the United States, though its provisions were modified to meet protests against "Europeanising" the party.[39] The decision was confirmed to call a midterm convention each off-year, offering the activists an opportunity to shape party policy. This idea derived from British party conferences, which now, even more than in the past, have become occasions for bitter factional battles that often do the party more harm than good in the electors' eyes. Yet so far these dangers have been avoided in the United States. To everyone's astonishment, the first mid-term convention, at Kansas City in 1974, provided not a blood-bath but an opportunity for Democrats to halt the feuding of the last six years and work out a compromise on which the party could come together in the 1976 election. The second, at Memphis, caused more trouble but was skillfully managed on the President's behalf; it allowed his liberal critics to win a few concessions (notably 50% representation for women), to express grievances and utter unheeded warnings without wholly disrupting party unity. By 1980 the anti-party tide was on the turn, and the four past chairmen of Democratic rules reform committees all agreed that the changes had gone much too far in the direction of dismantling the organisation.[40] The first sign of the new mood was the DNC's decision that the third mid-term convention (at Philadelphia in 1982) should be mainly composed of party or elected office-holders and not, as hitherto, of delegates especially chosen by the rank-and-file. Another rules reform committee, under Governor Hunt of North Carolina, went back on some of the earlier changes. It sought to limit the primary season and the length of presidential campaigns, abandon the proportional representation requirement, and ensure that party and public office-holders formed at least a seventh (many would have preferred a fourth) of the presidential nominating convention. The intention was to preserve a block of uncommitted votes in the hands of politically experienced delegates, in order, if the primaries were inconclusive, to restore the convention's role as a bargaining arena for selecting the candidate best able to win the election. Another hope was to give the contenders more incentive to assemble coalitions with other politicians before the nomination, which might help in government to revive some links between President and party. It is too soon to judge whether the changes will have the results intended, or instead, like so many earlier reforms, have entirely unexpected consequences.[41]

One striking set of reforms, however, remains and is likely to remain intact. The old cliché that America had a hundred state parties but no national party is now far from the truth. The Democratic National Committee consisted, until 1972, of two members from each state; it was trebled in size to give greater weight to populous states and those that vote Democratic, with some members added to represent various interest groups, from women and blacks to mayors and governors. National Convention delegate allocation reflects almost equally Democratic voting (47%) and state population (53%). The national organs of the party have laid down, and have been sustained by the courts in enforcing, rules to which state parties must conform on pain of exclusion from the convention.[42] Mississippi has been obliged to accept blacks into its state party, where they now play a major part. Illinois has been unable to flout the rules requiring timely and genuine access to the nominating process and an effort to encourage participation by disadvantaged groups. Wisconsin cannot continue to open its Democratic primary to any citizen, whether a Democratic voter or not. The Republicans have shunned changes of this kind but are moving on a different path to a similar destination.

National party influence has grown among the Democrats by way of changing formal rules, among the Republicans by operational changes giving party headquarters a bigger role in campaigns. The reasons are succinctly explained by Cotter and Bibby.

> As the national committees become more institutionalised they become less exclusively focused on presidential politics . . . The nationalisation process reflects the continuity of issues with which the party had to deal over the last thirty years . . . While the Democrats were coping with the problems caused by autonomous state party organisations, the Republicans found quite a different problem: how to survive as a strong competitive force against the electorally dominant Democrats . . . the problems . . . have caused the two parties to follow quite different routes towards nationalisation.[43]

COMPETITIVE PRESSURES

The Democrats now have most incentive to move further towards that goal. In the long run they may find it hard to regain or retain power unless they can contrive a more coherent coalition, with more genuine agreement on political aims than they have managed to present in the last couple of decades. The very extent of their reach is a handicap here, a party preferred by most voters from every social, geographical and ideological group in the country— as the Democrats were in 1977—is bound to alienate some professed supporters, whatever stand it takes.[44] Quarrels and defections are inevitable, and united acceptance of a single presidential candidate is all the harder when policy decisions and symbolic affirmations are embodied in the choice. Without such severe internal strains, the Republicans, in spite of their minority status, are sustained by many and growing assets. Their regular adherents are more likely to vote. Their ranks are regularly swollen by disaffected Democrats. They have easier access to money—and that advantage will increase if they can hold the Senate and attract the funds that business political action committees have hitherto more or less reluctantly given to the Democrats to ensure legislative goodwill for their interest. They have a far better organisation at the centre and better links with the party in the country. They will benefit at all levels— the electoral college, the House, above all the Senate—if they can keep their ascendancy in the west and south-west and continue their expansion in the south; for these areas are enhancing their political influence as the old industrial north-east and midwest decline through migration. The 1982 election disappointed these hopes in the south, but not necessarily permanently.

If the Republicans are seen to have failed by 1984, the Democrats may get back into office through the swing of the pendu-lum. They will then be faced by the same situation as in 1976, and if their reluctance or inability to organise any policy consensus is repeated, they will govern equally ineffectively and may well again be penalised. That is not necessarily inevitable. The Democrats have been accustomed to the status of a governing party for 50 years, and—unlike many Republicans or British Labour Party members—they prefer that role to preaching purity in the wilderness. If they draw the conclusion that survival requires some effort at policy agreement and some tightening of discipline, they are better placed to achieve it than ever before.

The policy and ideological disputes among them are serious, but except on the extreme fringes these are far less acute and over-riding than in earlier years. The machinery for party management exists for the first time. The National Committee has some legitimate authority over state parties and has been liberated at last (for how long?) from presidential dominance and manipulation. The politicians with a long-term interest in the party's survival—whether elected or not—have more chance to influence the choice of a standard-bearer who can win than they have had for 15 years (although their pre-1968 dominance has gone, doubtless for good). The congressional leaders have more practical means in their hands for making their leadership real and not merely nominal, in the form both of machinery for ensuring that a workable and acceptable policy is hammered out and of incentives to obtain compliance from their followers. The voters may react strongly against the consequences, neither announced nor expected, of their decision in 1980 to vote for a change; as in

1932, that reaction might give newly-elected congressmen a motive for supporting rather than sabotaging their nominal leaders, as indeed occurred with the Democrats swept into office by Truman's victory in 1948 and Johnson's landslide in 1964. But neither the DNC nor the Congress is well adapted to provide effective national leadership. As usual in the United States, it will have to come, if at all, from the executive branch. A presidential victory is almost a necessary, but by no means a sufficient, condition for any developments of this kind to take shape.

Even then, it is by no means certain to occur. Long-term survival as a party may point in that direction. But in the short run it may well seem easier to play the traditional game of seeking to mobilise separate and shifting coalitions, differently composed on successive issues and having no long-term mutual loyalty or institutional structure. Within the Democratic party the centrifugal pulls stem from distinct historical traditions, conflicting geographic interests, and ideological differences that may be greatly attenuated but have certainly not disappeared. Politics as usual may well resume, leading before long to public disillusionment as usual—with unforeseeable consequences that will not necessarily be usual at all.[45] But an alternative course is now at least conceivable. No one would expect American parties to become as disciplined and centralised as British ones, with some exaggeration, were supposed to be a few years ago. But, with the Republicans leading the way, they might begin to converge towards the looser but still recognisable form of unity that their British counterparts may be approaching from the other direction. If so, "institutional links to facilitate collective action in politics and government" might become possible. But such a party-in-government "most likely will follow the development and articulation of collective purpose in the country rather than cause it."[46]

The United States is not nearly there yet. But the sweeping generalisations inspired by the bipartisan politics of the issueless Eisenhower years were to prove inapplicable to the bitter ideological conflicts, within or between the parties, that dominated the next decade and a half. Already it seems unlikely that the conservative outlook and often fragmented politics of the later 1970s will prevail indefinitely. When the climate changes, and politicians sense and respond to a new mood in the electorate, some neglected institutional developments will reveal their latent potential. "Even as the parties have become weaker, the general realignment of the party system . . . makes both parties more homogeneous ideologically in the nation at large. This is reflected in the Congress and is a force for cohesion there in an era of individualism. Ideological kinship will also facilitate cooperation between presidents and their congressional party colleagues . . . of immense significance in the long run will be the destruction during the 1970s of old barriers to effective and responsive government. The obstacles to harmonious legislative-executive relations . . . have for the most part been overcome."[47] No doubt the old-style American parties have decayed, probably past the point of no return. No doubt there are continuing problems in the way of developing parties with a purpose, recognisable as such to European observers. But if Americans come to decide they need such parties, as has occasionally happened for short periods in the past, the political components are there waiting to be assembled and the main institutional obstructions have been removed. Neither condition has ever before been met in the history of the United States.

NOTES

1. As J. L. Sundquist points out, strong disciplined local party organisations often weakened the President's power to govern instead of strengthening it; see J. L. Fleishman, ed., *The Future of American Political Parties* (The American Assembly, Columbia U. P., 1982), p. 56.

2. J. L. James, *American Political Parties in Transition* (Harper & Row, 1974), pp. 23-25, cf. 77-79, 102. On Chicago, M. Rakove, *Don't Make No Waves, Don't Back No Losers* (Indiana U. P., 1975), p. 7.

3. S. M. Lipset, ed., *Party Coalitions in the 1980s* (Institute for Contemporary Studies, San Francisco, 1981), p. 427.

4. R. K. Scott and R. J. Hrebenar, *Parties in Crisis* (Wiley, 1979), pp. 61-69.

5. In Fleishman, *The Future of American Political Parties*, especially pp. 6-10.

6. W. Schneider in Lipset, *Party Coalitions in the 1980s*, pp. 218-23; J. Q. Wilson, *The Amateur Democrat* (U. of Chicago Press, 1962, 1966); A. Ware, "Why Amateur Politics Has Withered Away," *European J. of Political Research*, Sept. 1981, pp. 219-36.

7. For these contradictions see K. Janda in W. J. Crotty, ed., *Paths to Political Reform* (D. C. Heath, 1980), pp. 316-27.

8. For the congressional reforms see particularly Chapters 2 and 5 in L. C. Dodd & B. I. Oppenheimer, eds., *Congress Reconsidered*, 1st ed. (Praeger, 1977; CQ Press, 1981); R. H. Davidson, Ch. 4 in T. E. Mann & N. J. Ornstein, eds., *The New Congress* (AEI, 1981).

9. N. W. Polsby in Lipset, *Party Coalitions in the 1980s*, p. 167.

10. Dodd & Oppenheimer, *Congress Reconsidered*, 1st ed., pp. 47-48.

11. B. Hinckley, *Congressional Elections* (CQ Press 1981), pp. 28-29, 55-56, 106-9, 136; G. C. Jacobson, *Money in Congressional Elections* (Yale U.P.,

1980), pp. 122-3; D. Mayhew, *Congress: The Electoral Connection* (Yale U.P., 1974), p. 41.

12. See L. J. Sabato, *The Rise of Political Consultants* (Basic Books, 1981), pp. 225, 241, 283, 322-30.

13. J. F. Bibby in G. M. Pomper, ed., *Party Renewal in America* (Praeger, 1980), pp. 103-7; C. Longley in Crotty, *Paths to Political Reform*, pp. 175-9; J. S. Saloma & F. H. Sontag, *Parties* (Knopf, 1972), pp. 29-37.

14. Longley in Crotty, *Paths to Political Reform*, pp. 168-70; C. F. Casey in Pomper, *Party Renewal in America*, pp. 87-9; A. Ranney, *Curing the Mischiefs of Faction* (U. of California Press, 1975), pp. 20, 83, 180-4; J. G. Stewart, *One Last Chance* (Praeger, 1974), pp. 40-42. Two-thirds rule: R. L. Rubin, *Party Dynamics* (Oxford University Press, 1976), pp. 110-18.

15. The attack was directed equally at other powerful state parties which, like Illinois, achieved similar results by other means.

16. G. M. Pomper, ed., *The Election of 1980* (Chatham House Publishers, Chatham, N. J., 1981), pp. 2-3. On the politicians, see B. E. Shafer, "Anti-Party Politics," in *The Public Interest*, Spring 1981, pp. 95-110; and on the importance of rules such as PR, see J. I. Lengle & B. Shafer, "Primary Rules, Political Power and Social Change," in *Am. Pol. Sci. Rev.*, March 1976, pp. 25-36. A few states abandoned their primaries by 1984.

17. A. Ranney in A. King, ed., *The New American Political System* (AEI, 1978), pp. 230-6; whereas 44% of the population had an annual income of under $10,000 in 1970, and 12% over $20,000, the percentages for delegates to the Democratic Convention were 13 and 52 in 1972, 8 and 70 in 1976. E. Drew, *Portrait of an Election* (Routledge & Kegan Paul, 1981), p. 225, on politicians choosing to stay away.

18. M. Malbin in A. Ranney, *The American Elections of 1980* (AEI, 1981), p. 128; Drew, *Portrait of an Election*, pp. 224-25.

19. Malbin's chapter in Ranney, *The American Elections of 1980*, gives the fullest account.

20. G. M. Pomper, ed., *The Election of 1976* (Longman, 1977), pp. 12-16; and on 1980, Pomper, *The Election of 1980*, pp. 33-34. (Proportional representation could work differently, to check the front-runner's progress, but has not done so yet.)

21. Donald Fraser in August 1981, quoted Lipset, *Party Coalitions in the 1980s*, p. 437. Also A. L. Teasdale, "The Paradox of the Primaries," *Electoral Studies*, April 1982, pp. 43-63; and on the media, D. S. Broder in *Choosing Presidential Candidates* (AEI, 1980: AEI Forum no. 35), pp. 11-14.

22. Discussed sceptically by Saloma & Sontag, *Parties*, pp. 332-42, and enthusiastically by Howard Phillips of the Conservative Caucus in Lipset, *Party Coalitions in the 1980s*, pp. 395-403.

23. Broder, *Choosing Presidential Candidates*, pp. 7, 14, 17-18, 22.

24. Schneider in Lipset, *Party Coalitions in the 1980s*, pp. 223-24 (and in Ranney, *The American Elections of 1980*, p. 261).

25. As shown by W. R. Shaffer, *Party and Ideology in the U. S. Congress*

(University Press of America, 1980) and, on a state-by-state basis, by K. G. Armstrong, "Party, State and Ideology in the U. S. House 1967–76" (paper for APSA Annual Meeting, 1981; both use ACA or ADA scores over a decade) and evident at almost any election over that period (with most exceptions—perhaps a dozen altogether—in 1978).

26. J. L. Sundquist, in a similar assessment, writes that "the diversity within each party is lessening year by year": in Fleishman, *The Future of American Political Parties*, p. 58.

27. E. G. Carmines & J. A. Stimson, "Issue Evolution, Population Replacement, and Normal Partisan Change," in *Am. Pol. Sci. Rev.*, March 1981.

28. W. Schneider & G. Schnell, "The New Democrats," in *Public Opinion*, Nov–Dec. 1978, pp. 7–13; B. Sinclair in Mann & Ornstein, *The New Congress*, p. 206.

29. Lipset, *Party Coalitions in the 1980s*, p. 436. The figures are from *Congressional Quarterly*.

30. Pomper in L. Maisel & J. Cooper, eds., *The Impact of the Electoral Process* (Sage, 1977), p. 35: an excellent summary chapter.

31. *The New Republic*, 16 December 1978.

32. C. P. Cotter & J. F. Bibby, "The Institutional Development of Parties . . . ," *Political Science Quarterly*, Spring 1980, pp. 1–27 (figures on p. 5). In 1979 the *full-time* staffs were 55 and 9 respectively: Sabato, *The Rise of Political Consultants*, p. 295.

33. D. S. Broder in Lipset, *Party Coalitions in the 1980s*, pp. 10–11; he summarises the RNC operation, which is discussed more fully by Bibby in Pomper, *Party Renewal in America*, Ch. 7; by Sabato, *The Rise of Political Consultants*, pp. 290–97, 334–35; by Malbin (pp. 100–1) and by T. E. Mann and N. J. Ornstein in Ranney, *The American Elections of 1980*, pp. 263–67; by R. J. Huckshorn and J. F. Bibby (pp. 82–84) and by F. C. Arterton in Fleishman, *The Future of American Political Parties*, pp. 104–8; by Scott and Hrebenar, *Parties in Crisis*, pp. 275–77; by Longley in Crotty, *Paths to Political Reform*, pp. 188–209.

34. Longley in Crotty, *Paths to Political Reform*, p. 189.

35. Charles O. Jones in Ranney, *The American Elections of 1980*, pp. 88–94; Broder in Lipset, *Party Coalitions in the 1980s*, pp. 10–11; Huckshorn and Bibby in Fleishman, *The Future of American Political Parties*, pp. 92, 99. But note the warning by Arterton in *ibid.*, pp. 129–36.

36. Schneider in Lipset, *Party Coalitions in the 1980s*, p. 224.

37. Author's calculations. In 1982 the Republican leader in the House was almost beaten (favourable redistricting just saved him); senior senators lost badly in votes, though keeping their seats.

38. Pomper, *The Election of 1980*, p. 91; P. Caddell (Carter's pollster and strategist) in Lipset, *Party Coalitions in the 1980s*, p. 300.

39. Longley in Crotty, *Paths to Political Reform*, pp. 172–75; Stewart, *One Last Chance*, pp. 175–77.

40. Pomper, *The Election of 1980*, p. 31.

41. See *The New Republic*, 17 February and 10 March 1982.

42. Longley in Crotty, *Paths to Political Reform*, Ch. 5; Ranney, *Curing the Mischiefs of Faction*, pp. 181–86. Stewart, *One Last Chance*, p. 181 (DNC).
43. Cotter & Bibby, "The Institutional Development of Parties . . . ," pp. 25–26.
44. E. C. Ladd Jr., & C. D. Hadley, *Transformations of the American Party System* (Norton, 2nd ed., 1978), pp. 294–99.
45. W. D. Burnham's characteristically apocalyptic prediction in Lipset, *Party Coalitions in the 1980s*, p. 386.
46. E. C. Hargrove & M. Nelson in E. Sandoz & C. V. Crabb, eds., *A Tide of Discontent* (CQ Press, 1981), p. 62.
47. J. L. Sundquist, *The Decline and Resurgence of Congress* (AEI, 1981), pp. 478, 483.

3

REDISTRIBUTING POWER
IN BRITISH PARTIES

Leon D. Epstein

My attention is fixed on recent changes in candidate and leadership selection within British parties and most specifically on the Labour party's changes of 1980–81. I am more interested in the principles evoked and the trends suggested by that controversy than in the factional triumph that occurred. All of us surely understand that competing leadership groups, based on personal ambitions and economic interests as well as ideological preferences, are prime movers in debates concerning the distribution of power in any party. In the British Labour party no more than elsewhere are new rules adopted, nor old rules defended, purely because of principles. I shall not ignore Labour's power struggle, although I concentrate on the rhetoric of intra-party power redistribution.

The more or less rhetorical principles with which I am concerned are those labeled anti-elitist, anti-oligarchical, populist, participatory, or (in an American context) Jacksonian and progressive. I prefer "progressive," although it has not been a British term either for party reforms or for various nonparty governmental reforms. The closest British equivalent is probably "radical." But I apply the American term to principles used lately in British parties, as they have long been in American, to justify the transfer of power from an established leadership to a new one claiming a broader constituency. The claim, credible at least to its supporters, is readily contested. Opponents, as we shall see, counter with a still more "democratic" claim of their own in behalf of the established leadership. In our age, when legitimacy requires a popular mandate, it is understandable that the terms of debate should be thus defined once there is a challenge to party rules. But that such a challenge should only recently have substantially succeeded in Britain might well seem remarkable to Americans accustomed to a century of far-reaching progressive reforms of party organizations. At any rate, it seems remarkable to me. And I propose to treat British changes from that unabashedly parochial viewpoint.

AN AMERICAN PERSPECTIVE

I must amplify my particular perspective because it is unusual. For many decades, most political scientists have regarded British parties as more modern, meaning more highly developed, than ours.[1] No doubt, they are more modern, now as in much of this century, when measured by familiar criteria. We readily recognize the "advanced" nature of British parties with respect to their national electoral orientations, professional staffing, substantial national headquarters, parliamentary cohesion, regularized dues-paying memberships, and programmatic commitments. From that standpoint, certain recent American party developments, described elsewhere in this volume, represent advances in a British direction. I am thinking particularly of the growth of the Republican National Committee into a much larger and more active headquarters operation, and of the somewhat different Democratic development of an effective national party rule-making authority. One might also add the increasingly national nature of American electoral alignments at least in presidential contests, and, more uncertainly, a few indications of a more clear-cut ideological division between congressional parties. Even the newly successful direct-mail solicitation, notably by Republicans, of many modest contributions could be seen as the functional equivalent of long-standing British party support by numerous dues-payers. Although all of these American developments may well be overshadowed by the extent to which our increasingly candidate-centered politics takes us a greater distance from the British party model, I mention them because they illustrate the usual view of the direction of party modernization.

The reversal that I make here is to treat two important British changes as late and limited responses to claims that have been carried much farther in the United States. The changes themselves are not American, but their *direction* resembles that taken by American progressives when they began to reform parties. The results in the

United States, as we well know, are weak and porous party organizations that do not strike us as modern even though they are plainly characteristic of the United States in the late twentieth century. To be sure, they are not modern insofar as that term implies highly developed organizations. And whether they are modern in the sense of being better or more democratic than former American parties, or later British parties, is controversial. A considerable portion of the American public may like the results, but most political scientists do not. It is entirely possible that the successful claims of intra-party democracy lead to undemocratic results by way of a lessened collective responsibility of leaders to masses of unorganized voters. In the United States, as in Britain, participatory rhetoric may not produce participatory consequences even if such consequences should be genuinely intended by reformers.

Hence, I do not present the triumph of American progressivism in party affairs as the fulfillment of an entirely desirable democratic ideal that Britain either should or will now begin to approach. Like most American political scientists, I am dubious about the weakening of party organizations associated with progressivism. On the other hand, I think of the relevant American changes as "modern" in that they are designed to meet the expectations of many politically active citizens in our twentieth-century circumstances of high educational levels, considerable leisure, and general social mobility. Because such expectations in our time flow from a democratic ethos by no means limited to the United States, we can look with wonder, even awe, at the long resistance of British parliamentary parties and especially of their leaders to the effective, regularized sharing of their organizational power with other intra-party forces.[2] Perhaps it is the resistance, accompanied, to be sure, by occasional concessions, that we should have more explicitly admired during all of the many years that American political scientists looked enviously at British party models. We did recognize that the decidedly limited power of nonparliamentary participants and even of individual back-bench members of parliament (M.P.s) was crucial to the "responsible party government" vainly sought for the United States. But we did not so clearly link that limited power with an old order of insulated leadership. We thought that we were admiring a modern phenomenon instead of an institutional remnant—another of the monuments of the British past that American tourists appreciate.

So accustomed are we in political science to treat British parties as modern relative to American that my approach may strike scholars as annoyingly perverse. No doubt, it would be not merely perverse but wrong, as I have already conceded, to regard many familiar

American party characteristics as more modern than Britain's. And my view of the modernity of American candidate and leadership selection principles is carefully qualified so as not to suggest that particular American practices themselves provide an inevitably modern pattern any more than they fulfill the democratic ideals of their advocates. Accordingly, in the following brief summary of the relevant American practices, I shall try to emphasize the extent to which they are the product of special national experiences unlikely to be duplicated elsewhere. They remain, it is true, significant components of my comparative perspective but mainly because of the general principles that led to their establishment.

In selecting candidates, that is, in party nominations for Congress and most other nonpresidential offices, the widely accepted direct primary is itself so distinctively American that it seems more odd than modern to students of comparative politics. Only in the United States do mere party voters (and in some states, like mine, even voters who do not identify publicly as party voters) have the power under law to determine in government-run elections who shall bear party labels in subsequent general elections.[3] Note well that it is the state, not the party organization, that establishes the rules for both candidate eligibility and voter participation, and that the state runs the nominating contests as it does the general elections. Here as well as in related organizational respects, the party is converted into a quasi-governmental agency or a highly regulated public utility. However extraordinary such status is in the universe of comparative parties, it is part of the means by which the direct primary transfers a most consequential power from party leaders and also from party activists to a much more numerous and loosely defined body of participants.

In this light, it is well to recall that the direct primary was adopted in most places to replace the selection of party candidates by local caucuses and state conventions that had also, since Jacksonian times, been meant to be less plainly oligarchical and more open to party identifiers than either office-holding leadership caucuses or dues-paying membership organizations. Of course, local caucuses and state conventions, like direct primaries afterwards, often failed to function as popular participatory mechanisms, but the intention is unmistakable in nineteenth-century American experience. Rhetorically at any rate, democratic legitimacy has long been accorded only to relatively open methods of candidate selection. The direct primary, now by far the most widely accepted of those methods in the United States, is really an extreme alternative although a familiar one. Why American states went so far as to deprive party organizations of the power to assign their own labels is explicable only as a reaction to the strength and corruption characterizing the old American patronage parties—the machines—at the very time that states legally recognized parties by printing their names on government-provided ballots.

Equally extreme and distinctive is the American party's selection of its national leader through the post-1968 presidential nominating process. Here, too, the primary, in its preference form, has become dominant after over a half-century of varying influence in nominating contests. But even during most of the nineteenth century, before the primary played any role, the national nominating conventions were designedly broader party affairs than the congressional nominating caucuses that they had replaced. At these conventions, the state and local party leaders, who effectively bargained and thus settled nominations, acted as a confederative group that was by no means exclusively or even largely Washington-based. It has been a long time since anyone seriously proposed a return to nomination by congressional caucuses. Those who are now critical of the post-1968 plebiscitary system want only to include members of Congress along with state and local leaders in reviving something like the old convention bargaining possibilities. Most of the revivalists do not hope to abolish presidential primaries but merely to limit them, often in favor of open participatory caucuses. Hence, what Anthony King correctly calls "the peculiar features of America's way of selecting candidates for the country's highest office"[4] are likely to remain as part of the distant perspective with which I approach the relatively modest changes in British party practice. I shall separately discuss the changes in candidate selection and then those in leadership selection before trying to treat the two sets of changes as parts of broader British developments.

CANDIDATE SELECTION

The long-established and still unchallenged basic principle of British parliamentary candidate selection is that the party label is bestowed by the authority of an organized dues-paying membership in each constituency. As a branch of a national party, the constituency organization ordinarily consists of members loyal to that party's cause and thus responsive to its influence. The national organization's influence, however, is seldom exercised heavy-handedly, and only in unusual circumstances does a central headquarters seek to reverse a constituency association's selection of a candidate. Notably in the absence of an incumbent M.P. wanting to stand again under the given party label, a constituency association, whether Labour, Conservative, or Liberal, now as in the past exercises a substantial freedom of choice.[5] Party members, more particularly their local officers and activists, possess effective power antedating any recent changes. The legitimacy of that power has generally been taken for granted. As long as constituency associations have fairly numerous memberships (now often a dubious assumption), their democratic credentials seem sufficient and evidently better than those of the old American bosses or those of a national party headquarters acting on its own. To be sure, even a large association of a few thousand members is much smaller than the total of a party's voters in the constituency. But Britain is hardly unusual in excluding voters who do not want to join a party from a direct role in selecting its candidates.

Except, therefore, from the standpoint of the peculiar American progressive commitment to the direct primary, the democratic legitimacy of Britain's organizational control of candidate selection is more likely to be questioned because of limited membership participation in the process than because only members can participate. Oligarchical practices are readily apparent even, perhaps especially, when association memberships are large. Typically, small selection committees of ten to twenty local leaders produce short lists of three to seven likely candidates (from among many more applicants in an open seat); then, a larger body of 100 or more representatives of the membership (often its general management or executive committee) chooses one prospective candidate after a meeting when they hear the short-listed aspirants. Apart from a usually pro forma clearance with the national office, no other approval is required in the Labour party.[6] Conservative associations have general meetings in which all party members have the opportunity to accept (as they almost always do) or reject the choice of their representatives. But the consequential steps in the process—the short-listing and the subsequent selection of one candidate—are in both parties essentially private matters. They customarily take place without observers from the public or the news media.

In exceptional instances, however, the oligarchical features of candidate selection have been subjected to scrutiny and criticism well before the most recent debate over rules changes.[7] Significantly, these instances almost always involved a constituency association's attempt to use its power to replace its sitting M.P., for, unlike the association's largely unquestioned freedom to choose when selecting a candidate for an open seat, the rejection of an incumbent able and willing to stand again violated a widely cherished though not quite uniformly observed political convention. Astounding from an American standpoint, the convention holds that a constituency association should not deny readoption to its M.P. because it disagrees with the M.P.'s policy positions. Denial of readoption becomes less illegitimate, it is true, if an M.P.'s positions are also offensively at odds with those of his parliamentary party. Mainly, therefore, the convention protects M.P.s against the consequences of disagreements with their own local selectors. In this light, the convention looks like a residual Burkean principle in which M.P.s are no mere delegates but representatives entitled to exercise their own judgment of issues. But since M.P.s are expected, under another compelling convention, to vote most of the time, if not nearly all the time, with their parliamentary party, the Burkean principle is less than pure. It is further diluted by the tendency of M.P.s to answer constituency party attacks by appealing to the larger number of party voters who are not party members or activists.

As the previous paragraph implies, the convention favoring readoption has not always protected M.P.s even in the many years before the recent challenge to it in the Labour party. There were several well-publicized Conservative as well as Labour cases in each of the decades after World War II, and the M.P.s did not always survive.[8] Yet they were uncommon affairs in which personal attributes were often intertwined with policy considerations in influencing the outcomes. And they were portrayed in the national press as violations of a constitutional norm. They thus became political embarrassments to the party whose local branch had used its power to replace one M.P. with another (which, in practice, it does when the constituency is so safe for a given party that its candidate almost invariably wins the general election). Not only was it unusual to employ that power, but it was virtually illegitimate. It still is the latter in the Conservative party, although perhaps less unusual than it was in the past.

Only the Labour party has now officially reacted against the convention by changing its national rules so as to legitimize the substitution of a new candidate for a sitting M.P. Until 1980, Labour rules also sought to institutionalize the conventional protection of incumbents. The Conservative party merely stipulated, and it still stipulates, that a constituency association may not begin the process of selecting a new candidate without first refusing readoption to a sitting member by a majority vote taken at a special meeting to which all the association's dues-paying members are invited. The Labour party, however, had protected its incumbents by requiring a constituency party seeking to drop its M.P. against the M.P.'s wishes to follow a complicated procedure in which the proposed action was considered at three separate representative committee meetings, each of which the M.P. was to attend and from which he could appeal an adverse decision, on procedural grounds, to the party's National Executive Committee.[9] Such rules, like the convention on which they were based, did not prevent the most determined of constituency associations from displacing their M.P.s, but they made action both more difficult and less likely. To be sure, it is neither easy nor likely in the United States that an incumbent member of Congress can be denied renomination. But even the safest of American incumbents does not enjoy the institutionalized protection of the old British convention. It has always been entirely legitimate to try to dislodge a member of Congress in a primary or nominating (or endorsing) convention.

By changing its rules in 1980, Labour has now similarly legitimized party reselection challenges although in circumstances vastly different from the American.[10] In contrast to anything resembling a primary election, even of only party members, the same old candidate-selecting bodies have simply had their power effectively enlarged so as to allow a free choice despite the presence of a sitting M.P. The British terminology is confusing because the new procedure is called mandatory or automatic reselection. It does not mean, as the term might suggest, that an M.P.'s reselection is automatic in the old manner. On the contrary, mandatory reselection means that a Labour M.P. will be less automatically reselected than in pre-1980 times. Now the sitting M.P. who wants again to be Labour's candidate must be reselected in a process like that of selection for an open seat. In fact, constituency parties are required to short-list other aspiring candidates, if any, along with the M.P. It is not sufficient for a constituency party to decide to have no contest by voting to reselect its M.P. Something like that procedure—a compromise in which a party could opt for or against competitive reselection—had been rejected by the 1980 Labour Conference before it adopted its mandatory reselection rule. In practice, during 1981 and 1982 the new rule was dodged by the device of short-listing only the sitting M.P., but this has been officially discouraged as being against the spirit of the conference decision. Yet inevitably constituency parties without dissident movements against their M.P.s will do little more than go through the motions of reselection contests.[11]

By no means, however, does the new rule mean merely a formal change in every constituency. Often enough, it has the effect that its sponsors had intended: the displacement of moderate, centrist, or right-of-center M.P.s by left-wing candidates, and, short of that, the pressure of reselection threats to influence sitting M.P.s to follow left-wing preferences within the Parliamentary Labour Party (PLP) and the House itself. The rhetoric favoring the rule change was consistent with this left-wing factional purpose. As the final speaker said on behalf of the Conference change in 1980: "I ask you to support the enfranchisement of the people in the constituency parties. . . ."[12] Unconvincing though this rhetoric must be for those who regard the limited membership of constituency parties as unrepresentative of the electorate, it is not readily turned away by a reaffirmation of the status quo ante. After all, the constituency party bodies now given reselection powers are the same agencies long accepted as adequate selectors of candidates for open seats and thus of those candidates now serving as M.P.s. Unrepresentative or not, Labour's local party leaders and committees, like the Conservatives', exercise a well-established authority in choosing parliamentary candidates.

Nevertheless, it is in the last decade that the authority has been more frequently questioned, particularly in the Labour party. Several related circumstances account for the questioning. First, individual membership in the Labour party has declined so sharply since the early 1950s that by the late 1970s only about 250,000 to 300,000 direct dues-paying members remained, although over twice that number were officially recorded. Accordingly, only 13% of Labour's constituency parties had over 1,000 members, and more than half of the parties had fewer than 500 members. The Labour totals were considerably lower than the Conservative membership, which, though halved since the early 1950s, was still estimated in the range of 1 to 1.5 million.[13] The fact that Labour's direct individual membership is so low has relevance for the legitimacy of party candidate selection despite the indirect affiliation to Labour of over 6 million trade unionists. Trade unions are able not only to dominate national party conferences, but also, through their delegates on local party general management committees, to help determine the choice of parliamentary candidates in many places. Their power, exercised as it is by union leaders rather than directly by the rank-and-file, is not so obviously legitimate, in democratic terms, as the actions of individual dues-paying members. Thus with only limited numbers of direct duespayers in a local party the power that they employ, though often in conjunction with trade union leaders, is suspect.

Secondly, the power of Labour's constituency parties is specifically suspect because it had frequently been taken over by left-wing militants who thrive in already small membership organizations that they may make still smaller by discouraging moderate but less devoted Labour participants. Evidence from the 1970s indicates that Trotskyites and Marxists of other persuasions have thus successfully practiced "entryism" in permeating some local Labour parties.[14] But there has also been a more widespread if less spectacular takeover by nonrevolutionary socialists, who are nonetheless well to the left of the party's customary parliamentary leadership, and the majority of Labour M.P.s who have supported that leadership.[15] Among these socialists, with whom the still more militant entryists may choose to work in various situations, are Tribunites, an old left group supporting Aneurin Bevan in the 1950s as well as his heirs (including Michael Foot) in more recent years, and the followers of Tony Benn, the leading left-of-center champion of a socialist version of participatory democracy ever since the late 1960s. Benn himself was a potential beneficiary of the participatory campaign to change Labour's rules for candidate and leadership selection. His chance of becoming Labour's leader could have been improved by any reduction in the independent power of Parliamentary Labour Party (PLP) members. His popularity seemed greater among constituency activists and some left-wing trade unionists than among his fellow Labour M.P.s.

Hence, the third circumstance leading to questions about the legitimacy of the long-standing candidate-selecting authority of Labour's constituency associations was the increasingly evident use of that authority to choose Bennites or other left-wing candidates. Such use was not entirely new; for several decades and perhaps longer, left-wing candidates were advantaged in some Labour selections (as right-wing candidates were sometimes in Conservative selections). Thus, with left-wing Labour candidates chosen in many marginal seats, the number of left-wing Labour M.P.s rose as a result of the electoral swing to Labour in the elections of 1964 and 1966. But in the 1970s another phenomenon came to the fore. Left-wing Labour M.P.s tended to replace moderate Labour M.P.s, so that even when the party lost numerous marginal seats and so their disproportionately left-wing M.P.s, as it did in 1979, the total number of left-wing M.P.s did not decline appreciably. The replacement making for that result did not, however, follow from any large number of violations of the old convention concerning a sitting M.P. having to be reselected. The violations that did occur were dramatic, but more often associations merely replaced dead or retiring M.P.s with new, more left-wing candidates.[16] In short, the active constituency party members, however few, had begun more pointedly to use an established power to achieve their ends and those of their factional leaders. It is not a long step from that usage to the reselection rule change of 1980. The one almost as much as the other was ill-regarded by the defenders of the old order. They thus raised doubts even before 1980 about the legitimacy of selection by Labour's constituency parties.

Nevertheless, the rule change of 1980 made the doubts about the process more salient. It took only a limited number of purges of Labour M.P.s to raise concern. In 1981 and early 1982, there were but seven actual ousters, including one especially well-publicized action against a former cabinet minister who was also a former chairman of the national party. Significantly, however, a larger group of sitting Labour M.P.s withdraw from potential reselection contests and, in several instances, joined the new Social Democratic party that had seceded from Labour in 1981. Altogether, it is reasonably estimated that two to three dozen Labour M.P.s were thus affected by reselection through April 1982.[17]

In criticizing Labour constituency associations for their post-1980 actions against moderate M.P.s, as in criticizing earlier actions of a similar import, opponents emphasize the small and arguably unrepresentative character of the selectors. Although Labour's associations, like those of other parties, must vary considerably both in size and in participatory quality, many of them have an inherently oligarchical element often of crucial importance. The General Management Committee, serving as each association's highest governing authority, consists of members—ordinarily over 100—from the party's several local federated components, mainly ward units of individual dues-paying members *and* trade unions that affiliate their members locally as well as nationally. Principally because of their federative structure, accommodating the trade-union affiliation, Labour's constituency associations do not and apparently cannot conveniently have a general meeting of all their local "members." Most trade-union members indirectly affiliated to the party are not identifiable as individuals eligible to attend any such meeting. Hence, as noted earlier, Labour's General Management Committee is the final constituency-level candidate selector, in contrast to the Conservative arrangement in which a general meeting of all local members is given the opportunity to confirm or reject a committee choice.

The particular Conservative procedure, because it tends to be pro forma, does not often commend itself to critics of Labour's selection practices. But the basis on which it rests, an exclusively direct individual membership, does appeal to critics. Specifically, moderate Labour M.P.s, calling themselves the Manifesto Group, proposed in the 1970s that their party's constituency associations should cease to be federations of delegates, governing as General Management Committees, and become instead general membership bodies.[18] Such bodies could then select candidates, but not necessarily by the Conservative-style meeting. Instead, dues-paying members could cast ballots by mail or at polling places operated by the party.

From a democratizing standpoint, the balloting proposal is unquestionably attractive, especially when coupled with the Manifesto Group's hope that membership would rise once the association's structure had been changed. But changing that structure did not look politically feasible in the 1970s. Nor does it look so now. As Dennis Kavanagh has said, "the British Labour Party, because of its adherence to delegatory democracy, has to reject the principle of one man one vote."[19] Nevertheless, the Manifesto Group's unviable proposal is significant in terms of the British debate over candidate selection in the Labour party as well as outside it (where one person one vote is feasible). The proposal was a not untypical means by which established leaders seek in a democratic age to counter the professedly democratic challenge of their factional opponents. Rather than merely defending the old order, which had satisfied many moderate Labour M.P.s as long as they were rarely rejected by the small leadership groups that had selected them in the first place, they moved a notch beyond their challengers by suggesting a more fully participatory arrangement under which they could expect to fare better than they would under the challengers' preferred method. Their slogan might well be the old American progressive cry: the cure for the defects of democracy is more democracy.

The same observation can be made about another British candidate-selection proposal to emerge in the late 1970s. The Hansard Society's Commission on Electoral Reform, going much farther in the American direction than the Manifesto Group and addressing itself to all British parties, suggested that the law require that "registered members" (apparently meaning official dues-payers) have the opportunity to cast secret ballots, financed from public sources, so as to determine their party's candidate. Interestingly, the Commission did not want the procedure normally applied to sitting M.P.s, but otherwise it was proposing in the British context a highly progressive step (or, as the British would say, a radical step).[20] The proposed step was still well short of the American direct primary in two vital respects. It did not open candidate selection to ordinary non-dues–paying party voters, and it did not establish a government-run primary election. On the other hand, the Commission did suggest governmental action to the extent of a law requiring parties to conduct elections under certain stipulated rules and with publicly provided funds.

One can detect a resemblance to late nineteenth-century American statutory efforts to regulate party candidate selection before their apparent ineffectiveness led to the imposition of the direct primary. But the failure of those old American efforts is probably irrelevant in contemporary Britain. The Hansard Commission's regulations could work in parties with regular dues-paying members, as the American regulations could not in the absence of such memberships. Difficulties, of course, might still arise even apart from those posed by Labour's confederative structure. A dues-paying membership, when defined by a party, leaves room for padding the rolls, and certainly for charges that rolls are packed. The problem has surfaced in Australian experience when parties, on their own, have selected candidates by conducting "plebiscites" of their members.[21]

Neither the Hansard proposal, nor anything else approximating the American direct primary, is a serious short-run possibility in either the Labour or the Conservative party. Nor is it for the Liberals and the new Social Democratic party, although both (like the Conservatives) have entirely individual dues-paying memberships that may well play influential roles in selecting candidates. The Social Democrats once proposed that members belong to area associations covering several parliamentary constituencies, and that members of these area units select the candidates.[22] Whatever balloting mechanism is finally adopted by the new party as well as by older parties, the direction of any change—however small—is familiar in light of American experience. Saying this about the Labour change is, I know, at odds with the public perception of oligarchical groups, narrower than before, that have increased their power to select candidates. But, as I have argued, advocates of the change claim, however mistakenly, a participatory mandate that their opponents now contest by suggesting more participatory procedures.

LEADERSHIP SELECTION

A progressive pattern of development is similarly evident in leadership selection. Here, too, recent British changes and serious proposals for further changes are indeed modest by comparison with practices in the United States. The changes, however, constitute significant steps away from the long-established British practice in which only

M.P.s have selected their party's national leader. That practice, still accepted by the Conservative party, resembles no American leadership-selection method used since the abandonment after 1824 of the congressional party caucus's nomination of presidential candidates. Much as that abandonment confirmed the constitutional separation of executive and legislative branches, leaving the legislative parties only the power to select their own leaders, so the contrasting British practice can be regarded as the product of a parliamentary system in which a party's leadership in the House of Commons is also its actual or potential executive leadership. Given that system's constitutional principle of executive responsibility to a Commons majority, that is, ordinarily to a majority party, it follows that the members of the majority should choose the leader who heads the executive.[23] However impeccable this British constitutional argument, it excludes the more numerous dues-paying party members, activist or not, from the actual leadership selection. Although they might nevertheless exert an indirect influence on the outcome, they have under the traditional doctrine no more of a right to vote in the process than have ordinary electoral party identifiers.

Despite the force of the British constitutional argument on behalf of leadership selection exclusively by parliamentary parties, it is nevertheless remarkable that the practice was not seriously challenged before the 1970s. So it seems from my American perspective—derived from the United States—and also from a broader North American perspective based partly on Canadian experience. For Canada's major party leaders, who also become prime ministers, have for over half a century been chosen by national conventions of delegates mainly from constituency associations. That practice, though probably derived from the United States, has turned out to be compatible with the working of a parliamentary system and even of one largely adapted from Britain. Like U.S. leadership selection, the Canadian method tends to widen the choice so as to include candidates with little or no national legislative experience.[24] British practice, on the other hand, has surely narrowed the choice to old and experienced parliamentary hands. In this respect, Britain differs not only from Canada but also in some degree from certain nations whose parliamentary parties have retained the authority to choose their national leaders. And by no means have all parliamentary parties even outside North America kept the same full leadership-selection authority that has characterized traditional British practice. Although parties in Australia and New Zealand have on this score closely resembled their British counterparts, many elsewhere (West Germany, for example) have in one way or another institutionalized the participation of extraparliamentary organizations in the process of selecting leaders.[25]

The old British leadership-selection method, however, appears less extreme at its end of a broad comparative spectrum than does the American method of nominating presidential candidates at the other end. Thus, Anthony King understandably treats the British method as closer to a comparative norm when he analyzes the American nominations of 1976 and 1980 alongside the British experience in the 1970s—the Conservative contest won by Margaret Thatcher in 1975 and the Labour contest (still within the parliamentary party) won by James Callaghan in 1976. Written against the background of widespread dissatisfaction with the American choices of Carter and Reagan in 1980, King's discussion suggests the relative virtues of the long-standing British system and notably of its peer review of aspiring leaders by their experienced governmental and parliamentary colleagues.[26] Those virtues were conspicuously absent from the new American plebiscitary method that had by 1976 virtually eliminated the decisive role of state and local leaders as well as of members of Congress, and that came close to transforming a party affair into a general public process. Many of us, therefore, yearn for something closer to the old British order in which the power to choose leaders was firmly in the hands of those most familiar with the debating performance, political knowledge, ministerial ability, and personal character of the contenders. One can acknowledge the advantages of peer review in these respects while arguing that members of a parliamentary party may have no stronger claims than nonparliamentary activists in judging the electoral appeal of potential leaders.

Interestingly, until 1965 peer review was conducted by the British Conservative party in a different manner from its now established system, resembling Labour's pre-1980 system, in which the 200 to 400 M.P.s of a major party vote to choose their leader. When holding a parliamentary majority, the Conservatives before 1965 had no election when their leader and prime minister died or resigned, but relied on consultation among their elder statesmen to produce an emergent consensual choice to be recommended to the monarch and subsequently accepted by the party. And, when out of power, the pre-1965 Conservatives also relied heavily on informal consultations rather than on an election to settle on a leader.[27] Certainly the process qualified as peer review, even as peer review by the few more highly qualified by knowledge, experience, and competence than were the whole body of M.P.s. Back-bench M.P.s were nevertheless taken into account, since the support of most of them for a particular leader was ultimately necessary.

But so indirect a selection process, despite its genuinely high level of peer review, yielded finally to the more evidently democratic method by which Conservative M.P.s now choose their party leader—through successive ballots, if necessary, to produce a majority winner. The Conservative process, with some elaboration and change since 1965, formally at least can be said to have broadened participation beyond Labour's pre-1980 arrangement in that a provision was made for ascertaining the preferences of Conservative constituency associations.[28] The decision-making power, however, has remained firmly lodged in the parliamentary party. Even so, the 1965 switch was a consequential if modest participatory step. Of the two Conservative leaders chosen by voting in the parliamentary party, the first, Edward Heath in 1965, might have emerged under the old system, but the second, Margaret Thatcher in 1975, is believed to be the product of a back-bench rebellion against the established leadership. Successful rebellions against Conservative leaders, particularly those losing general elections, were not new, but they had tended in the past to be managed by established figures who put one of their own in power. Margaret Thatcher, despite her considerable national experience, was a new and surprising choice in her party.[29]

However consequential the post-1965 Conservative change in leadership-selection method, it cannot be seen as a precursor of Labour's rule change in 1980–81. At most, the new Conservative practice provided the kind of intraparliamentary party participation that Labour had long had. It was the Liberal party that pioneered before 1980 in going beyond the constituency of M.P.s in its leadership selection—specifically by having its organized membership choose a national leader in 1976. To be sure, with barely more than a dozen M.P.s, the Liberal party was in a sharply different situation from that of a major party. Liberals had a special reason to seek a broader mandate. Yet they had not similarly responded to that reason during the previous 30 years, when they had had only six to 14 M.P.s. As late as 1967, a dozen Liberal M.P.s chose Jeremy Thorpe. But when Thorpe's forced resignation in 1976 again created a vacancy in the leadership, the Liberals quickly adopted a broader election method that they had been contemplating over previous months.[30] This timing is so close to the years when Labour began seriously to discuss changes in its leadership selection that it suggests a common participatory or progressive spirit that the admittedly great differences in intentions and in results should not entirely conceal.

The new Liberal method left only the proposing of candidates for the leadership in the hands of M.P.s; a candidate had to be an M.P. and to be nominated by three M.P.s. The election itself was by Liberal constituency parties, each of which held a meeting of its individual members to assign its leadership votes. The number of votes allotted to each constituency party had been fixed by a formula that included bonuses in proportion to votes cast for the constituency's Liberal candidate in the previous general election. Results from each constituency party were delivered to a central counting service that tabulated and announced the winner—David Steel—after a three-week campaign against a substantial opponent. No subsequent election was held as of 1983, and none is required as long as there is no vacancy. Nevertheless, the method is evidently accepted in the Liberal party. It reflects the antiestablishment spirit that the new party has sought to represent in the last few decades. As a close professional observer who is himself a staunch Liberal said, the "demand for this more democratic method reflected the growing strength of the newer members . . . determined to apply within the party the sort of participatory democracy that they were preaching in government and industry."[31]

The similarity of the Liberal rhetoric to that of the Labour left in its challenge to the old rules is worth noticing, although the one party probably did not influence the other. The campaign to change Labour's leadership selection method, like the related campaign to change candidate selection practices, was an internal affair that required no Liberal, Conservative, or other party models. So much can be acknowledged while still insisting on the rough parallelism of the movements for change elsewhere in Britain during the last decade or two.

Let us look more closely at the way Labour changed its leadership selection. The crucial period ran from October 1980 through January 1981, because it took two party conferences, the usual annual one in October and a special conference in January, to establish a new method.[32] The October conference, the same one that finally instituted mandatory reselection of parliamentary candidates, voted to widen the leadership electorate beyond the parliamentary party, but it rejected each proposed widening formula and hence required the January conference to settle the question. Before that special conference was assembled at Wembley, the PLP had one more opportunity to choose a leader; its rules required an election at the beginning of a new annual parliamentary session in November. And instead of the usual unchallenged reelection, there was a contest among several contenders seeking to succeed the retiring leader, James Callaghan. The PLP's choice of the personally popular leader of the old left, Michael Foot, over the moderate Denis Healey, who had earlier been expected to win, is calculated to have been marginally but decisively influenced by M.P.s who wanted to avoid choosing anyone who would seem provocative to a newly constituted body of leadership selectors.[33] Healey, however, became deputy leader—a position that, like the leadership itself, would soon be subject to selection by a larger Labour party constituency than the PLP.

Determining how that constituency would be polled was complicated by Labour's federative structure as well as by a desire to retain a substantial role for the PLP. Nothing so simple and straightforward as "one member (one dues-paying member), one vote" could fit that structure as it had the Liberal party's membership and as it could the Conservative party's. As in candidate selection so in leadership selection, Labour's participation had to be largely indirect unless the party drastically revamped its basic organizational structure. Such revamping was not a serious possibility at the Wembley conference; no more than about 5 to 6% of the delegates favored any method involving individual membership ballots.[34] Overwhelmingly, the delegates opted for an electoral college where the votes of affiliated trade unions, constituency parties, and the PLP would be recorded at annual party conferences. Each of these components would have its own mechanism for ascertaining the leadership preferences of its members—by ballot of all M.P.s in the PLP but probably through representative committees or elected officials in unions and in many constituency parties. The well-known oligarchical tendencies of unions and constituency parties might not preclude considerable membership participation and consultation in some units. In any case, such tendencies, though readily dramatized as boss rule in the leadership selection process, were hardly new in Labour's decision-making process—for example, in dealing with policy resolutions. Block voting, notably by the leaders of the largest trade unions, had long dominated Labour conferences. For example, at the 1980 conference, trade unions cast almost 7 million votes and constituency parties fewer than 700,000.

The closely contested issue at Wembley was not, therefore, about the principle of indirect representation and so of the practice of block voting. So much was widely accepted for leadership selection, as it had always been for conference decisions generally. The contentious matter was the weighting of each of the three components in the new electoral college. In particular, what percentage of the college's vote—30, 50, 75, or something in-between—should the PLP have? Labour's new leader, Michael Foot, argued for a compromise relatively favorable to the PLP: 50% for it, and 25% each for the unions and the constituency parties. But he lost to more astute tacticians who, despite an apparent majority for at least the 50% figure, succeeded in securing a formula that gave the unions 40% and the PLP and constituency parties each 30%.[35] Whether these percentages will remain fixed is uncertain, but their short-run impact led to the presentation of Labour in the news media as a party that had transferred its leadership selection from M.P.s to trade-union bosses. Another consequence was to encourage the withdrawal of the moderates who had most openly fought the transfer and who within a couple of months had founded the new Social Democratic party.

Labour's first use of its new electoral college occurred in October 1981. Foot's leadership itself was not contested, but Healey as deputy leader was challenged by two M.P.s to his left, Tony Benn and John Silkin. Benn, with considerably more support outside than inside the PLP, became the major opponent. On a second ballot, required because none of the three had a majority on the first, Benn nearly won with 49.6% of the vote to Healey's 50.4%. He had outpolled Healey by nearly four to one in the constituency parties while losing by a little less than two to one in the PLP and by only five to three among unions.[36] The new leadership selection rule, in its 40–30–30 representational form, worked very nearly as Benn and his supporters had hoped. Benn himself could not benefit from the party's second use of the 40–30–30 formula to choose, in October 1983, both its leader and deputy leader in succession to Foot and Healey. Having failed to win a parliamentary seat in the general election of May 1983, Benn was not a contender. Instead, the beneficiary was Neil Kinnock, a younger and more widely acceptable left-of-center M.P. who won the leadership with 71% of the electoral-college vote and with majorities in each of its three sections—unions, constituency parties, and PLP. Moreover, his chief rival, the centrist Roy Hattersley, subsequently won the deputy leadership, with 67% of the vote, over a Bennite candidate. Enough trade-union votes, as well as others, were so cast as to produce relatively consensual and healing results. Hence, the 1983 leadership-selection experience hardly supports an argument, within the Labour Party, for abandoning the new system. Re-establishing anything like the old PLP monopoly appears even less realistic than it did before.

There is a much better chance for proposals to provide more meaningful extraparliamentary participation in leadership selection than the new rule now provides. Even at the time of the Wembley conference, such proposals were debated. The most drastic of them, as we have seen, was overwhelmingly rejected at least partly because it required direct individual voting in an otherwise federative structure. But even that proposal for one member, one vote is worth further notice as an illustration of escalating, or ratcheting, democratization once the established order is effectively challenged.

Specifically, the election of the party leader by all Labour party dues-paying members was advocated by David Owen, a prominent PLP moderate who opposed the Bennite reforms at Wembley before becoming one of the "gang of four" who subsequently formed the Social Democratic party.[37] Not all of his fellow moderates may have embraced Owen's radical alternative; some apparently adhered to the old PLP monopoly or to a relatively slight sharing of its power. Owen himself asserted that he had favored "one member, one vote" during pre-Wembley discussions in the PLP's shadow cabinet, and his commitment could well have been genuinely principled and not merely a last-minute expedient to forestall the substitution of the block-voting electoral college for the cherished full PLP authority. It is, however, fair to say that not much, if anything, had been heard of Owen's one member, one vote alternative before it became likely that the PLP would lose its sole power. But at Wembley the proposal rhetorically outflanked Bennite democratization. "No socialist party in Western Europe," Owen declared, "has a block vote." Moreover, he argued that the day the block-vote system is used to elect a prime minister (as it would be when a leader had to be chosen for a Labour parliamentary majority), "the whole country will be watching the procedures, and then these procedures will be shown to be undemocratic."[38]

Unpersuasive at Wembley, where Owen's direct membership selection was bound to be perceived as a last-ditch opposition to Bennism, the proposal later became the available alternative for the new Social Democratic party to use instead of M.P. selection. But in the Labour context of 1981 Owen's proposal was a more meaningful alternative to the electoral college system being adopted. Why, one might ask, would moderate, centrist, and right-wing Labour M.P.s have then preferred the direct over the indirect method of extraparliamentary balloting? Apart from possibly thinking it more democratic in principle, they could perhaps have found it politically more attractive on the not unusual assumption that they had greater support among a relatively inactive party majority than among militant activists dominating many local associations and perhaps now certain unions as well. The perception is familiar in the United States, where pragmatic politicians have been known to favor presidential primaries among ordinary party voters as an escape from issue-oriented activists capable of controlling open caucuses.[39] Such politicians might really have preferred the old and manipulated closed caucuses, but when going back to them had become as unlikely as the restoration of the PLP monopoly was for Labour moderates, the primaries looked better than open caucuses. And, like primaries in relation to caucuses, Owen's "one member, one vote" option also looked clearly more democratic than the militants' preferred arrangements.

This is not to say that Owen's proposal, or anything like it, could now have greater appeal in the Labour party than it had at Wembley. In fact, it must have become even less of a live option once Owen and his fellow moderates departed to form the Social Democratic party. One suspects that these moderates took with them most of the little intraparty support for a sharp break with Labour's federative structure now further institutionalized in the electoral college. Nevertheless, the progressively democratic escalation represented by Owen's proposal may well remain and flourish in a more general sense. It would be reasonable to expect intraparty pressure for the involvement of larger numbers of constituency association members and perhaps of trade-union members too in the processes that their units use to determine electoral college votes. These processes, it might be argued, could even include individual ballots at the local level, or meetings in the manner of the Liberal party, without destroying the federative structure. Whether there are any seriously considered proposals of this kind, I do not know. I have heard only a little about the desire of constituency party members for broader consultation within their units before leadership preferences are settled. The point, however, is that numerous participatory means can be advanced—and, I believe, will be advanced—by way of efforts to modify the apparently oligarchical features of Labour's electoral college.

My thesis here is in accord with the arguments, if not with all the power-struggling intentions, of the Labour activists who originally insisted on broadening the party's leadership selectorate. Those who made the arguments might, I grant, now resist the advocacy of further changes less well-suited to their factional purpose than are the rules now adopted. But others with a different purpose, perhaps one farther left, can readily adapt the rhetoric of democratic participation to serve their interest. Note, therefore, a few examples of that rhetoric from speakers at the 1980 conference, which first resolved to break the PLP's sole power over leadership selection: "Our movement is awakening. Our people will no longer be denied their rightful place in our movement. . . . We have to extend participation and accountability. . . . For the party to have any credibility we first have to let our party workers play a meaningful part." Or another delegate, himself an M.P. who said that he had consulted his constituency party before Callaghan's election as leader: "Why should not good strong Labour parties in Tory seats have some say in the selection of their Leader?" The same speaker added the interesting observation that "all these newspapers who are telling us what an outrageous thing it would be for Labour party members to have some sort of say in the election of the Leader are not saying that there is something outrageous about the delegates from the United States deciding who will be the Democratic candidate and possibly the President of the United States." And he concluded: "It is a question of ending an anachronism, of ending what is an elitist procedure and applying a modern democratic principle for a modern democratic socialist party." Still another M.P., speaking for the N.E.C., observed: "Most of our social democratic and socialist comrades in all the European countries, in and out of the Common Market, have a wider franchise than us."[40]

It is easy to view that rhetoric as being at odds with reality when the case for democratization was being made on behalf of a shrinking individual party membership and a notoriously nonparticipatory set of trade union organizations. Certainly the proposed new leadership selectorate is far removed from the American nominating method invoked to support the change in Labour's rules. These points were indeed scored by moderate Labour M.P.s and their allies when the change was debated in 1980–81. But to score them, I have argued, an important contingent of moderates moved beyond their opponents to champion a further—and in their argument truer—democratization of the selection process. Significantly, too, that contingent's "one member, one vote" formula was eventually used in 1982 by the Social Democratic party, which became the new political home of many of the old moderates.

The SDP's adoption of the formula is itself a neat example of escalating progressivism. After all, most of the Labour moderates who became SDP leaders had begun the fight that took them out of their old party as defenders of the power of M.P.s to select their own leader. And some, unlike David Owen, had not embraced the "one member, one vote" alternative even at Wembley. Furthermore, the SDP's first draft constitution of September 1981 adhered to the parliamentary tradition of having M.P.s select their leader.[41] That provision was not greatly diluted by another that gave dues-paying members the power to elect the party's "president." But the draft constitution's provisions for leadership selection, it was immediately understood, were subject to change in a more partici-patory direction. As a discerning critic observed in November 1981, "Ironically, the party seems to be pushed towards more democracy, and more say for the local activists, by the same currents of opinion which pushed the party leaders out of the Labour party in the first place."[42] A few months later, in February 1982, delegates at the SDP's constitutional convention heavily favored switching the leadership selection to the "one member, one vote" formula.[43] That switch was championed, as it had been earlier, by David Owen, but opposed by Roy Jenkins who, as the SDP's senior statesman, was soon to win a parliamentary by-election and then become the likely choice of the slightly more than two dozen SDP M.P.s.[44] The last word on the leadership selection method was not the SDP conven-tion's but rather the party's individual members'—all 78,000 being given the opportunity in a postal ballot to decide on the method.[45] The result was that the SDP's first leadership selection in June and July 1982 used this same kind of postal ballot. The contest was between Jenkins and Owen, each an M.P. nominated according to the rules by five other M.P.s. After a campaign involving press releases and interviews, but, by a curiously discreet agreement, no competitive appearances on the same public platform or broadcast program, Jenkins won by a narrower margin (56 to 44%) than he would probably have had among fellow M.P.s.[46]

Compared with past British major party practices and even with present Labour party methods, the SDP's leadership selection in 1982 is a radical departure. It resembles the Liberal party's 1976 procedure, except that SDP members vote directly on a national basis rather than at meetings of local parties, which then translate individual preferences into their respective constituency allotments. The SDP method is thus a slightly purer version of the "one member, one vote" principle. It may, however, have been adopted because of the absence of conventional local organizations in the still new SDP.[47] Also, as in the Liberal case, membership participation of one kind or another might have been attractive as long as the party had only a small number of M.P.s. But for the SDP as well as the Liberals, it is hard to believe that more M.P.s at a later date would permanently reverse the transfer of power to the larger membership. The particular means for membership participation—the postal ballot or the Liberal kind of local meeting—are more likely subjects for change. From the North American perspective, British parties are far from exhausting the mechanisms for participation and particularly for participation of members defined by less restrictive criteria than dues-paying. Canadian nominating conventions suggest other feasible possibilities.[48]

THE BROADER PICTURE

Fastening attention as I have on changes only in the selection of candidates and leaders has, I hope, served to emphasize the late arrival of limited versions of the institutional progressivism familiar to Americans. But the focus should not suggest that the particular changes have occurred independently of broader political and social developments in British society. Even within the confines of recent Labour party controversy, a third established practice was challenged. At the same conferences that adopted new rules for candidate and leadership selection, the Bennites and their allies also raised the older controversial question of the extent of the extra-parliamentary party's power, through its annual conference and elected National Executive Committee, to impose policy preferences on the PLP and its leadership. I have put the issue aside not primarily because it remained unresolved as of mid-1983, but because this proposed change does not, unlike the candidate and leadership selection changes, represent a step in an American direction. Nor is it so novel a thrust for power in the Labour party. It could well be argued that even without any new Bennite enlargement of its authority the extraparliamentary Labour party has already had a larger policy-making role than any activist organization has in relation to a major party's governmental officeholders in the United States. Labour's constitution has long provided a means for conference policy resolutions to become part of the party's election program, which the National Executive Committee and the PLP leadership are supposed to join in drafting before a general election.[49] And, like the Conservative program produced by a less encumbered parliamentary leadership, Labour's election program—its manifesto—has been a more politically meaningful set of commitments than those of an American party platform. It is true that the PLP, or effectively a Labour government, is allowed by party rules to decide on the timing of legislation designed to carry out manifesto policies and that, as a result, some policies have been put aside indefinitely.[50] It has also been possible for the PLP leadership, notably for a Labour prime minister, to dominate manifesto-making so as to omit or dilute certain favorite resolutions of the party conference and the NEC.

It was, in fact, Prime Minister Callaghan's success in writing the manifesto for the May 1979 election, but his failure to win the election, that aroused the proponents of extraparliamentary party power to insist that in future the NEC should write Labour's election manifesto. They secured a bare majority for that principle at the October 1979 conference, lost by an equally slim margin when the question was taken up again in 1980, and won once more on principle in 1981 but lost on the crucial resolution that would have amended the party constitution to give the NEC the means of implementing the principle.[51] No matter how the particular question is finally resolved, there can be no doubt about the general importance of extraparliamentary party policymaking in the canons of Bennism. As Benn himself has written, Labour's existing constitutional provision for conference policy decisions is "the hinge that joins the people to their party and it must be seen as a crucial element in the commitment of the party to democratic change."[52] The manifesto-writing proposal thus appears designed to oil that hinge. And the same might be said for the new candidate and leadership selection rules, since they are surely meant to make the PLP more directly responsive to the policy preferences of the organized extraparliamentary party membership. But, unlike the manifesto-writing proposal, the changes in candidate and leadership selection are institutional departures that American experience would have led us to expect at an earlier date.

All three Bennite proposals may also be thought of as part of a broader set of challenges to British political institutions. Not all of the challenges are on behalf of extraparliamentary parties. M.P.s themselves, even without constituency party pressures, have become notably more restive followers of their party in parliamentary voting. Conservative and Labour M.P.s, while still constituting high cohesive forces by American congressional party standards, ceased in the 1970s to be so nearly uniform in their loyalty as they had been in preceding decades.[53] Hence, the parliamentary leaders even of a governing majority no longer command the kind of disciplined troops that used to guarantee Commons approval of their policies once established as party policies—to be sure, often only after compromises had been struck. Moreover, back-benchers now have departmental Select Committees [subject-matter standing committees] in the House of Commons that may be used to exert a degree of independent legislative power against the long-established domination of the executive. Conceivably, in committees or on the House floor, the newly asserted freedom of M.P.s from the most stringent parliamentary party discpline will allow not only more individually independent judgments but also a greater reflection of constituency interests, be they of their selecting associations or of their larger local electorates. In the past, M.P.s have been insulated to a large extent from the latter as well as the former.[54] Perhaps that, too, may now change and M.P.s more nearly resemble American legislators in displaying a greater responsiveness to their own constituents than to their national parties.

There is a still broader front on which established British leadership can be perceived as being under attack during the last decade or so. Within Britain's highly developed and bureaucratized trade unions, for example, there has been a decentralization of power to particular industrial establishments and to the shop floor. Numerous analogous illustrations from various sectors of British society, including government and politics, are cited by Samuel Beer in a book that stresses the effects of class decomposition, the collapse of deference, the romantic revolt of the 1960s, and the new populism represented by Tony Benn.[55] Beer's brilliant exposition provides an understanding of the social context in which the institutional changes, which I have discussed, could finally occur. At the same time that Beer sees these changes, much as I have, as late steps in a direction long since taken in the United States, he is able to assure the British that "the Americanization of their politics is still far from complete."[56]

I should like to underline the same point. Britain has remained notably immune so far to the cardinal accomplishment of American progressivism: the use of the state and its primaries to transfer the selection of candidates, now even presidential candidates, from party organizations to ordinary party voters. Nothing about the new Labour, Liberal, and SDP practices, any more than about the Conservatives, makes either candidate or leadership selection other than a private associational matter open only to a well-defined membership or, in the Labour case, its putative representatives. Nor has there so far been even a live proposal, despite the escalating progressivity I have noted, to substitute party voters for party members as selectors of candidates or leaders. To do so would, as in the United States, almost certainly require a government-run primary election that British parties would not welcome any more than they do the very idea of letting ordinary voters participate in the process. They have until now escaped not only government-run primaries but virtually all of the legally regulated status to which American parties have become accustomed in the twentieth century. British parties are not treated as quasi-public agencies, or regulated public utilities, and they might well be able to resist the relatively slight regulation suggested in the Hansard Commission's proposal for legally required but party-conducted primaries.[57] Whether they could also resist the governmental regulation accompanying the public funding suggested elsewhere in this volume is more doubtful, but such regulation, when accompanying public funding in continental Europe, has not resembled the American governmental control of nominations and related organizational affairs.

Having now emphasized how far short of American methods the redistribution of power in British parties is almost certain to remain, I am obliged to restate and justify the American perspective that I used to examine British changes. It should not have led anyone to expect particular progressive reforms, notably a transplanted direct primary. American historical circumstances, I have not merely granted but insisted, are responsible for institutional developments ill-suited not only to Britain but to other nations as well. But the rhetoric of American progressivism, in contrast to progressive devices, is a more nearly universal currency of reform in a democratic age.

Here, I trust, I have made the case for reversing, in matters of candidate and leadership selection, the customary twentieth-century view of political scientists that British party developments are advanced models for Americans eventually to follow. Advanced as they may be in other important respects, they are surely late in redistributing crucial powers from insulated leaders to other participants. I say this without being at all sure that the redistribution in its British Labour form or in its more radical American form makes for more satisfactory representative government. Ideologically, I sympathize with the moderates who resisted Bennism, as I did with the American critics of several McGovern–Fraser reforms, but I recognize the need to accommodate new and growing participatory demands. It can be hoped that British parties will accommodate the demands without the antiorganizational American results.

NOTES

1. In the late nineteenth century, however, the then large-scale American party organizations were customarily perceived as highly developed, even over-developed, in relation to the still emerging mass parties in Britain and elsewhere in Europe.

2. For a similar but broader interpretation of the impact of these expectations, see Samuel H. Beer, *Britain Against Itself: The Political Contradictions of Collectivism* (New York: W. W. Norton, 1982), chaps. 3-5. I take his broader interpretation into account at the end of my chapter.

3. Austin Ranney, "Candidate Selection," in *Democracy at the Polls: A Comparative Study of Competitive National Elections*, ed. David Butler, Howard R. Penniman, and Austin Ranney (Washington, D. C.: American Enterprise Institute, 1981), pp. 75-106.

4. Anthony King, "How Not to Select Presidential Candidates: A View from Europe," in *The American Elections of 1980*, ed. Austin Ranney (Washington D. C.: American Enterprise Institute, 1981), pp. 303-28, at p. 307.

5. Austin Ranney described the usual British candidate-selection practices in *Pathways to Parliament* (Madison: University of Wisconsin Press, 1965) and in "Selecting the Candidates," in *Britain at the Polls: the Parliamentary Elections of 1974*, ed. Howard R. Penniman (Washington, D. C.: American Enterprise Institute, 1975), pp. 33-60.

6. In each party, the national organization maintains a long list of persons, from which local associations may choose prospective candidates. Thus there is some prior screening for eligibility.

7. I explored a cluster of these instances in the late 1950s in *British Politics in the Suez Crisis* (Urbana: University of Illinois Press, 1964), chap. 6. An example from the early 1970s is provided by Dick Taverne in recounting his experience, *The Future of the Left: Lincoln and After* (London: Jonathan Cape, 1974), part 1.

8. Ibid. Taverne, reelected as an M.P. despite deselection by his local Labour party, finally lost his seat in October 1974. His book had been published earlier in 1974.

9. Ranney, "Selecting the Candidates," in *Britain at the Polls*, pp. 40-41.

10. The change in 1980 involved an amendment to the party constitution implementing the reselection principle adopted by Labour's 1979 conference.

11. British Politics Group, *Newsletter* (Spring 1982), pp. 3-5.

12. *Report of the Annual Conference and Special Conference of the Labour Party 1980* (London: Labour Party, 1980), p. 142.

13. The Conservative national membership estimates are not official, but, rough as they are, they are commonly cited in comparison to a figure of about 3 million in the early 1950s. For a Labour total of only 250,000 in 1978, when the party officially tabulated 675,000, see Paul Whiteley, "The Decline of Labour's Local Party Membership and Electoral Base, 1945-79," in *The Politics of the Labour Party*, ed. Dennis Kavanagh (London: George Allen & Unwin, 1982), pp. 111-34, at p. 115.

14. S. E. Finer, *The Changing British Party System, 1945-1979* (Washington, D. C.: American Enterprise Institute, 1980), pp. 99-100.

15. The entryists from the revolutionary Left have been most prominent in London parties, from which one should be wary of generalizing to the rest of the country. A careful study of a sample of Labour activists in

1978 described the dominant tendency as Left but "not a simple-minded doctrinaire Left: rather it is a highly educated, disproportionately middle-class Left." Paul Whiteley, "Who are the Labour Activists?" *Political Quarterly* 52 (1981): 160-70, at 170.

16. Hugh Berrington, "The Labour Left in Parliament: Maintenance, Erosion and Renewal," in *The Politics of the Labour Party*, ed. Dennis Kavanagh (London: George Allen & Unwin, 1982), pp. 69-94, at pp. 83-84, 91.

17. British Politics Group, *Newsletter* (Spring 1982), pp. 3-5. Of the seven actual ousters, three occurred where redistricting will cause the relevant constituencies to disappear. The well-publicized case was Fred Mulley. *New York Times*, March 5, 1982, p. 3.

18. Finer, *The Changing British Party System*, p. 115.

19. Dennis Kavanagh, "Representation in the Labour Party," in *The Politics of the Labour Party*, ed. Dennis Kavanagh (London: George Allen & Unwin, 1982), pp. 202-22, at p. 216.

20. *Report of the Hansard Society Commission on Electoral Reform* (London: Hansard Society, June 1976), p. 19. The ballot would not apply to sitting M.P.s unless 20% of a party's members signed a declaration that they wanted a ballot.

21. Leon D. Epstein, "A Comparative Study of Australian Parties," *British Journal of Political Science* 7 (1977): 1-21, at 16-18.

22. Henry Drucker, "Social Democrats and Their Members," *New Society*, November 26, 1981, pp. 362-65.

23. It has even been argued that the unwritten British constitution stands in the way of leadership selection by a nonparliamentary party because it might produce a prime minister lacking the support of his or her *parliamentary* party majority. That unhappy contingency has somehow been avoided in the Canadian experience described below.

24. John C. Courtney, *The Selection of National Party Leaders in Canada* (Toronto: Macmillan of Canada, 1973). Canadian constituency parties choose convention delegates in relatively open meetings that are often well attended by identifiable party activists and their followers—not by the more numerous party voters of an American primary. The delegates, when assembled in convention, may be influenced by their M.P. or other local leaders, but they cast individual secret ballots rather than in consti-tuency blocks. The Canadians use neither the British-style card vote nor the U.S.-type state delegation roll-call (Courtney, p. 227).

25. Various national patterns of leadership selection are discussed by Anthony King, "Executives," in *Handbook of Political Science*, ed. Fred I. Greenstein and Nelson W. Polsby (Reading, Mass.: Addison-Wesley, 1976), vol. 5, pp. 173-256, and by Stanley Henig and John Pinder, eds., *European Political Parties* (London: George Allen & Unwin, 1969).

26. King, "How Not to Select Presidential Candidates," in *The American Elections of 1980.*

27. Robert McKenzie, *British Political Parties* (London: Heinemann, 1963), chap. 2.

28. Finer, *The Changing British Party System*, p. 79.

29. David Butler and Dennis Kavanagh, *The British General Election of 1979* (London: Macmillan, 1980), pp. 63–64.

30. Michael Steed, "Foreword," in *Liberal Politics in Britain*, by Arthur Cyr (New Brunswick, N. J.: Transaction, 1977), pp. 11–35, at pp. 31–34.

31. Ibid., p. 32.

32. A change in leadership had also been proposed but defeated at the 1979 conference.

33. Henry Drucker, "Changes in the Labour Party Leadership," *Parliamentary Affairs* 34 (1981); 369–91, at 384–87.

34. Kavanagh, "Representation in the Labour Party," in *The Politics of the Labour Party*, p. 220.

35. Drucker, "Changes in the Labour Party Leadership," *Parliamentary Affairs*, p. 387.

36. British Politics Group, *Newsletter* (Fall 1981), pp. 3–4. *The Times* (London), October 1, 1981, p. 4.

37. In addition to Owen, the four were William Rodgers (also an M.P. and a former Labour minister), Shirley Williams, and Roy Jenkins. Both Mrs. Williams and Jenkins, though ex-M.P.s as well as ex-ministers in 1980, reentered the House in 1981 and 1982 by winning by-elections as Social Democrats, Rodgers and Mrs. Williams, however, lost their seats in the 1983 general election.

38. *The Times* (London), January 26, 1981, p. 4.

39. James W. Ceaser, *Presidential Selection: Theory and Development* (Princeton, N.J.: Princeton University Press, 1979), p. 263, suggests that such a preference by regulars and moderates provides one possible explanation for the increase in presidential primaries in the early and middle 1970s. Some supporting evidence is in the files of the Democratic National Committee.

40. *Report of the Annual Conference*, pp. 149, 150, 151, 152.

41. *The Economist*, September 26, 1981, p. 56.

42. Drucker, "Social Democrats and Their Members," *New Society*, p. 363.

43. *The Economist*, February 20, 1982, p. 32.

44. Most of the 28 SDP M.P.s in the spring of 1982 had been elected as Labour candidates in 1979. One was a defecting Conservative.

45. Slightly fewer than half of the 78,000 returned ballots, and fewer than a third of them favored having M.P.s now select the SDP leader. The other voting members, however, left the way open for selection by M.P.s either by favoring it after a general election or, in larger numbers, by voting to have the procedure reviewed again after three years. The ballot cost £30,000. *The Guardian* (London), May 10, 1982, p. 1.

46. *The Times* (London), June 7, 1982, p. 2, and July 3, 1982, p. 1. In this postal ballot, the turnout, over 75% of the SDP membership, was much higher than in the previous ballot on the method of leadership selection.

47. Unlike other British parties, however, the SDP has had an up-to-date national list of individual members and their addresses. Thus it could run a national contest when other parties probably could not.

48. Courtney, *Selection of National Party Leaders.*

49. McKenzie, *British Political Parties*, pp. 486-516.
50. Lewis Minkin, *The Labour Party Conference* (London: Allen Lane, 1978), p. 314.
51. John E. Turner, "The Labour Party: Riding Two Horses," *International Studies Quarterly* 25 (1981): 385-437, at 429-30, and *The Times* (London), October 2, 1981, pp. 1, 4.
52. Tony Benn, *Arguments for Socialism* (London: Jonathan Cape, 1979), p. 41.
53. Philip Norton, *Dissension in the House of Commons 1974-1979* (Oxford: Clarendon Press, 1980), and *Dissension in the House of Commons 1945-1974* (London: Macmillan, 1975).
54. Jorgen Rasmussen discusses this point in a not yet published paper, "Is Parliament Revolting?" So does L. J. Sharpe, "The Labour Party and the Geography of Inequality: A Puzzle," in *The Politics of the Labour Party*, ed. Dennis Kavanagh (London: George Allen & Unwin), pp. 135-70.
55. Beer, *Britain Against Itself*, chaps. 3-5.
56. Ibid., p. 169.
57. *Report of the Hansard Society Commission on Electoral Reform*, p. 19.

4

PARTY AND PUBLIC
IN BRITAIN
AND THE UNITED STATES

Ivor Crewe

> The electorate requires . . . something
> that can be loved and trusted, and
> which can be recognised at successive
> elections as being the same thing that
> was loved and trusted before; and
> party is such a thing.
>
> Graham Wallas, *Human Nature in
> Politics*, p. 83.

That sentence was written in 1910, on the eve of Britain's emergence
as a mass democracy. In retrospect it seems an odd assertion. At that
time, the majority of adults had never voted, being unenfranchised;
no national party explicitly represented urban workers; mass party
organisations were barely a generation old; and no effective means of
nationwide mass communication was available to politicians. Today
the conditions for strong party allegiances would seem more favourable. Almost all adults will have been entitled to vote throughout
their adult lives; the Liberals have been replaced by Labour, ostensibly
devoted to the material interests of workers; and television has
emerged as a powerful means of mass communication, partly at the
disposal of the parties. Yet there is now overwhelming evidence that,
at least in Britain and the United States, the major parties are not
loved and trusted, and they have become progressively less loved
and trusted over the past 20 to 30 years. The first part of the paper

documents this growing disenchantment and the second explores some possible consequences for party politics, the party system, and the democratic order in both countries. First, the facts.

SOME FACTS

In one obvious but crucial sense the established parties continue to receive all the public support they need. Their capacity to carry out their primary function of forming a government remains unimpaired. In the United States, the Democrats' and Republicans' duopoly of seats in Congress and the state legislatures is not remotely threatened, and it is barely conceivable to think of a mayor or governor, let alone a president, obtaining office without nomination by one of the two parties. From time to time third parties have erupted (and disrupted) but have always subsided. In Britain the Conservative and Labour parties' dominance of Parliament and the council chambers has been less complete, especially in the 1970s; but they continue to take over 90% of parliamentary and local seats. The Nationalists have entered Parliament, the Liberals have slightly strengthened their presence, and most recently the SDP has established itself as a parliamentary party, but the post-war period has been only three and a half years of minority government (1974 and 1976–79). Single-party government faced by a single-party alternative government remains the norm.

Nonetheless, the popular base of the major parties has been steadily eroding since at least the early 1960s. This crumbling has been less spectacular in Britain than in the United States but potentially no less significant. Whichever indicator one chooses reveals the same trend: the public's allegiance to the established parties has become looser, more conditional and less predictable. The British and American electorates are undergoing a "partisan dealignment." To ram the point home, some summary statistics and commentary follow.

The Major-Party Vote

The single most telling statistic of a party's popularity is its share of the total *electorate* (see Table 4.1). In 1951 the two-party grip in Britain was at its tightest: four out of five electors (80%) turned out to vote Labour or Conservative. In the quarter-century that

Table 4.1

Proportion of electorate voting for either major party in general elections (Britain) and presidential elections (United States), 1950–1980

Great Britain Percentage of the electorate voting either Conservative or Labour		United States Percentage of the resident voting-age population voting for either the Democratic or Republican presidential candidate	
1950	75.5		
1951	80.3		
		1952	61.0
1955	74.3		
		1956	58.7
1959	73.8		
		1960	62.8
1964	67.7	1964	61.9
1966	68.7		
		1968	52.4
1970	64.8		
		1972	54.9
Feb. 1974	60.7		
Oct. 1974	56.1		
		1976	53.2
1979	62.9		
		1980	47.8
1983	50.5		

followed, the proportion declined unremittingly: by October 1974 it was little over half (56%); 1979 saw a reversal, but not a reversion: at 63% two-party support was still lower than at any election between 1945 and 1970. And by 1983 it had slumped to its lowest level since the modern two-party system was established: 50.5%. For every elector voting Conservative or Labour, another was not.

Exact parallels between the United States and Britain are difficult to draw. In the United States electors disaffected from the Democratic and Republican parties rarely have the opportunity to vote for a non-fringe alternative. The only regular alternative, in fact, has been abstention—which has steadily increased since 1960. In presidential races turnout (i.e., voters as a proportion of the voting-age resident population) fell from 62% in 1952 to 52% in

1980 (and in off-year House races from 42% in 1950 to 38% in 1978). It is this growth in abstention that largely accounts for the fact that under one-half of the voting-age population bothered to turn out for either Carter or Reagan—the worst performance by the two parties' nominees since the 1920s.

The Party Leaders' Popularity

The decline in the vote for the two parties might reflect a growing disenchantment with their capacity to govern, but not with their capacity to produce leaders. The electorates both of Britain and of the United States do not appraise the party and its leader identically. This is particularly evident in the United States, where first executives as well as legislators are elected directly. The American voter therefore has the opportunity to distinguish between the personal qualities of a prospective president, governor or mayor and the policy and record of that candidate's party in the legislature. They have the option of "splitting their ticket," and there is ample evidence that in recent years they have been doing so in growing numbers. In Britain, where the majority party's leader and the first executive is the same person, the popularity of a party and its leader are more closely bound together. However, the monthly opinion polls reveal that they are not the same: approval of a party leader, especially the Prime Minister, nearly always runs ahead of voting support for the leader's party.

Nonetheless, although leaders and parties are not identically assessed, their popularity over the last quarter-century has fallen more or less in tandem. Table 4.2 shows how the "combined approval score" for the prime minister and the opposition leader in Britain dropped by a quarter between the mid-1960s and the early 1980s. By the second half of 1981, the prime minister's "approval rating" was below that of any of her predecessors (except for Harold Wilson for a brief period in 1968), and the Opposition Leader's *markedly* lower than any of his, since Gallup first asked the question over 30 years ago. By late 1982, after "winning" the Falklands War, Mrs. Thatcher's popularity was less than that of Conservative prime ministers in the 1950s and early 1960s, including Sir Antony Eden's after he had "lost" the Suez War. Parallel figures do not exist for the United States, where there is no precise equivalent to the party leader in Britain, but it is clear that public esteem for the presidential candidates of 1980 was the lowest, in combination, since at least 1948.[1]

Table 4.2

Approval for leaders of the two major parties, 1955–82, Gallup poll (in percentages)

Parliament	Prime Minister	Opposition leader	Combined approval
1955–59	55	44	99
1959–64	51	51	102
1964–66	59	41	100
1966–70	41	33	74
1970–74	36	47	83
1974	46	34	80
1974–79	46	41	87
1979–83 (April)	39	33	72

Note: All figures are average (mean) monthly ratings.

Source: Reproduced (with permission) from Richard Rose, "Why won't we play follow-my-leader?" *New Society*, 4 November 1982, p. 210, with additional material taken from Social Surveys (Gallup Poll) Ltd., *Gallup Political Index*, Nos. 265–273 (August 1982–April 1983).

Party Membership

In the United States there is no equivalent to the dues-paying individual member of a British party. In Britain current national membership figures are unavailable from the Conservative party and notoriously unreliable for all other parties. But there is no doubt that membership of political parties has fallen sharply since the war. The best estimates—unofficial but independently corroborated ones—are that Conservative party membership has dropped from 2.8 million in 1953 to about 1.5 million in the mid-1970s and that Labour party membership has fallen from just over a million in 1953 to 250,000–300,000 over the same period.[2] Thus the two big parties have lost over two million individual members during a period in which the electorate has expanded by 15 million and leisure time and voluntary association membership has grown considerably. These losses cannot be due to increasing membership of the minor parties, which altogether stood at 400,000 in the mid-1970s (to which the 60,000 members of the SDP can now be added). There are few grounds for believing that this trend will go into sustained reversal, although there are signs that Labour party membership has revived a little in the last few years.

Party Identification

Party membership, however, is a suspect measure of partisan commitment. Some campaign activists are not members, and the majority of members are not activists. A superior indicator is the direction and strength of an elector's self-declared party identification. Both in Britain and in the United States, this has consistently proved to be the best single correlate of long-term partisan loyalty and of party political involvement, including turnout. Exact comparisons between the two countries are hampered by the slightly different ways in which the party identification questions are asked and the answers categorised. In Britain no provision is made for Independents, and the strength component is divided into three ("very," "fairly" and "not very" strong) rather than two.[3]

But the basic facts about partisan dealignment in the two countries stand out clearly enough (see Tables 4.3 and 4.4). In Britain, the electorate's willingness to identify with a party has, despite a slight drop, remained very high throughout the last 15 years, and there has been only a modest fall—from 81% to 70%—in the proportion identifying with the Conservative and Labour parties. In the United States major party identification has fallen further and from a lower starting level. In 1952, when party identification was first measured, 75% of American electors thought of themselves as Republicans or Democrats. That proportion stayed the same until 1964, after which it dropped continuously to 60% in 1978 and again in 1980. The proportion calling themselves Independents simultaneously rose from 23% in 1952 (and again in 1964) to 38% in both 1978 and 1980 to become the biggest "party." The seriousness of this dealignment should not be exaggerated, however, since over half the Independents, when subjected to further questioning, turn out to "lean" towards the Republicans or Democrats, and research has shown that such "leaners" are usually as partisan in their attitudes and behaviour as those who describe themselves as "weak" Republicans or Democrats.[4] In 1976 "independent Independents" still amounted to only 15%. Thus in both Britain and the United States residual attachments to the two big parties remain widespread.

But the point to stress is that they *are* residual. For what has markedly declined in both countries is the *strength* of partisan attachments. "Strong" Democrats and Republicans made up 36%

Table 4.3

Trends in the incidence and strength of major party identification in Great Britain (in percentages)

	1964	1966	1970	Feb. & Oct. 1974 (average)	1979	1983
Percentage of electorate with						
a party identification	93	91	90	90	90	86
a Conservative or Labour identification	81	81	82	75	76	70
a *'very strong'* Conservative/Labour identification	38	40	40	25	19	23
a *'fairly strong'* Conservative/Labour identification	34	32	33	35	39	29
a *'not very strong'* Conservative/Labour identification	9	9	9	15	18	18

Sources: Re-analysis of data from Butler and Stokes' 1964, 1966 and 1970 cross-sectional surveys, and the February 1974, October 1974 and 1979 British Election Study cross-sectional surveys and the 1983 BBC/Gallup election survey.

of the American electorate in 1952 (and 38% in 1964), but only 23% by 1978. In Britain the weakening has been even more pronounced, the proportion of "very strong" Labour and Conservative identifiers in the electorate having halved from 38% in 1964 to 19% in 1979, but having apparently crept up to 23% in 1983.[5] Thus in both countries only one elector in five can now be described as truly committed—as the kind of unswerving loyalist who could be relied upon to turn out for his party in bad times as well as good.

Moreover, this dilution of partisanship has occurred irrespective of party and with remarkable evenness across the social and demographic spectrum of both countries: men and women, rich and poor, blue-collar and white-collar, Protestant and Catholic, Northerner

Table 4.4

Trends in the incidence and strength of major party identification in the United States (in percentages)

	1952	*1956*	*1960*	*1964*	*1968*	*1972*	*1976*	*1980*
Percentage of electorate who are								
Independents*	23	23	23	23	30	35	37	38
('independent' Independents)	(6)	(9)	(10)	(8)	(11)	(13)	(15)	(n.a.)
Republicans or Democrats	75	73	75	77	70	64	63	61
'strong' Democrats or Republicans	36	36	36	38	30	25	24	(n.a.)

Sources:

1952–76: Warren Miller et al., *American National Election Studies Data Sourcebook* (Cambridge, Mass.: Harvard University Press, 1980), p. 81.

1980: NORC General Social Survey

*Includes those "leaning" to the Republicans or Democrats.

and Southerner have been gradually distancing themselves from the main parties at about the same rate. But there are two exceptions, both of which hint at the probability of further partisan weakening for some time to come. The first is that in both Britain and the United States partisan dealignment has proceeded faster and further amongst the younger generation of university graduates and professional people than in any other group. According to late 1980 Gallup polls in the United States, 50% of college graduates under 30 described themselves as Independents. These groups are likely to be the opinion leaders and agenda setters of the next three decades and as such the *avant-garde* of the political culture of the 1990s. Secondly, in both countries the incidence and strength of partisanship is directly related to age (as indeed, it always appears to have been). The younger the age category, the higher its proportion of Independents and weak partisans. Moreover, the partisanship of each "entry" cohort of new electors has got progressively weaker since 1964. The reasons for this differ in subtle ways between the two countries,[6] but the probable consequences for the future do not. In the absence of a sharp reversal of this trend among future entry cohorts, the overall proportion of strong partisans in the American and British electorates respectively is likely to continue falling as older generations die out.

Electoral Volatility

One result of a weakening of partisan ties is that considerations other than habitual party loyalty will influence the voting decisions of more and more electors. In particular, campaign-specific factors—the outgoing government's record, the major issues of the day, the party leaders' personal qualities, specific incidents and events—will come to have greater impact. And as electors look at the political world through less partisan spectacles, these considerations are likely to make them more hesitant and fickle in their choice or, to use the fashionable umbrella term, more volatile. One manifestation in both countries is that final voting decisions are increasingly left to the last week or two of the campaign. In Britain the proportion leaving it that late has risen from 17% in 1964 to 28% in 1979; in the United States from 11% in 1952 to 34% in 1980; in fact, in 1980 one in four voters postponed their decision to the last week (waiting for the Carter–Reagan debate?) and 10% to polling day itself.[7] Another example is the proportion of British electors reporting that they had "seriously thought of voting for a different party during the campaign." In the five elections from 1964 to October 1974, this was always in the range of 21-24%; in 1979 it rose to 31%. The committed electorate has been replaced by the hesitant electorate (see Tables 4.5 and 4.6).

The weakening of partisan ties and the enhanced importance of the campaign period have, in turn, produced more party switching between elections. In 1952, only 29% of American electors claimed to have voted for different parties for president at some time in the past; by 1976, 53% did. In Britain panel data, which are more reliable, show that in the three elections of 1964, 1966 and 1970 an average of 32% switched between parties or to or from abstention between two successive elections; in the three elections of February 1974, October 1974 and 1979 the average was 37%.[8] Over the four elections of the 1970s—a mere nine years—only half (51%) of electors eligible to vote on all four occasions were perfectly consistent in their party choice (or in abstaining). Much of this switching cancels out, but not all: the Labour and Conservative parties have experienced steadily sharper oscillation of support, not only in general elections, but also in local elections, by-elections and in the

Table 4.5

Hesitancy and wavering in voting decisions in Britain

	1964	1966	1970	Feb. & Oct. 1974 (average)	1979
Percentage of respondents who left decision on how to vote to the campaign period	17	14	11	22	28

Sources: Butler and Stokes 1964, 1966 and 1970 cross-sectional surveys; BES February 1974, October 1974 and 1979 cross-sectional surveys. The question was: "How long ago did you decide that you would definitely vote the way you did—a long time ago, some time this year or during the campaign?" (1974, 1979); "How long ago did you decide to vote that way?" (1964, 1966, 1970).

opinion polls since the late 1950s.[9] Thus the "swing" at general elections (i.e., the average of the Conservative percentage point gain in the vote and the Labour percentage point loss) has steadily risen, from 1.1% in 1955-59, to 2.9% in 1959-64, 3.1% in 1964-66, 4.7% in 1966-70 and 5.2% in October 1974-79.[10] In the United States swings in presidential elections are higher but have also risen by leaps and bounds over most of the same period: 2.5% in 1952-56, 6.9% in 1956-60, 9.8% in 1960-64, 10.8% in 1964-68, 11.1% in 1968-72, 12.7% in 1972-76 (but only 6.0% in 1976-80).

These swings of electoral mood, moreover, appear to be moved by the forces of repulsion, not attraction. Allegiance to one's preferred party might be weakening, but rejection of the other might not. Large numbers of voters in recent elections have voted against one party (usually the government party) rather than for the other. In November 1980 a CBS/New York Times poll asked: "Did you decide on your candidate mainly because you liked him, or because you did not like the others?" Only 50% said "because they liked him." A similar pattern was found by the BBC/Gallup election day poll in June 1983: 55% of Conservative voters (and 63% of those who *switched* to the Conservatives, and 85% of those who only decided to vote Conservative in the final week) said they disliked the Labour party more than they liked the Conservative party. Valid trend data do not exist, but one suspects that negative motivations play a stronger role in elections nowadays than in the past—that elections have become *un*popularity contests. And as British and American

Table 4.6

Hesitancy and wavering in voting decisions in the United States

	1952	1956	1960	1964	1968	1972	1976	1980
Percentage who left decision on how to vote until last fortnight of campaign	11	10	12	13	22	13	24	34

Sources: For 1952-78—Warren Miller et al., *American National Election Studies Data Source Book 1952-78*, p. 380. The question was "How long before the election did you decide that you were going to vote the way you did?" (Knew all along/During convention/Post-convention/Last two weeks of campaign/Election day). The 1980 figure, not available from the 1980 CPS study, is taken from a post-election Roper poll (Gallup's estimate is even higher–37%). See Ladd, 'The Brittle Mandate,' p. 22.

governments are widely regarded to have failed in their major objectives over the last two decades, so they have found it harder to get re-elected. The 1983 election was the first for almost a quarter century to return the governing party to office after a full term. No president has served two full terms since Eisenhower (although it was not electoral defeat that stopped Nixon). As party loyalists weaken and the campaign becomes more important, as elections come to resemble periodic referenda on the government's record, so governments will find it harder to protect themselves from the inevitable disappointments that office brings.

The dramatic fortunes of the Social Democratic Party since its formation in March 1981 offer a recent and telling example of electoral volatility. Almost immediately after its creation, it led the two established parties in the opinion polls, with about 40% of the intended vote, a level of support confirmed by its (or its Liberal partner's) impressive performances in the parliamentary and local by-elections during the rest of the year.[11] There had been Liberal surges in the past; but no eruption of support for any party of such suddeness and force had occurred since the war. Indeed, the long-term pattern of popular support for third, moderate parties in Britain resembles an upwardly spiralling cycle: at each of the four post-war cycles both the peak and subsequent trough have been higher than their predecessors.

However, the opinion polls of 1981–82 also revealed that support for the SDP (singly or in alliance with the Liberals) was as shallow as it was wide. Identification with the SDP was even weaker than it was with the Conservative and Labour parties. Unlike the two main parties, the SDP did not draw its support from any distinctive and organised social group, on whose loyalty it could rely in times of national unpopularity. Its supporters were attracted not by the party's political principles or policy positions (which were invisible to most electors) but by such short-lived factors as its leadership, its image of freshness and moderation, and its sheer novelty. Consequently the SDP–Liberal Alliance was particularly vulnerable to an equally rapid ebbing-away of support, as happened during the Falklands War when the Conservatives could take over from the SDP the claim to be the party of national purpose, far-sighted principle and, above all, success. Thus the eruption and subsequent subsiding of support for the SDP–Liberal Alliance was a symptom of, but not an answer to, the partisan dealignment in the British electorate.

SOME IMPLICATIONS

Evidence of partisan dealignment tends to be greeted—especially in the United States—with a wringing of hands.[12] The broad assumption is that it threatens the effectiveness and stability of the established party system and, by implication, the democratic order. More specifically, a dealigning electorate is alleged to involve four distinct dangers. Supposedly, it:

1. impairs the quality of the electoral process;
2. encourages weak government;
3. challenges the domination of the two major parties;
4. undermines the public's commitment to competitive party politics as a system of representation.

The Quality of the Electoral Process

The argument here is that election results come to depend too heavily on the brief campaign period, which is an inadequate basis on which to judge the parties and candidates. As a growing proportion of electors postpone their voting decision to the last moment, so the campaign assumes undue importance. The effect of the concentrated politicking of the campaign is to "blot out" memories of the government's overall record and to give exaggerated emphasis to the trivial and fleeting. Minor incidents, verbal gaffes, tiny items of news, PR stunts—all have an electoral impact out of all proportion to their intrinsic significance. This is not only because of the quality of the media's campaign reporting, but because a wavering, hesitant electorate will be more easily swayed by the immediate and transient than the strongly partisan.

These arguments are not wholly convincing. One can point to campaign events that have clearly been decisive such as the Carter-Reagan television debate, but the impact of most campaign events is usually greatly exaggerated. Moreover, it is hard to accept that the automatic party voting engendered by strong partisanship had much merit in it as a way of "deciding" how to vote, especially when the occasion that originally gave rise to the partisanship may have long since lost all political significance.

Weak Government

The argument here is that widespread and entrenched party loyalties in the mass electorate are a pre-requisite for any system of account-able yet responsible government. Strong partisanship is a form of electoral credit upon which governments can draw when running into popular deficit or wishing to invest in long-term risk. It allows governments to pursue unpopular policies or long-term strategies with no immediate electoral pay-off. It gives parties time to mobilise their usual supporters behind new ideas, different interests or changes of course (contrast, for example, the Conservative party's success in reconciling its supporters to the loss of Empire and embrace of Europe with Carter's failure to carry Democratic voters on his energy policy campaign). But once party loyalties weaken, the argument goes, it becomes impossible for governments to ignore short-term electoral considerations. An impatient electorate inflicts revenge on the government at the next round of the Congressional and local elections. The opposition party comes to dominate Capitol Hill and the town and county halls, and their resistance to the White House or Whitehall gets bolder. The government supporters' morale in Congress or the Commons backbenches is dented, and, especially in the United States, they begin to place electoral survival before party loyalty. In the eyes of organised interests, the admini-stration's staying power begins to be questioned, its policies lose credibility, and obstruction becomes legitimate as well as practicable politics: the delaying tactics of Conservative local councils under the last government and, increasingly, Labour councils under this one are cases in point.

Yet this argument, too, is not entirely convincing. What a volatile electorate can take away in mid-term it can give back by the next campaign. The very knowledge that rapid recoveries of fortune are possible in the months prior to the election may stiffen rather than weaken the government's resolve to persist with unpopular measures; such would certainly seem to have been the thinking of the present Conservative government.

Two-Party Domination

In a dealigning period more electors are "up for grabs." This does not necessarily destroy the two-party system, since the established parties may do the grabbing from each other. If they take turns, landslide election results become more frequent (as has happened in the United States since World War II). If one party grabs and then manages to keep the hitherto unaligned, as the Democrats did so successfully in 1932 and 1936, the party system undergoes an enduring realignment.

But it is becoming clear that a dealigned electorate rarely results in such a neat and tidy re-adjustment of the two-party system. The more common pattern is for new, minor and sometimes short-lived parties to benefit, thereby robbing the political system of the unique benefits that two-party politics allegedly bestows. Moreover, it is argued, non-partisans are particularly vulnerable to the appeals of "flash" parties and extreme movements: favourite examples include the Nazi party, Poujadism in the 4th Republic in France, Glistrup's Progress Party in Denmark and Wallace's support in the 1960s. And even if the new beneficiaries are impeccably moderate (e.g. the Scottish Nationalists in 1974), their emergence increases the probability of coalition governments in which small, often single-interest parties wield strategic and thus undue power. The direct line of accountability between government, party and electorate is snarled up.

This is not the place to judge the familiar arguments between advocates and opponents of the two-party system. But two points are in order. First, the existence of a strongly partisan electorate does not preclude, and sometimes encourages, the growth of extremism. When McCarthyism briefly held sway, American electors were very firmly aligned; and it was "strong" Republicans, not Independents, who were the most fervent adherents (and later came to be the John Birch Society's most likely recruits). Similarly, the "entryist" strategy of the Trotskyites in the Labour party is crucially dependent on the willingness of ordinary Labour partisans, whose own views are far removed, to continue casting an unquestioning Labour vote.

Secondly, the historical function of minor parties has frequently been to ease an adjustment in the two-party system: Governor Wallace's candidacy provided Southern whites with a stepping-stone from the Democrats to the Republicans (at presidential elections); the Scottish Nationalists forced Labour to become a devolutionist party; ecology parties may play a similar kind of role in the Europe of the 1980s. A dealigned electorate can allow two-party systems to adapt in less direct and dramatic ways than the classical realignments of 1852–56, 1896 and 1932–36.

The Public's Commitment to Competitive Party Politics and the Political System

This final qualm about the consequences of partisan dealignment is the most serious. The argument is that a firm party allegiance binds the elector to the competitive party system by giving him a psychological stake in its outcome. Surveys have consistently found, for both countries, that the strongly partisan are the most likely to vote, to be politically active and to take an interest in public affairs; the most likely to believe in the effectiveness of the electoral process and the solvability of recurrent problems by conventional political means; and the most likely to think well of politicians and the party system of representation.[13] It would seem to follow that an overall weakening of partisan commitment in the electorate would adversely affect its enthusiasm, not only for the party system, but for the wider democratic order.

However, the true state of people's feelings towards the political system is notoriously difficult to fathom. The main reason is that many electors do not possess such feelings in the first place. The typical citizen, with only a limited interest in politics, forms political views in relation to the concrete, particular and personal, not in relation to the abstract and general. Thus "political system" and "democratic order" are terms that, although familiar to the academic student of politics, have virtually no meaning to many electors. Their views about political institutions will be changeable rather than stable, ambivalent rather than consistent, fragmentary rather than systematic, and easily subject to suggestion rather than independent of it. Thus surveys designed to gauge mass attitudes to the political system are particularly liable to elicit "non-attitudes"[14] rather than true convictions.

Interpretation of the results of such surveys is beset by unusual difficulties. The first is apparent contradiction: a substantial number of respondents will be found to endorse propositions that, on the face of it, are plainly contradictory.[15] The second is "partisan contamination": whether a respondent is a partisan of the party in government or the party in opposition will often explain his supposed support for or opposition to the political order. This is because many respondents do not distinguish between regime and government—or because survey researchers have failed to phrase questions that make the difference clear. A third difficulty is the weak relationship between attitudes and behaviour. Substantial proportions of the alienated do not engage in anything that might be described as "anti-system" behaviour, withdrawing into apathy and passivity instead; and large numbers of those involved in illegal, coercive or violent political activities hold attitudes that appear to endorse established democratic institutions. A final obstacle to interpretation might be dubbed the "half-filled bottle problem." In the absence of historical or international baselines the assessment of any single set of figures must be arbitrary. If, as a survey of attitudes to Parliament found in 1972, 40% agreed that either "several" or "drastic" changes needed to be made for "Parliament to work well," should one say "only 40%" or "as many as 40%"? Is a half-filled bottle half empty or half full?[16]

These problems of interpretation can be partially overcome by long-term trend data. Even if the validity and reliability of an indicator is less than ideal and its precise meaning is open to dispute, regular observations of the mass public at least reveal the direction in which its mood is changing. In the case of the United States time series evidence of this kind exists and justifies the fear that partisan dealignment is linked with a growing scepticism about the effectiveness and integrity of the United States' democratic institutions.

Over the period of partisan dealignment—roughly from 1960 to 1980—disaffection with almost all aspects of the political system has conspicuously increased. The most telling "hard" indicator has already been mentioned: the steady drop in turnout at presidential elections from 63% to 52%, despite the easing of registration requirements, the almost complete enfranchisement of blacks, and the massive expansion of higher education over these 20 years. A recent study of turnout rates across the world shows that out of 20 comparable democracies, the average post-war turnout in the United States (at presidential elections) ranks twentieth, lower even than India's.[17]

But this decline in turnout is a muted echo of the spectacular change in popular attitudes towards the political system. Figures 4.1, 4.2 and 4.3 display a summary selection of trend data drawn from biennial national election surveys conducted by the Center for Political Studies at Michigan. And what it reveals for the period 1960–80 is, quite simply, a massive deterioration of faith in the conventional democratic process.

Limited space requires a staccato description. First, there has been a growing scepticism about the capacity of public opinion, parties, elections and elected representatives to ensure that governments remain responsive to the views of the ordinary elector. In 1964 respondents were asked "How much do you feel that political parties help to make the government pay attention to what the people think?"—to which 41% said "a good deal" and 13% "not much." (The rest replied "some" or "don't know"). By 1978, in answer to the identical question, opinions were much more evenly divided: 21% said "a good deal" and 22% "not much." To a similar question about the amount of attention paid by Congressmen, the "good deal"/"not much" ratio changed from 42:15 in 1964 to 17:21 in 1978. Even elections—the institutional and symbolic core of the democratic credo—began to inspire less faith: the "good deal"/"not much" ratio slipped from 65%:7% in 1964 to 56%:10% 14 years later.

Secondly, the American public has become far more cynical about the way central government works, and in particular about its honesty, competence and fairness. Trust in the capacity of the federal government "to do what is right most of the time" plummeted from 62% in 1964 to 27% in 1978. Agreement that the government is run by "a few big interests looking out for themselves" (rather than "for the benefit of the people") rose sharply from 29% to 67% over the same period. The belief that the government "wastes a lot of money we pay in taxes" jumped from 47% to 77%. Faith that "almost all of the people running the government are smart people who usually know what they are doing" fell from 69% to 41%. And the suspicion that "quite a lot of the people running the government are a little crooked" rose from 29% to 40%. The CPS constructed a three-point "Trust in Government" scale based on these five questions. In 1964, 61% were at the trusting end and 19% at the cynical end; by 1978 the proportions were almost reversed, with 52% dubbed cynical and only 19% trusting.

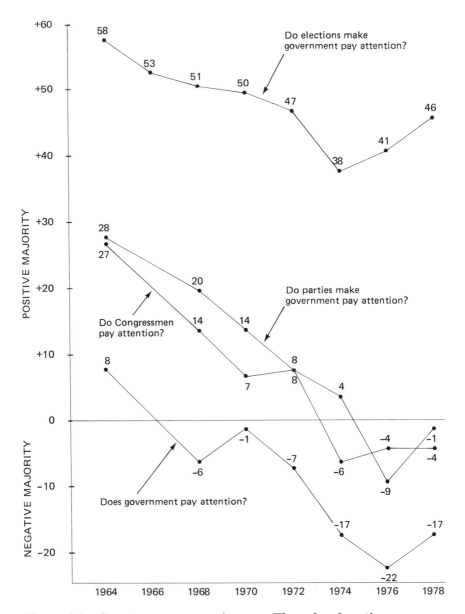

Figure 4.1. Government responsiveness: The role of parties, congressmen and elections, United States 1964–78

Note: Each score represents percentage of those responding "A good deal" *minus* percentage responding "Not much."

Source: Warren Miller et al., *American National Election Studies Data Sourcebook 1952–1978* (Cambridge, Mass.: Harvard University Press, 1980), pp. 261–62.

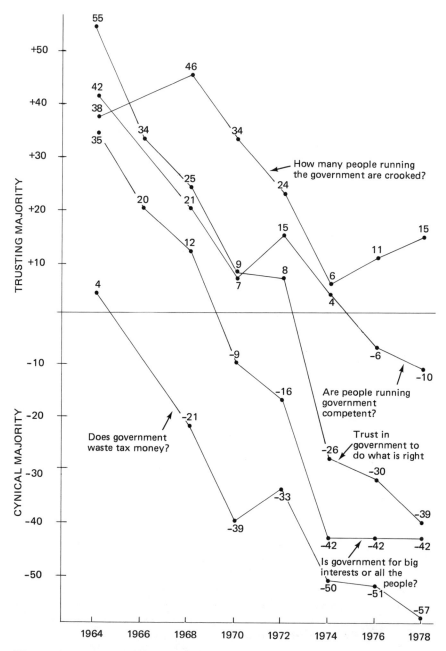

Figure 4.2 Trust in government, United States 1964-78

Note: Each score in the Figure is the "Percentage Difference Index" (PDI) used by the CPS. For details see Miller et al., *American National Election Studies Data Sourcebook, 1952-78*, pp. 257-59.

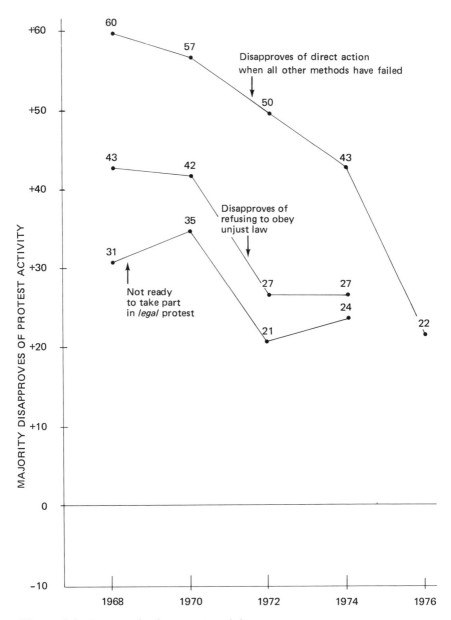

Figure 4.3 Approval of protest activity

Note: For two of the items data are not available for 1976. The scores are the percentage 'disapproving' *minus* the percentage 'approving' (respondents also had the option of answering "it depends"). For further details, see Miller et al., *American National Election Studies Data Sourcebook 1952–78*, pp. 266–67.

This disenchantment with the democratic "myth" reveals itself in a growing approval of various forms of protest action (for which trend data are available for a shorter period only). Between 1968 and 1974 disapproval of legal protest marches and meetings fell from 49% to 40%, whereas at least qualified approval went up from 43% to 58%. Disapproval of breaking laws one strongly feels to be unjust dropped from 56% to 42% over the same six years. And the rejection of "sit-ins, mass meetings and demonstrations" when "all other methods have failed" plummeted from 67% in 1968 to 29% in 1976. By the mid-1970s there was majority approval for forms of political pressure that by-passed the "normal channels" provided by the party system.

Two items of background information should be added. First, this transformation in public attitudes has been common to all the electorate and has proceeded at an even rate across the social, demographic and political spectrum. It is not, for example, a generational phenomenon or one confined to the college-educated. The most disenchanted groups are the poor and manual workers, but this was so in 1964 as much as now. It is amongst these same groups, incidentally, that turnout has declined most over this period.[18] Second, these changes of attitude cannot be attributed to a general growth of cynicism and mistrust in society. Throughout the period the stable and majority view was that "most people" could be trusted, tried to be helpful and were fair. What had changed was not the general culture but the political culture. Whether partisan dealignment led to this change of culture or vice versa is a separate and probably unanswerable question.

In Britain, too, strength of partisan commitment appears to be related to strength of commitment to the wider political system. This is convincingly shown in Louis Moss, *Some Attitudes towards Government*, the most thorough survey-based investigation of the subject so far. Moss constructed a scale (INST) to measure people's acceptance of positive conventional wisdom about the role of M.P.s, the parties and Parliament. A high level of acceptance is linked with trust of the government and politicians, interest and involvement in politics, and a favourable image of public institutions. He shows that electors' position on the scale is unaffected by their social or demographic attributes (age, sex, class, education etc.) or even by their party preference. It is affected, however, by their degree of attachment to one or other of the major parties and by how much they care which party wins an election (see Table 4.7).

Whether the weakening of partisanship in Britain over the last two decades has led to a weakening of respect for democratic institu-

Table 4.7

Partisan commitment and acceptance of positive conventional wisdom about MPs, party system, and parliament (INST scale) (in percentages)

Acceptance of positive conventional wisdom (INST score)	Low	Medium	High	Total	(N)
Supports Con. or Lab.	22	50	29	100	(816)
Leans to Con or Lab.	29	51	20	100	(178)
Supports or leans to Lib.	26	52	23	100	(81)
Supports or leans to no party	42	44	14	100	(229)
All	27	48	25	100	(1,304)

Source: Re-constructed from Louis Moss, *Some Attitudes Towards Government: A Survey of Opinion in England & Wales, May/June 1978* (London: Birkbeck College, December 1980), p. 212. I am grateful to Louis Moss for giving me permission to quote his work.

Notes: The INST scale is based on twelve questions about "selected current institutional beliefs" about M.P.s, the party system and Parliament, most of which fall into pairs of positively and negatively slanted questions. The scale accords equal weight to opinions on M.P.s, the party system and Parliament. For further details, see Moss, op. cit., p. 202. The partisan commitment questions were: "Generally speaking, would you usually think of yourself as supporting any one of the political parties? (Which?) *IF NONE:* Would you think of yourself as *closer* to any of them than to others?"

tions is less certain. Unfortunately, the rich store of trend data for the United States has no equivalent in Britain. Almost the only information at hand is an irregular scattering of variously phrased, one-off questions in the opinion polls and the occasional academic survey. But a flavour of public attitudes in Britain, and how they have moved over time, can be obtained from Table 4.8, which presents the answers to the only questions for which, to my knowledge, trend data exist.

All three questions suggest a substantial but not overwhelming degree of scepticism and dissatisfaction—as do most of the one-off questions that are asked in the opinion polls. There appears to have been a growth of disaffection, but a slow one, stretching back to the

Table 4.8

Three indications of attitudes to the wider democratic order: Post-war trends

Q. "Do you think that British politicians are mainly out for themselves, for their party, or to do the best for the country?" (Gallup)

	July 1979	May 1978	July 1972	June 1944
Themselves	48	46	38	36
Party	24	24	22	22
Country	18	19	28	36
DK	11	11	13	6

Q. "Do you think there is any real important differences [sic] between the political parties or are they all much of a muchness?" (Gallup)

	Oct. 1977	Aug. 1972	June 1970	June 1962	Nov. 1952
Important differences	50	47	50	46	59
Much of a muchness	46	48	44	45	32
DK	4	5	6	9	9

Q. "On the whole, are you very satisfied, fairly satisfied, not very satisfied or not at all satisfied with the way democracy works in Britain?" (Eurobarometer)

	Oct. 1980	Oct. 1979	Sept. 1973
Very/fairly satisfied	51	52	44
Not very/not at all satisfied	43	41	54

war rather than concentrated in the 1970s. The June 1944 responses to the first question are particularly revealing: considering that 1944 was a year in which a popular war was being successfully prosecuted by an all-party coalition, the degree of public cynicism about the patriotism of British politicians is remarkable, a reminder that such attitudes are well entrenched in the popular consciousness.

One should not, however, exaggerate the degree of public disillusionment with parties. In neither country has a minor party managed to make a decisive, sustained breakthrough; in neither is there widespread support for anti-party ideologies (despite the occasional hankering in Britain for all-party coalitions), let alone for a new system of government in which parties have no place. There is grumbling and scepticism, certainly; resigned acceptance, perhaps; but seething indignation and deep-bitten alienation, no. Such a mood is not necessarily unwelcome. It may reflect badly on the parties, but not on the public: the new realism is healthier than the old credulousness. On further reflection, in fact, the remarks by Graham Wallas appear less odd. They were written before the state had assumed responsibility for economic growth, social welfare and, in the United States, international order; before parties' governing capacities in these respects had been fully tested; and in an era still marked (at least in Britain) by extensive social and political deference. They were written in an age of mass innocence about parties, and that age has now passed.

NOTES

1. A week before the 1980 presidential election the Gallup Poll reported that the percentage of respondents giving Reagan and Carter "highly favourable ratings" was only 23% and 30%, respectively. Since Gallup first undertook the ratings in 1952 there have been elections in which one or other candidate fared even worse (Goldwater in 1964, McGovern in 1972), but none in which the combined ratings were so unfavourable. See *The New York Times*, October 31, 1980, p. A 18.
2. See Dick Leonard, *Paying for Party Politics: The Case for Public Subsidies*, PEP, Vol. XLI Broadsheet No. 555 (London: Political and Economic Planning, September 1975), pp. 2–3; *Report of the Committee on Financial Aid to Political Parties* (Houghton Report) (London: HMSO Cmnd 6601, August 1976), pp. 31–32, and "Are More People Joining The Parties?" *New Society*, April 16, 1981, p. 103.

3. The exact wording of the questions is:
   United States (SRC surveys): "Generally speaking, do you think of yourself as a Republican, Democrat, Independent or what?" Those who classify themselves as Republicans or Democrats are then asked: "Would you call yourself a strong (Republican, Democrat) or a not very strong (Republican, Democrat)?" Those who called themselves Independents were then asked: "Do you generally think of yourself as closer to the Republican or Democratic party?"
   Great Britain: "Generally speaking, do you usually think of yourself as Conservative, Labour, Liberal (in Scotland/Wales since 1974: Nationalist/ Plaid Cymru), or what?" This is followed by: "and how strongly (Conservative, Labour etc.) do you generally feel—very strongly, fairly strongly, or not very strongly?" (In February and October 1974 and 1979 the wording was slightly varied to: "Would you call yourself a very strong Conservative (Labour etc.), fairly strong, or not very strong?") Respondents answering "none" or "don't know" to the first question are asked: "Do you generally think of yourself as a little closer to one of the parties than the others?"

4. This has been established by Petrocik, "An Analysis of Intransitivities in the Index of Party Identification," *Political Methodology*, 1(1974), pp. 31-48.

5. There is a technical reason for believing that the real trend may not have reversed at all. Self-declared strength of party identification tends to be higher in surveys conducted close to general elections in mid-term. (See David Butler and Donald Stokes, *Political Change in Britain* (London: Macmillan, 1974), p. 470). The interviewing for the election surveys in 1964, 1966, 1970, 1974 and 1979 was done a few weeks after the general election, whereas that for the 1983 election was done on the eve and day of polling. Moreover, measures of party identification based on differently worded questions suggest that its incidence and strength is lower still. For example, in answer to Gallup's weekly question "Do you consider yourself to be close to any particular party? If so, do you feel yourself to be very close to this party, fairly close or are you merely a sympathiser?" over half said they were not close to any party, and a further one-fifth described themselves as 'merely a sympathiser'. (See Ivor Crewe, "Is Britain's Two-Party System Really About to Crumble?" *Electoral Studies* 1982, 1, p. 290"). In the United States, however, a review of various polls taken in mid-1982 suggests that the proportion describing themselves as Independents had dropped to about 31%. (See "Opinion Round-Up", *Public Opinion*, August/September 1982, p. 29.)

6. In the United States the persistent weakening of partisanship among successive entry cohorts appears to be a *generational* phenomenon, i.e., confined largely to those first entering the electorate since the 1960s. In Britain it appears to be the result of a *period* effect—of the prevailing social and political forces of the period—rather than of any disruption of the normal processes of intergenerational socialisation. Further details are given in Ivor Crewe, "Prospects for Party Realignment: An Anglo-American Comparison," *Comparative Politics*, July 1980, pp. 379-99. Both patterns

are likely *ceteris paribus* to result in the continued partisan de-alignment of the electorate as a whole, but the rate at which it continues to occur is sharper when the cause is generational rather than periodic.

7. See Everett C. Ladd, "The Brittle Mandate: Electoral Dealignment and the 1980 Presidential Election," *Political Science Quarterly* 96, No. 1 (Spring 1981), pp. 1–30. The figures are taken from the CPS studies and, in the case of 1980, from a CBS/*New York Times* election day poll. See also, "Opinion Roundup," *Public Opinion*, December/January 1981, p. 26.

8. See Bo Sarlvik and Ivor Crewe, *Decade of Dealignment* (Cambridge: Cambridge University Press, 1983), Table 2.18. In the BBC/Gallup eve-of-election survey in 1979, 28% of those entitled to vote at both the October 1974 and 1979 elections claimed to have switched; in the BBC/Gallup survey for 1983 the proportion was 36%. It therefore seems reasonable to conclude that the actual amount of switching, including movements to and from abstention, as measured by a panel survey, was higher in 1983 than in 1979.

9. On trends in by-election and opinion poll fluctuations, see Ivor Crewe, "Electoral Volatility in Britain since 1945," paper presented to the Workshop on Electoral Volatility in Western Democracies, ECPR Joint Sessions, University of Lancaster, March/April 1981. The mean fall in the governing party's vote share at by-elections, compared with the same constituencies at the preceding general election, rose from 2% in the 1950–51 and 1955–59 governments, to 9% in 1955–59, 14% in 1960–64 and 17% in 1966–70. The figures subsided a little in the 1970s, but when adjustment is made for the lower general election base against which by-election support is compared, the anti-government swing in by-elections turns out to be more serious in the 1970s, not less. In the three governments of the 1950s the average annual fluctuation (range) in opinion poll support for each major party was 11%, 9% and 14% respectively; in the three governments of the 1960s, 11%, 18% and 19%; in the three governments of the 1970s, 15%, 23% and 26%.

10. Between 1970 and February 1974 the swing was technically 2.1%, but this apparent stability was based in fact on exceptionally high rates of defection from *both* parties: the 8.2% fall in the Conservative share of the poll was the largest suffered by any party since the war; Labour's loss of 5.8% was its worst since 1931. Between 1979 and 1983 the swing was technically 4.2%, but once again the figure is misleading because both major parties saw their share of the vote fall, the Conservatives' by 1.1%, but Labour's by 9.3%, a figure that surpasses the Conservatives' post-war record slump in 1974. No major opposition party had lost so much support at a single election since the Liberals in 1924.

11. These two paragraphs are based on a more detailed analysis in Ivor Crewe, "Is Britain's Two-Party System Really About to Crumble?" loc cit.

12. A typical recent example is William J. Crotty and Gary C. Jacobson, *American Parties in Decline* (Boston, Mass.: Little, Brown, 1980.) Apocalyptic forebodings can also be found in the prolific writings of

W. Dean Burnham on the subject; see, for example, "American Politics in the 1970s: Beyond Party?" in Louis Maisel and Paul M. Sacks, eds., *The Future of Political Parties* (Beverly Hills, Calif.: Sage, 1975) and "Revitalisation and Decay: Looking toward the Third Century of American Electoral Politics," *Journal of Politics*, 38 (August 1976), pp. 145–72.

13. See Ivor Crewe et al., "Non-voting in British General Elections 1966–October 1974," in Colin Crouch, ed., *British Political Sociology Yearbook* (London: Croom Helm, 1977), especially pp. 63–79.

14. See Philip Converse, "Attitudes and Non-Attitudes: Continuation of a Dialogue," in Edward R. Tufte, ed., *The Quantitative Analysis of Social Problems* (Reading, Mass.: Addison-Wesley, 1970) for the classical account of non-attitudes.

15. Some excellent examples of such inconsistency can be found in Louis Moss, *Some Attitudes towards Government: A Survey of Opinion in England and Wales May/June 1978* (London: Birckbeck College, 1980), pp. 196–99. Moss found that on six pairs of oppositely slanted propositions the proportion of his respondents giving inconsistent answers varied from a third to a half.

16. See Moss, op. cit., p. 177.

17. See Ivor Crewe, "Electoral Participation," in David Butler et al. (eds.), *Democracy at the Polls* (Washington, D.C.: American Enterprise Institute, 1981), pp. 216–63, esp. Table 10.3.

18. See Walter Dean Burnham, "The Appearance and Disappearance of the American Voter." In Richard Rose, ed., *Electoral Participation* (Beverly Hills, Calif.: Sage, 1980), pp. 35–73, esp. p. 64 (Table 12).

5

ANTIPARTISANSHIP
IN AMERICA

William Schneider

The year 1964 appears to have been a major watershed in American politics. The period from the late 1940s through the early 1960s—"the Eisenhower era," "the fifties"—is conventionally depicted as a time of affluence and conformism. One leading scholar, in an article published in 1965, found in the data a trend of steadily increasing public confidence in the American system and its institutions, or what he labeled "the politics of consensus in the age of affluence."[1] Another characterized the years between 1952 and 1964 as a "steady state" period in American politics, when the balance of partisan forces in the electorate was maintained at a roughly constant level through the normal working of the political life-cycle.[2]

The period since 1964, however, has been marked by political turbulence, ideological polarization, conflict, confrontation, scandal, distrust, and malaise. In their analysis of "the changing American voter," Nie, Verba, and Petrocik present evidence of a sharp rise in ideological consistency in the American electorate, beginning in 1964. This was followed by increasing political distrust, growing alienation from political parties, higher levels of political independence, and greater instability in voting behavior.[3] Voter turnout in the United States also began a long-term decline in 1964, eight years before the national voting age was lowered.

Nor is the evidence of decline limited to the political sphere. The mid-1960s saw antibusiness and antilabor sentiment rising more or less in tandem with disaffection from government. Indeed, confidence in every major institution of American society, including education, religion, the military, and the press, suffered serious deterioration after 1964.[4] Moreover, there is no evidence to date of any decisive reversal in these negative trends. Political distrust was at its highest point ever in the fall of 1980, and the average level of public confidence in the leaders of major institutions reached an all-time low in the fall of 1982.[5]

In the area of politics, it is possible to differentiate two somewhat different types of change in the post-1964 period. One is the increase in ideological polarization and issue voting in the electorate, accompanied by sharper ideological differences between the two major parties. "There is much evidence," reports one study published in 1976, "that over the last two decades issues have gradually become as important as party loyalties in predicting voting behavior in Presidential elections."[6] Another study, applying the same scale of political beliefs to samples of the American electorate in 1956 and 1973, finds a decline from 41 to 27% in the proportion holding "centrist" beliefs, while voters whose beliefs can be described as consistently "rightist" or "leftist" increased from 25 to 44%.[7] An analysis of aggregate Presidential election returns by state reveals a sudden sharpening of the ideological contours of the vote in 1964, with the Democratic vote becoming more clearly liberal and the republican vote more distinctly conservative.[8]

The second important change after 1964 is the rise of disaffection from, and disaffiliation with, political institutions, or what is commonly called the "dealignment" of the electorate. Its most obvious manifestation is the growing proportion of Independents, who began to outnumber Republicans in 1966 and who have lately increased to close to 40% of the electorate, which is within striking distance of the historically dominant Democrats. Both parties have lost supporters, while the relative proportion of Democrats to Republicans has remained fairly constant. Related expressions of dealignment include the growth of political distrust and the decline in voter turnout.

Nie, Verba, and Petrocik document both types of changes but find them surprisingly unrelated:

> The rise in the proportion of Independents is found on the left, on the right, and in the center. The same is true for the proportion who express negative views about the parties. The proportion expressing such views goes up across the political spectrum. ... In short, though the increase of political distrust and the weakening of party ties comes on the heels of the increase in the coherence of political

attitudes, there is no clear evidence that distrust and the abandonment of parties takes place among those who have developed those coherent attitudes.[9]

The argument of this paper is that the two trends are separate and distinct. Since 1964, two things have been happening at the same time. There has been a gradual realignment of voter support for the two major parties: the Democrats have moved to the left and the Republicans to the right, and they have traded supporters accordingly. At the same time, large numbers of voters have come to feel that their political leaders are incompetent and their institutions ineffective. This sort of disaffection is not an ideological sentiment. It is a response to what the public perceives as a failure of performance. Things have gone from bad to worse since 1964, and the public's response is to show mounting distrust toward powerholders in all sectors of society.

The first change, realignment, means that the parties have shifted their bases of support, even if their strength relative to each other is stable or declining. "A realignment," according to one study, "occurs when the measurable party bias of identifiable segments of the population changes in such a way that the social group profile of the parties—the party coalitions—is altered."[10] The second change, dealignment, entails the overall weakening of public support for political parties—which, it will be argued, is one manifestation of the more general decline of confidence in institutions.

The two trends are distinct because they are caused by different kinds of issues. Realignment results from conflict over position issues, that is, issues such as civil rights or military interventionism or government spending, on which there are legitimate opposing sides. Powerful position issues—most notably, race and foreign policy—polarized the electorate during the late 1960s and early 1970s and generated a deep antipathy between liberals and conservatives. The "moderate" Establishments of both major parties were opposed by major protest movements on the left and right. These ideological insurgencies, which aimed to displace the party Establishments, made important changes in party rules and procedures and ultimately forced an accommodation with each party—in other words, a realignment.

Valence issues involve "some condition that is positively or negatively valued by the electorate."[11] Candidates and parties compete by claiming to stand for the same, universally desired values (peace, prosperity, competence—i.e., positive valence issues) or by associating their opponents with universally rejected values (corruption, incompetence, inflation—all issues with a negative valence). Valence issues are not divisive. They do not realign party support because they do not create group conflict: no one is "for" corruption or "against" prosperity the way many people are for government regulation or against military intervention. Valence issues are responsible for the normal electoral phenomenon called "swing" in the British context, or "switching" in the classic study of American voting behavior by Key.[12] In bad times, voters swing against the incumbent party and switch to the "outs." Voter support is affected across the board. As a result, valence issues have a powerful effect on a party's overall performance but leave the underlying correlates of the vote—the "social group profiles" of the parties—essentially undisturbed.

In order for swing to take place, the voters must be able to differentiate the parties in terms of valence issues; that is, the electorate must be able to perceive a choice. A choice in valence issue terms is simply the anticipation that one party can solve the problems created by the other, and that it therefore makes sense to change governments. If the Democrats have the country embroiled in a tragic and wasteful foreign war, voting for the Republicans makes sense only if people believe the Republican Party can end the war. If the Republicans create a major depression, the Democrats must try to make voters believe that they can return the country to prosperity. If such a choice is not perceived, if the voters become disillusioned and cynical about the possibility of effective leadership, then the result is widespread alienation and its behavioural consequences—apathy, rejection of parties, volatility, and support for unconventional and sometimes extremist alternatives.

Protest occurs when a group with a strongly defined issue position—antiwar, anti-civil rights, anti-abortion—believes that the party system offers them no real choice on the issue that matters to them. In a two-party system, both parties have a natural inclination to avoid highly divisive issues. Protest creates pressure on the parties to "take a position" and thereby realign the basis of party support. Thus the Democratic Party 1960–64, under pressure from the civil rights movement, became firmly identified with the cause of racial equality. The Republican Party in 1976–80 came to embrace the social conservatism of the New Right. Alienation, on the other hand, results in dealignment, that is, defection from traditional partisanship as an expression of no confidence in the conventional alternatives. Realignment is a process of ideological change. Dealignment is not ideological but repudiative.

Both developments have been in evidence in American politics since 1964. Their causes are distinct, though not necessarily unrelated. Thus, stronger ideological differences may make the choice between parties less meaningful in valence-issue terms: both parties may be seen as too extreme and too divisive to offer effective, pragmatic solutions to the country's problems. Moreover, the two trends are difficult to disentangle because they both assume the same mode of expression, namely, *antipartisanship*. Protesters reject parties because the parties do not take a stand on important issue conflicts. Alienated voters disaffiliate from the parties because they are seen as incompetent or irrelevant with respect to society's pressing needs. Thus, separate processes with separate causes have the same ultimate effect—that is, to sustain the revolt against parties and to promote anti-Establishment hostility as a dominant motif in American political life.

DEALIGNMENT

A number of studies in recent years have attempted to identify the forces that produce partisan stability and partisan change in the American electorate. These have focused on three kinds of effects: those associated with the life-cycle, or aging, in which individuals alter their attitudes and behavior as they grow older; generational effects, which occur when an age-cohort enters the electorate with distinctive political attitudes that persist throughout the life-cycle; and period effects, which result from historical forces that affect all voters at all age levels simultaneously. These studies display considerable disagreement over the relative role of generational and life-cycle effects in accounting for partisan change in the postwar period. But there is general agreement on two points: (1) that fundamentally different explanations are needed to account for partisan stability during the 1952–64 "steady state" period and partisan decline after 1964, and (2) that period effects are of paramount importance in explaining the post-1964 dealignment.[13]

Thus, according to one study, "That the aggregate level of partisanship has declined since 1964 is beyond doubt. That period effects are primarily responsible for this decline is not disputed."[14] Another study reports:

> Our findings indicate that the decline in partisanship occurred throughout the American electorate, which suggests the importance

of period forces on dealignment. Hardly any age cohort escaped party erosion from 1964 through 1976. Although the young failed to acquire partisan ties to a degree which had been commonplace in the past, voters with acquired ties to a considerable degree abandoned them.[15]

These post-1964 period effects gave rise to party desertion among older voters, abnormally low levels of partisanship among new voters, and the suppression of normal gains in partisanship as voters aged. In short, the last 18 years of American politics have been unusually inhospitable to political parties as far as the mass electorate is concerned. While period forces are often treated as temporary conditions, these have persisted for almost a generation and show no signs of abating. Indeed, even if confidence in parties were somehow suddenly restored, the post-1964 political generation would very likely remain distinctively hostile to political parties.

What accounts for this sudden, pervasive, and persistent antipathy toward parties?

We can look for an answer by examining an index of antipartisanship based on questions asked in the 1980 American National Election Survey conducted by the Center for Political Studies at the University of Michigan.[16] Question R4 in the September–October wave of interviews presented respondents with five statements aimed at eliciting their attitudes toward political parties. Respondents were asked to react to each statement by indicating their position on a seven-point scale, ranging from position (1), "disagree very strongly," to position (7), "agree very strongly." The five statements, with responses 5, 6 and 7 grouped as "agree" and responses 1, 2, and 3 grouped as "disagree," were as follows:

"The best rule in voting is to pick a candidate regardless of party label" (71% agree, 18% disagree)

"The parties do more to confuse the issues than to provide a clear choice on issues" (52% agree, 22% disagree)

"It is better to be a firm party supporter than to be a political independent" (51% disagree, 30% agree)

"It would be better if, in all elections, we put no party labels on the ballot" (45% agree, 36% disagree)

"The truth is we probably don't need political parties in America any more" (30% agree, 52% disagree)

Since this question was asked for the first time in 1980, there is no basis for gauging trends over time. However, the high level of hostility toward political parties is evident from the 1980 responses. In every case except the last—which implied sympathy for the abolition of political parties—more respondents endorsed the antiparty than the pro-party position. Indeed, a plurality took the fairly extreme view that "it would be better if, in all elections, we put no party labels on the ballot."

The five items were combined into a simple additive index, with each respondent given an "antipartisanship" score.[17] The index was then trichotomized, with the one third of the sample scoring highest labeled "antiparty" and the one third scoring lowest labeled "pro-party."

The data show quite clearly that antipartisanship as measured by this index is closely associated with the abandonment of party identification. Strong partisans in the 1980 CPS survey came out 61% pro-party and 11% antiparty. Weak partisans were evenly balanced, 33% pro-party and 32% antiparty. Independents were strongly antipartisan. Indeed, Independents who felt closer to one of the two parties and Independents with no party leanings came out exactly the same on the antipartisanship scale—14% pro-party and 53% antiparty.[18] Although there are important differences in other areas between "pure" Independents and Independent-leaners, as will be shown below, they are completely alike in their attitudes toward political parties. Calling oneself an Independent is, in short, an expression of antipartisanship.

There are grounds, therefore, for assuming that the documented rise in independence after 1964 was an expression of mounting antipartisanship in the electorate. Wattenberg, however, has offered a different interpretation. He uses an index that summarizes the number of positive and negative comments respondents make about each political party in response to a battery of questions asked in every CPS election-year survey:

> "Is there anything in particular that you like about the Democratic Party? What is that? Anything else?" (Up to five replies coded)
>
> "Is there anything in particular that you don't like about the Democratic Party? What is that? Anything else?" (Up to five replies coded)
>
> (and similarly for the Republican Party)

Wattenberg finds "that the increase in alienation towards the parties has been minimal. The major change which has taken place in the public's evaluation of the parties has been towards a neutral rather than a negative attitude."[19]

The principal evidence for this conclusion is the fact that, from 1952 to 1980, the proportion of respondents presenting a net neutral attitude toward both major parties has increased steadily, from 13% in 1952 to 36.5% in 1980. The proportion offering overall negative views of both parties, as well as the proportion expressing negative views of one party and a neutral attitude toward the other, has shown no tendency to increase.[20] Wattenberg argues, therefore, that the trend has not been one of increasing negativism or antipartisanship, but growing neutrality toward political parties, that is, a "reduction of salience" of the parties as political objects.

Table 5.1a reconstructs the Wattenberg index using data from the 1980 CPS survey and correlates it with independence and antipartisanship. Independence and antipartisanship are both associated with neutral as well as negative attitudes toward the two parties. The highest level of independence (51%) is exhibited by people who are neutral in their feelings about both Democrats and Republicans. Antipartisanship is highest (48%) among those with negative attitudes toward both parties, but it is almost as high (43%) among those with neutral or negative-neutral attitudes. A positive attitude toward either or both parties has the effect of reducing independence and antipartisanship.

These findings suggest that neutralism, as measured by the Wattenberg index, is as much associated with antipartisanship as negativism is. That conclusion comes across even more clearly in Table 5.1b, which shows the distribution of Wattenberg's index by antipartisanship. As antipartisanship rises, so does a net *neutral* attitude toward both major parties. The explanation lies in the character of Wattenberg's index. "Neutrals" were overwhelmingly people who had nothing to say either positive or negative about either party. Thus, in the 1980 survey, 94% of Wattenberg's "neutral-neutrals" said there was nothing they liked and nothing they disliked about the Democratic Party; 96% had no comments positive or negative about the Republican Party. But, as the antipartisanship index reveals, they had plenty to say that was critical of political parties in general.

Strong partisans, on the other hand, were the most likely to offer both positive and negative comments about the parties—positive about their own party, negative about the other party. Wattenberg's index is based on questions relating to the Democratic and Republican parties specifically, not parties in general. Strong feelings about

Table 5.1

Public evaluations of the political parties, 1980: The Wattenberg
Index (in percentages)

A. Independence and antipartisanship by evaluation of parties	Independent (%)	Antipartisan (%)	(N)
Neutral–Neutral	51	43	(549)
Negative–Negative	40	48	(80)
Negative–Neutral	39	43	(140)
Positive–Positive	32	22	(79)
Positive–Neutral	24	26	(287)
Positive–Negative	22	24	(442)

B. Evaluation of parties by antipartisanship	Proparty (%)	Middle (%)	Antiparty (%)
Neutral–Neutral	22	37	45
Negative–Negative	4	4	7
Negative–Neutral	6	10	11
Positive–Positive	6	6	3
Positive–Neutral	23	17	14
Positive–Negative	39	26	20
	100	100	100
(N)	(513)	(500)	(516)

Note: The Wattenberg Index measures attitudes toward the Democratic and
Republican parties, based on responses to open-ended questions concerning
things liked and disliked about each party. Index shows the balance of negative
or positive comments about the two parties; neutral means that the number of
negative and positive comments was the same. See text and n.20 for further
details.

Source: Center for Political Studies, University of Michigan, 1980 American
National Election Survey, N = 1,614.

specific parties are most common among strong partisans, not antipartisans. Antipartisans are "antiparty," not anti-Democratic or
anti-Republican. Moreover, the increase in neutralism reported by
Wattenberg began in the 1950s, during the "steady state" period of
partisanship and before the post-1964 dealignment. Wattenberg's
"growing neutrality" probably does reflect a long-term decline in the

salience of parties since the emergence of the New Deal party system in the 1930s. But it does not explain the sudden abandonment of partisanship after 1964. In that case, antipartisanship—negative attitudes toward parties in general—is more likely to have been involved.

But what exactly does antipartisanship mean? It means, to a considerable extent, a distrust of large and powerful institutions. It was noted earlier that confidence in all institutions, political and nonpolitical, began to decline after 1964. Antipartisanship, it is hypothesized, was associated with that decline. Two pieces of evidence support this hypothesis.

The first is the fact that in the 1980 CPS survey, antipartisanship is correlated with distrust of government. A distrust of government index was created using four standard political trust questions that have been asked regularly in CPS election surveys since 1958.[21] Respondents who have distrusting answers to all four questions (32% of the sample) were labeled "high" on distrust of government. The proportion showing "high" distrust increased with antipartisanship, from 27% among the pro-party third of the sample, to 29% in the middle third, to 43% in the antiparty third.

Since antipartisanship is correlated with independence and political distrust, and since both of the latter have been rising since 1964, one may presume that antipartisanship has also been rising. There is one missing connection in this triad, however: distrust of government is virtually uncorrelated with independence. In the 1980 survey, 31% of strong partisans scored "high" in political distrust, compared with 32% of weak partisans, 36% of Independent-leaners, and 32% of "pure" Independents. Wattenberg tested this relationship in every CPS survey between 1958 and 1980 and found no relationship in any of them except 1968, when there was a modest correlation of .11 between strength of partisanship and trust in government. He thus found no evidence "that the rise in cynicism towards the government has been responsible for the decline of partisanship. It must therefore be concluded that the growth of cynicism and political independence are roughly parallel trends but which have little relationship to each other."[22]

The reason for this finding, or lack of one, is not difficult to discern. It is that distrust of government is strongly influenced by *direction* of partisanship. Partisans of the political party currently in control of the government always express greater confidence in government than partisans of the "out" party. Thus, in 1976, when the Republicans held the White House, Republicans showed the highest levels of political trust.[23] In 1980, when the Democrats were in office, this relationship reversed: the percentages "high" in distrust were 28 for Democrats, 35 for Independents, and 37 for Republicans. By comparison, on the antipartisanship index, Democrats and Republicans were both 23% antiparty, while Independents were 53% antiparty.

The relationship between direction of partisanship and trust in government can be seen even more clearly in Figure 5.1, reproduced from the Center for Political Studies' *American National Election Studies Data Sourcebook.* Changes of Administration are apparent as between 1960 and 1962, Democrats became more trusting and Republicans less so, while between 1968 and 1970, Republicans moved up in trust and Democrats down as control of the White House switched hands. Between 1976 and 1978, Democrats once again

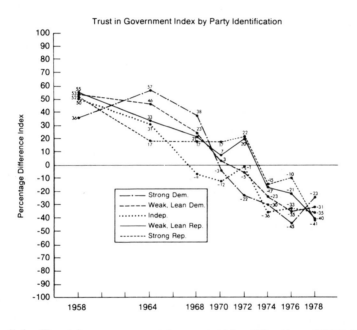

Figure 5.1. Trust in government by party identification, 1958–78

Note: Percentage Difference Index represents the proportion of "most trusting" minus the proportion of "least trusting." Negative values indicate a preponderance of cynical responses, whereas positive values indicate a preponderance of trusting responses. The questions included in the index are the same as those cited in n. 21.

Source: Warren E. Miller, Arthur H. Miller, and Edward J. Schneider, *American National Election Studies Data Sourcebook,* 1952–1978 (Cambridge, Mass.: Harvard University Press, 1980), p. 272.

became more trusting than Republicans. Data from the 1982 CPS survey reveal another reversal after Ronald Reagan took office. Between 1980 and 1982, political trust rose sharply among Republicans but only modestly among Democrats and Independents.[24] Apparently, respondents do not take seriously the introductory admonition read to them just before the sequence of political trust questions is asked: "These ideas don't refer to Democrats or Republicans in particular, but just to the government in general."

Still, the overall impression of Figure 5.1 is that of a continuous slide from the mid-1960s to the late 1970s. Every partisan group was politically trusting in 1964, and every category had become, on balance, distrusting ten years later. The timing of the shifts varied with partisanship. But once a partisan group lost faith in government, usually when its party was out of office, that faith was not fully regained, even when its party was returned to office. Political trust was not a "steady state" variable after 1964; once lost, it was never restored.

In any given year, direction of partisanship tends to overwhelm strength of partisanship as a cause of political distrust. However, distrust is consistently related to antipartisanship within every category of party identification. It would therefore be plausible to argue that, over time, rising political distrust has been associated with rising antiparty feeling, and that the abandonment of parties—dealignment—has been a consequence of this growing antipartisanship. Increasing cynicism toward government has thus been indirectly responsible for the decline of partisanship.

A second piece of evidence suggesting this conclusion comes from the General Social Surveys conducted almost every year by the National Opinion Research Center. These surveys included a sequence of questions gauging confidence in the leaders of different institutions: "As far as the people running [various institutions] are concerned, would you say you have a great deal of confidence, only some confidence, or hardly any confidence at all in them?" Twelve institutions were regularly tested: medicine, education, major companies, organized religion, the executive branch of the federal government, the U.S. Supreme Court, Congress, organized labor, the press, television, the military, and the scientific community. A general index of confidence in institutions was constructed for the combined sample or respondents in five NORC General Social Surveys, 1973-1977.[25]

Figure 5.2 shows the relationship between party identification and the general index of confidence in institutions (which did *not* include political parties). The pattern is clearly curvilinear. Independents who had no leanings toward either party exhibited the

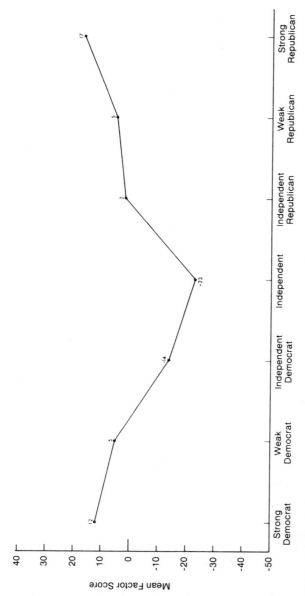

Figure 5.2. Confidence in institutions by party identification

Note: Factor score represents a composite index of confidence in twelve institutions (medicine, education, major companies, organized labor, the executive branch of the federal government, the U.S. Supreme Court, Congress, organized religion, the press, TV, the military, and the scientific community). Mean factor score = 0, standard deviation = 100. A higher score indicates a higher general level of confidence in institutions. Data are the combined General Social Surveys, 1973–77, of the National Opinion Research Center, University of Chicago (N = 7,500).

Source: Seymour Martin Lipset and William Schneider, *The Confidence Gap: Business, Labor, and Government in the Public Mind* (New York: Free Press, 1983), p. 103.

lowest level of confidence in institutions. Positive sentiments about institutions rose steadily as party identification became stronger in either the Republican or the Democratic direction. Thus, Independents with party leanings were higher in confidence than "pure" Independents, weak partisans were higher in confidence than Independent-learners, and strong partisans, both Republicans and Democrats, showed the highest confidence of all.

Strength of partisanship is thus related to more general feelings of institutional trust and identification. The decline of parties seems to be tied in to the broader trend of declining confidence in government, business, and other major social and economic institutions. Evidence cited earlier from Nie, Verba, and Petrocik indicated that the decline of trust in government during the 1960s and 1970s could be detected in all partisan groups, among highly committed Democrats and Republicans as well as Independents. Direction of partisanship affected mainly the timing of the decline. It appears that voters turned away from the political parties after 1964 for the same reasons that they soured on business, government, and labor.

What were those reasons? The explanation for the general decline of confidence after 1964 is the subject of a recent study published by Lipset and Schneider, the principal results of which can be summarized here.[26]

The study found no evidence of any substantial increase in the personal dissatisfaction or unhappiness of the American public after 1964. Americans have consistently rated their own personal well-being and their own expectations for the future significantly higher than their comparable judgments about the country. During the 1970s, there was some increase in people's frustration with their financial situations, which is hardly surprising given the economic dislocations of that decade. However, the decline in people's estimates of their personal well-being was modest in comparison with the sharp fall-off in their evaluations of the country's well-being. It would be difficult, therefore, to argue that a decline in personal trust and satisfaction accounts for the decline in public confidence.

The data did show a relationship during the 1970s between faith in institutions and the condition of the economy. Rising inflation and unemployment were found to depress trust in the people running various institutions and to lower the public's estimate of the way things were going in the country. Interestingly, economic conditions had a much weaker effect on people's assessments of their own lives and their own personal futures. The correct causal sequence would not appear to be that worsening economic conditions cause a declining sense of personal well-being, which in turn produces lower confidence in the country. Rather, it appears that a troubled economy primarily affects people's conceptions of how things are going in the country and only secondarily their sense of personal well-being and optimism.

While the condition of the economy does a fairly good job of accounting for fluctuations in confidence during the 1970s, it does not explain most of the substantial decline from the mid-1960s to the early 1970s. That was the period of sharpest deterioration, according to several measures. It was also a period of relative prosperity. Inflation and unemployment appear to function as a kind of "bad news." When the economy turns downward, what collapses most readily is the public's estimate of how things are going in the country and their faith in leaders and institutions, long before any sense of personal desperation sets in.

This interpretation is bolstered by Kinder's research concerning Presidential popularity between 1972 and 1978, a period that spans the major economic downturn of the 1970s. Kinder correlated Presidential popularity with two types of economic indicators: "pocketbook economic discontents"—that is, people's sense of financial well-being and their experiences with unemployment—and what he labeled "sociotropic economic judgments," their evaluation of the economic situation of the country as a whole and the economic performance of the government. Kinder found that "sociotropic judgements" had a stronger and more consistent impact on Presidential job ratings. The public exhibits a "bending toward the social," as opposed to the purely personal, in making political judgments. Even in a period of severe economic decline such as the 1970s, Kinder found that "in evaluating the President, citizens seem to pay principal attention to the nation's economic predicament, and comparatively little to their own."[27]

Thus, the period effect associated with the post-1964 dealignment was the widespread perception of "bad times." Confidence in institutions seems to be mostly a response to events, a reaction to the way things are going in the country. The downturn in the economy after 1973 should be treated as one of a long sequence of events interpreted by the public as "bad news." The sheer quantity of "bad news" increased rapidly beginning in the mid-1960s. Between the mid-1960s and the early 1970s, most of the "bad news" was noneconomic in nature—a disastrous foreign war, racial strife, and social conflict. That was also true in the early 1970s, when the Watergate scandal cut short the country's efforts to return to normal. Finally, from the time of the oil embargo of late 1973, "bad news" about the economy began to monopolize the country's attention—

albeit with a regular smattering of social unrest, foreign policy failures, and political scandal. Moreover, to a considerable extent, the "bad news" of the past 18 years has been presented in the context of implicit or explicit criticism of the country's leaders and institutions. Not only have things not been going well, but it almost always seemed to be someone's fault—that of the President, or the oil companies, or the press, or Congress, or big business, or the military.[28]

"Bad news" in this sense functioned as an unremitting sequence of negative valence issues. Most Americans were not unhappy for ideological reasons, that is, because government did not conform to their ideological preferences. They were unhappy because political leadership was proving ineffective in dealing with massive social problems such as war, race relations, the energy crisis, and the economy. Sundquist has labeled the situation, aptly, a "crisis of competence" rather than a "crisis of confidence":

> A succession of adverse events has produced a generalized feeling about government far more negative than was the case fifteen or twenty years ago. . . . The people expect the government to control events. After all, candidates for office keep promising that it can do so. They go on insisting that elections make a difference. So each time an election does not, it adds to the disillusionment.[29]

What Sundquist is describing is a failure of choice in valence-issue terms, resulting in widespread alienation and partisan dealignment. The behavioural consequences of dealignment include increasing voter apathy, growing volatility, and greater interest in unconventional political alternatives. It is well known that Independents exhibit these characteristics and that the proportion of Independents has been growing steadily since 1964. Table 5.2 indicates that antipartisanship may be the agent responsible for these trends. Antipartisanship was shown to be highly correlated with independence, but, according to Table 5.2, within every category of party identification, antipartisanship consistently produces: (1) lower support for the candidate of one's own party, (2) higher support for a third party alternative, and (3) a substantially higher level of nonvoting.

REALIGNMENT

The dealignment of the American electorate is shown by the growing number of Independents. But Independents have played a key role in the realignment of the electorate as well. That can be seen in

Table 5.2

Presidential vote by antipartisanship, controlling party identification, 1980

	Reagan (Rep.) (%)	Carter (Dem.) (%)	Anderson (Ind.) (%)	Non-voter (%)	(%)	(N)
Democrats:						
Proparty	12	61	2	25	= 100	(234)
Middle	18	50	5	27	= 100	(169)
Antiparty	22	40	6	32	= 100	(117)
Independents:						
Proparty	44	22	6	28	= 100	(64)
Middle	45	18	7	29	= 100	(152)
Antiparty	32	16	12	41	= 100	(232)
Republicans:						
Proparty	76	4	4	16	= 100	(139)
Middle	72	4	4	20	= 100	(110)
Antiparty	65	3	10	23	= 100	(71)

Source: Center for Political Studies, University of Michigan, 1980 American National Election Survey, N = 1,614.

Table 5.3, which examines the characteristics of Independents who felt closer to one or the other party or to neither party in 1980.

All Independents share two characteristics, both of which mark the impact of dealignment. One is that they tend to be relatively young. Table 5.3 displays the familiar relationship between age and strength of partisanship, with the representation of younger voters diminishing steadily as partisan commitment increases. Dealignment, of course, has its strongest impact on new voters who enter the electorate at a time when partisan forces are weak.[30] As noted earlier, all Independents also tend to be relatively antipartisan. Calling oneself an Independent, whether or not one feels closer to one of the major parties, expresses an intention to disaffiliate with the traditional party system.

Education divides Independents into two disparate types: Independents who feel closer to one of the major parties are quite well educated, while Independents with no party inclinations are, despite their relative youth, the worst-educated category in the

Table 5.3

Characteristics of party identifiers, 1980 (in percentages)

	Anti-partisan (%)	*Under 30 years of age (%)*	*College edu-cated (%)*	*Liberal (%)*	*Mode-rate, DK (%)*	*Conser-vative (%)*	*(N)*
Democrats							
Strong	11	16	28	32	44	24	(286)
Weak	33	28	33	26	44	30	(372)
Independents							
Lean Dem.	*59*	*39*	*49*	37	37	26	(183)
Lean Neither	*53*	*41*	24	18	*48*	33	(208)
Lean Rep.	*46*	*33*	*43*	10	33	*56*	(165)
Republicans							
Weak	29	28	49	12	32	56	(225)
Strong	12	19	49	7	16	77	(136)
All	37	29	37	22	38	40	(1,575)

Source: Center for Political Studies, University of Michigan, American National Election Study, 1980.

party identification scale. When ideology is taken into account, however, the Independent-leaners are split apart. Independents who feel closer to the Democratic Party are the most liberal category in the electorate, while Independents leaning toward the Republican Party are strongly conservative. Independent-leaners, in other words, tend to be young and well educated and to fit the ideological inclinations of the parties they lean toward quite well. Independents who lean toward neither party, on the other hand, are poorly educated and undistinctive in ideology (heavily moderate or "don't know" in their ideological views). The latter seem to fit the traditional stereotype of "apolitical" Independents.

Petrocik has examined the characteristics of Independent-leaners in order to ascertain whether they should be treated as "closet partisans," that is, as voters who behave almost the same as partisans but who eschew partisan labels because party loyalty has gone out of style. The evidence for this hypothesis is, he finds, largely limited to Presidential voting, where Independent-leaners have traditionally been more supportive of "their party's" candidate than weak partisans have been. In gubernatorial, Senatorial, and Congressional contests, however, Independent-leaners are less likely than weak partisans to follow the party line. Moreover, Independent-leaners exhibit less favorability toward the party they feel close to than weak partisans do. Petrocik concludes that, although Independent-leaners resemble partisans in some aspects of their voting behavior (mainly Presidential voting), "they do not, as some observers assume, display a stronger partisanship than the weak identifiers."[31] That conclusion is substantiated by the sharp differences in antipartisanship between Independent-leaners and weak partisans in Table 5.3.

What results, then, is the phenomenon of young, well-educated, relatively ideological voters who distrust the traditional parties and reject formal ties to them, but whose voting support, particularly at the Presidential level, is quite strong. It may be argued that their support for a party is ideological, not partisan. It is *contingent* upon the party's nominating candidates with the right ideological cast. For instance, Independent Democrats are quite liberal and usually vote Democratic because the Democratic party nearly always puts up the more liberal candidate, particularly for President. They have a counterpart among Independent Republicans who display a similar contingent loyalty to the Republican Party. The critical test comes when, as sometimes happens at the state or local level, the Democratic candidate is more conservative than the Republican. Partisans tend to stick with their party's nominee; Independents follow their ideology. The contingent nature of these voters' loyalty shows up well in the 1980 data, when the race for President included an Independent candidate, John B. Anderson, who was generally regarded as more liberal than the Democratic nominee. Independent Democrats deserted the Democratic Party in large numbers; only 48% of them voted for Jimmy Carter, compared with 60% of weak Democrats. Independent Democrats gave Anderson 21% of their vote, however, which was considerably stronger than his showing in any other category.

An ideological interpretation of the realignment process helps to explain where these Independent voters fit in. The political alignment that has been emerging in the United States since the mid-1960s is essentially two-dimensional in nature. The traditional partisan alignment represents the "New Deal system" of partisanship, with the Democratic and Republican parties differentiated primarily in class terms but with a strong overlay of religious and regional loyalties long antedating the New Deal. During the 1960s, a new dimension of ideological conflict was introduced into American politics.[32] This was a period of intense national polarization over race and foreign policy. The civil rights movement, the antiwar movement, and the law-and-order backlash were its earliest manifestations. These issues all died down in the 1970s and were replaced by narrower conflicts over women's rights, environmentalism, abortion, busing, nuclear power, and so on.

The old cleavages of class, religion, and partisanship associated with the New Deal did not disappear. The new ideological axis of conflict was superimposed on the old cleavages. Indeed, the new ideological conflicts *cut across* the old cleavages. During the 1960s and 1970s, middle-class voters divided into liberal (McCarthy, McGovern) and conservative (Goldwater, Reagan) segments. White working-class voters also split into left (Humphrey) and right (Wallace) tendencies. Protestants came to include some of the most conservative (Moral Majority) and some of the most liberal (National Council of Churches) elements in the elctorate. Right-wing and left-wing Catholic factions also came into prominence. Even Jews split, although in their case the split was between "New Left" and "Old Left" tendencies (New Politics liberalism versus neoconservatism).

Southern whites divided in a somewhat different way. During the New Deal, Southern whites maintained a solid front on the race issue behind the Democrats as the party of white supremacy. That became impossible once the Democratic Party was decisively identified with the civil rights movement in the early 1960s. As a result, Southern white voters were liberated from the tyranny of the race issue and began to divide along long-suppressed class lines. About the only group that became more unified as a result of the realignment of the 1960s was blacks. Blacks had been predominantly Democratic during the New Deal for reasons of class interest. They became solidly Democratic in the 1960s when racial interest was added in. Today, black voters must be counted as the Democratic Party's hard-core base.

The parties have been trading supporters as a result of the ideological realignment. Democrats have made substantial inroads among affluent upper-middle-class suburban voters outside the South. These New Politics voters, many of whom, like John Anderson, were traditionally Republican, cannot abide the reactionary social conservatism of the new Republican Party. They are attracted to New Politics liberals like George McGovern and Morris Udall, not old-fashioned Democrats like Henry Jackson or moderates like Jimmy Carter.

On the other hand, the Democratic Party has been losing much of its traditional support among white Southerners, conservative Catholics, and blue-collar voters who feel threatened by social and cultural change.[33] Conservative Democrats are not attracted to moderate Republicans like Gerald Ford but to right-wing Republicans like Ronald Reagan. Strom Thurmond, Jesse Helms, S. I. Hayakawa, John Connally, and Ronald Reagan all used to be Democrats, and all of them, as conservatives, found themselves out of place in their party. They "realigned" and took many of their supporters with them.

The mid-1970s temporarily reversed this realignment trend. There were three reasons: (1) Watergate, (2) the most severe recession since the 1930s in 1974–75, presided over by a Republican Administration, and (3) the nomination in 1976 of a Democratic candidate who was culturally conservative—and, as it turns out, out of step with his party.

Between 1964 and 1972, most white working-class voters were cross-pressured between economic insecurity and racial fear. Racial fear predominated during this earlier period, and so many of them defected from their traditional Democratic partisanship to vote for law-and-order Republicans and backlash candidates. In 1974 and 1976, economic insecurity brought most blue-collar whites back to the Democratic Party, a move made easier in the Presidential election because Jimmy Carter did not seem threatening to them on social and cultural issues. The return of many renegade Southerners and "white ethnics" seemed to give the old New Deal party a fresh breath of life.

The larger realignment trend was confirmed by the 1980 election, however. Voting differences by class and religion—the traditional bases of the New Deal alignment—were lower in 1980 than in any year since 1952. And despite the renomination of Jimmy Carter, the South went Republican once again. While Ronald Reagan did well in almost all categories of the electorate (blacks being the conspicuous exception), his gains (relative to Ford's 1976 vote) were greatest in the more conservative categories—Southerners, union members, older voters, and lower-status voters. Reagan showed the smallest gains in liberal-inclined groups like young voters, professionals, the college-educated, Northeasterners, and blacks.[34] Of course, Carter also lost liberal votes—but to John Anderson.

The system of class politics associated with the New Deal remains strong and, in fact, has been revitalized by the primacy of economic issues since 1973 and, currently, by the policies of the Reagan Administration. Overlying that dimension are the newer ideological cleavages associated with the social, cultural, and foreign policy conflicts of the past two decades. Thus, Ronald Reagan retains the antigovernment economic conservatism of the traditional Republican Party, but he adds to it the vigorous social conservatism of the New Right, which first brought him to prominence in California in the 1960s as a law-and-order candidate. Edward Kennedy represents a similar melding of old and new liberal traditions on the left. Thus, the current realignment has been in the direction of *ideological consistency*, with the Republican Party becoming socially as well as economically conservative and the Democratic Party moving toward social as well as economic liberalism.

One consequence has been to drive many traditional party supporters away from their respective parties. Conservative Democrats felt homeless in 1968, when the Democratic Party was firmly identified with the cause of racial equality; this group rallied behind the Independent candidacy of George Wallace. Liberal Republicans felt similarly homeless in 1980 and rallied behind the Independent candidacy of John Anderson. Some of these homeless voters—casualties of realignment, so to speak—have switched parties, but many have simply swelled the ranks of self-described Independents.

The Independent category includes many of these "realigning" voters who do not feel they can fully trust the old parties. Many liberal and conservative activists share the antiparty—indeed, anti-institutional—bias of the times and remain outside the ranks of the Democratic and Republican parties, even though, when forced to make a choice, they regularly support one of them. Thus, the Independent classification appears to be a haven for diverse groups of voters who are on their way into and out of the major parties, but who are currently immobilized by antipartisanship. In the 1980 CPS survey, liberal Democrats and conservative Republicans were the two most pro-party political categories. Their party preferences were fully consonant with their ideological inclinations. Liberal and conservative Independents, however, were the strongest antipartisans. The critical election has not yet happened that would drive conservative Democrats and Independents firmly into the arms of the Republican Party and liberal Republicans and Independents firmly into the Democratic fold.

Moreover, a realignment in the direction of ideological consistency may create *sociological inconsistencies*. As much survey research has shown, lower-status voters tend to be liberal on economic issues and conservative on social issues, while higher-status voters tend to be just the reverse. Thus, the typical voter is probably ideologically *in*consistent and therefore feels cross-pressured by the realignment trends in the party system. Many working-class voters seek economic protection from the Democratic Party but do not trust its social liberalism. Middle-class suburbanites favor Reagan's fiscal conservatism but are disturbed by the Moral Majoritarian, antienvironmental, and interventionist signals on foreign policy that sometimes emanate from the Reagan Administration. In many ways, the New Deal party system, with its ideologically inconsistent parties, may have been better adapted to the electorate. The problem with the realigned party system, in short, is that it leaves many voters with no comfortable home.

CONCLUSION

This essay has attempted to describe two different sources of antipartisan sentiment in the American electorate. One is the extensive distrust of leaders and institutions that began to characterize American public opinion after 1964. That development was brought about by the widespread belief that the system was not under control and that traditional powerholders were proving incompetent in handling the major problems facing society. It was, in short, a valence-issue discontent. Its most prominent characteristic was its generalized quality and the absence of any clear ideological or sociological underpinnings.

The second source of antipartisanship is ideological. It results from the protest sentiment that emerged in American politics during the late 1960s and early 1970s and created pressure on both major parties to realign. Conservative Democrats and liberal Republicans found themselves increasingly squeezed out of their respective parties and mounted the two major Independent Presidential candidacies of the past 30 years. Many liberal and conservative activists continue to distrust the traditional parties and to show, at best, contingent support based on ideological calculations. Thus, the Independent category collects large numbers of protest voters who feel that the party system does not fully accommodate their views. The realignment process appears to be stalled and will probably continue to be so until a sustained period of effective leadership—of "good news"—dispels the prevailing mood of anti-institutional cynicism.

These trends have come together at one point, namely, the striking success of *anti-Establishment* themes in American politics over the past 20 years. Anti-Establishment politics originated with the protest movements of the 1960s. In 1964, Barry Goldwater mobilized conservative activists to attend Republican caucuses and wrest party control from the party's moderate Eastern Establishment. The left protest movement sprang up with the antiwar candidacy of Eugene McCarthy in 1968. McCarthy's followers challenged the Democratic Party Establishment in the primaries and on the streets of Chicago that year. In 1972, party activists mobilized their strength in the primaries and caucuses in order to defeat the party Establishment that had "stolen" the Presidential nomination from them four years earlier. Thus, both conservatives and liberals waged war against their respective party Establishments. And, despite many setbacks and defeats, both protest factions have become dominant influences in their respective parties, rewriting party rules and procedures in order to "open up" the political process and pushing the parties farther apart ideologically.

The success of anti-Establishment themes can also be seen in the election victories of Jimmy Carter and Ronald Reagan in 1976 and 1980. Both ran anti-Washington campaigns, promising to shake up the system and change the way the country is run. Carter's failure in office must in some measure be attributed to the fact that he lacked an ideological program and so was perceived to be weak and inconsistent. During his first two years in office, precisely the opposite criticism was leveled at Reagan—that his strong ideological convictins made him divisive and inflexible. Thus, both major parties have managed to find campaign styles that accommodate to the anti-Establishment mood of the electorate, but neither has found an effective anti-Establishment formula for governing. The experiences of Carter and Reagan draw attention to a central problem of anti-Establishment politics: opposition to the Establishment is usually linked to an ideology, and that tends to limit its appeal.

Both George Wallace and John Anderson attempted to broaden their support by appealing to valence-issue sentiments in order to form a coalition of discontent. Wallace fashioned himself the candidate of "the little man" and "the forgotten American," while Anderson formally presented himself as the "National Unity" candidate. Neither succeeded, partly because the winner-take-all rules of American politics ruthlessly suppress third-party movements. But both candidates were also limited by a fairly clear ideological base, Wallace on the right and Anderson on the left. Voters who sympathized with their anti-Establishment point of view found themselves in disagreement with what the candidates actually stood for.

Antipartisanship is certainly not a uniquely American phenomenon. The Liberal Party in Great Britain made considerable gains in 1974, when antiparty feeling was strong in that country. The current Liberal–Social Democratic Party Alliance represents an effort to institutionalize that sentiment and develop a base in the political center. The problem is that anti-Establishment politics requires some degree of radicalism to be credible—that is, to appear anti-institutional and antisystem—and radicalism is not usually found in the political center. The Green Party in West Germany, a more genuinely radical phenomenon, has met with some success at the state level by appealing to broad antisystem frustrations. "We are the antiparty party," its leader has declared, and the Greens have proved their point by refusing to be drawn into a coalition with any of the conventional German parties.

The ideological character of most anti-Establishment politics tends to protect the political system. It is difficult to imagine an anti-party movement that would be both radical and nondivisive—in other words, one that would effectively mobilize the broad currents of valence-issue discontent that generates antipartisan feeling in the United States and elsewhere. In a very short time, Independents may be the largest political "party" in the United States. But as much as antipartisan feeling unites Independents, ideological differences divide them. It would require a major crisis of the system for voters to discard their ideological preferences and turn antipartisanship into effective political action.

NOTES

1. Robert E. Lane, "The Politics of Consensus in an Age of Affluence," *American Political Science Review*, Vol. 59 (December 1965), pp. 874-75.
2. Philip E. Converse, *The Dynamics of Party Support: Cohort-Analyzing Party Identification* (Beverly Hills, Calif.: Sage Publications, 1976), pp. 33-39.
3. Norman H. Nie, Sidney Verba, & John R. Petrocik, *The Changing American Voter* (Cambridge, Mass.: Harvard University Press, 1976), pp. 281-84. They also identified certain changes that were antecedent to 1964—most notably, an increase in political interest and campaign activity in 1960.
4. For a review of these trends, see Seymour Martin Lipset & William Schneider, *The Confidence Gap: Business, Labor, and Government in the Public Mind* (New York: The Free Press, 1983), Chapters 1 and 2.
5. Lipset & Schneider, pp. 33, 53. The Center for Political Studies, 1982 survey showed an increase in political trust in the American electorate for the first time in eighteen years. See Arthur Miller, "Is Confidence Rebounding?" *Public Opinion*, Vol. 6 (June/July 1983), pp. 16-20. The gain was small, however, and appears to have been ideological in origin. Anti-government conservatives—that is, people who shared the Reagan

Administration's ideological outlook—showed the greatest improvements in political trust. Other surveys that asked less ideologically loaded questions reported no rebound of confidence in late 1982 or 1983. A Gallup poll taken in August 1983, for example, revealed the lowest level of confidence in institutions since 1973, when this series began. See Seymour Martin Lipset and William Schneider, "Confidence in Confidence Measures," *Public Opinion*, Vol. 6 (August/September 1983), pp. 42-44.

6. Warren E. Miller & Teresa E. Levitin, *Leadership and Change: The New Politics and the American Electorate* (Cambridge, Mass.: Winthrop Publishers, Inc., 1976), pp. 6-7. See the symposium on "issue voting" in the *American Political Science Review*, Vol. 66 (June 1972), pp. 415-70. The article by Gerald M. Pomper, "From Confusion to Clarity: Issues and the American Voter, 1956-1968," pp. 415-28, gives evidence of the increasing clarification of party images.

7. Nie, Verba, & Petrocik, p. 143.

8. William Schneider, "Democrats and Republicans, Liberals and Conservatives," chapter 9 in S. M. Lipset, ed., *Party Coalitions in the 1980s* (San Francisco: Institute for Contemporary Studies, 1981), pp. 183-95.

9. Nie, Verba, & Petrocik, p. 286.

10. John R. Petrocik, *Party Coalitions: Realignments and the Decline of the New Deal Party System* (Chicago: The University of Chicago Press, 1981), p. 15.

11. Donald E. Stokes, "Spatial Models of Party Competition," chapter 9 in Angus Campbell, Philip E. Converse, Warren E. Miller, & Donald E. Stokes, *Elections and the Political Order* (New York: John Wiley, 1966), pp. 170-71.

12. V. O. Key, Jr., *The Responsible Electorate* (New York: Vintage Books, 1966).

13. See, for instance, Converse, *Dynamics of Party Support*; Paul R. Abramson, "Developing Party Identification: A Further Examination of Life-Cycle, Generational, and Period Effects," *American Journal of Political Science*, Vol. 23 (February 1979), pp. 78-96; Philip E. Converse, "Rejoinder to Abramson," *American Journal of Political Science*, Vol. 23 (February 1979), pp. 97-100; William Claggett, "Partisan Acquisition versus Partisan Intensity: Life-Cycle, Generation, and Period Effects, 1952-1976," *American Journal of Political Science*, Vol. 25 (May 1981), pp. 193-214; Helmut Norpoth & Jerrold Rusk, "Partisan Dealignment in the American Electorate: Itemizing the Deductions since 1964," *American Political Science Review*, Vol. 76 (September 1982), pp. 522-37.

14. Claggett, p. 209.

15. Norpoth & Rusk, p. 535.

16. $N = 1,614$. The data were made available by the Inter-University Consortium for Political and Social Research. The data for the American National Election Study, 1980, were originally collected by the Center for Political Studies of the Institute for Social Research, the University

of Michigan, under a grant from the National Science Foundation. Neither the original collectors of the data nor the Consortium bear any responsibility for the analyses or interpretations presented here.

17. Correlation analysis revealed that the five items were all positively intercorrelated (average $r = .26$). A principal components analysis showed the items to be basically unidimensional. The first factor extracted had an eigenvalue of 2.0, accounting for 40% of the total variance. A second factor had an eigenvalue less than 1.0.

18. It should be noted that one of the five items in the antipartisanship scale mentions the word "independent" explicitly: "It is better to be a firm party supporter than to be a political independent." Removing this item from the scale, however, does not diminish the relationship with party identification. All five items tested separately showed approximately the same correlation with party identification.

19. Martin P. Wattenberg, "The Decline of Political Partisanship in the United States: Negativity or Neutrality?" *American Political Science Review*, Vol. 75 (December 1981), p. 941.

20. See Wattenberg, Table 3, p. 946. Wattenberg creates his index by subtracting the number of negative comments from the number of positive ones. Thus a "net neutral" attitude means that the respondent makes the same number of positive and negative comments about a party—including zero "likes" and zero "dislikes." A net positive attitude means that the number of "likes" exceeds the number of "dislikes," while a net negative attitude signifies the reverse. In another article, Wattenberg carries out a similar exercise using data from Britain, Canada, and Australia. See Martin P. Wattenberg, "Party Identification and Party Images: A Comparison of Britain, Canada, Australia, and the United States," *Comparative Politics*, Vol. 15 (October 1982), pp. 23–40.

21. Questions U1-U4 in the 1980 CPS election survey;
    "How much of the time do you think you can trust the government in Washington to do what is right—just about always, most of the time, or only some of the time?" (Distrusting response = only some [or none] of the time = 73% in 1980, up from 22% in 1964).
    "Would you say the government is pretty much run by a few big interests looking out for themselves or that it is run for the benefit of all the people?" (Few big interests = 70% in 1980, 29% in 1964).
    "Do you think that people in the government waste a lot of the money we pay in taxes, waste some of it, or don't waste very much of it?" (Waste a lot = 78% in 1980, 47% in 1964).
    "Do you think that quite a few of the people running the government are crooked, not very many are, or do you think that hardly any of them are crooked?" (Quite a few = 47% in 1980, 29% in 1964).

22. Wattenberg, "Decline of Political Partisanship," pp. 943–44.

23. Lipset & Schneider, *The Confidence Gap*, Figure 10-6, p. 325.

24. See Miller, p. 18.

25. Lipset & Schneider, *The Confidence Gap*, pp. 98–99.

26. See ibid., chapter 5, for a more complete discussion of these results.
27. Donald R. Kinder, "Presidents, Prosperity, and Public Opinion," *Public Opinion Quarterly*, Vol. 45 (Spring 1981), p. 17.
28. The period after 1964 also witnessed the emergence of a variety of mass movements and citizen action groups whose business it was to expose social inequities and make the public more sensitive to social concerns. Leaders of such groups had a strong incentive to emphasize the continuing defects of society and government, not the progress being made or the victories won. Thus the volume of criticism of institutions may have been sustained by the enlargement of social and political conflict. It is also possible that the mass media played an independent role in re-enforcing the public's impression of deteriorating social conditions. Research has shown linkages between the amount of criticism and conflict reported by the media and the level of political trust shown by those exposed to such information. Television in particular—which, after 1963, became the principal news medium of the American public—has been accused of over-emphasizing "bad news." See Lipset & Schneider, *The Confidence Gap*, pp. 401-6.
29. James L. Sundquist, "The Crisis of Competence in Government," in Joseph A. Pechman, ed., *Setting National Priorities: Agenda for the 1980s* (Washington, D.C.: The Brookings Institution, 1980), pp. 534-35.
30. See Norpoth & Rusk, p. 536.
31. Petrocik, *Party Coalitions*, p. 159. Also see John R. Petrocik, "Contextual Sources of Voting Behaviour: The Changeable American Voter," chapter 13 in John C. Pierce & John L. Sullivan, eds., *The Electorate Reconsidered* (Beverly Hills, Calif.: Sage Publications, 1980), pp. 265-67.
32. Factor analysis of election returns shows that this occurred precisely in 1964, when the Republican Party nominated Barry Goldwater and the Democrats became clearly identified with civil rights liberalism. See Schneider, "Democrats and Republicans, Liberals and Conservatives," pp. 183-95.
33. Petrocik presents statistical evidence showing significant shifts in the social group characteristics of the Republican and Democratic parties from the 1950s to the 1970s. The strongest movements were those of Southern whites toward the Republican Party and blacks and Northern White Protestants toward the Democratic Party. See Petrocik, *Party Coalitions*, chapter 6.
34. Data can be found in William Schneider, "The November 4 Vote for President: What Did It Mean?" chapter 7 in Austin Ranney, ed., *The American Elections of 1980* (Washington, D.C.: American Enterprise Institute for Public Policy Research, 1981), pp. 253-56.

6

FINANCING POLITICAL PARTIES IN BRITAIN

Vernon Bogdanor

INTRODUCTION

Methods of political finance can be crucial in the shaping of a country's party system. The rules that regulate the getting and spending of political money will do much to determine the nature and limits of party competition. They will also affect the manner in which parties fulfil their various functions—offering a basis for electoral choice, representing the main segments of opinion in a country, recruiting candidates for office, and acting as channels for political participation. To chart the pattern of political finance in a country, therefore, is also to illuminate the nature of its political system.

It would be surprising if the issues raised by the study of political finance in Britain and the United States were precisely the same. Britain enjoys a highly organized party system, and one in which the parties are regulated largely through conventions and informal agreements rather than statutory rules. Party leaders dominate both the electoral campaign and also parliamentary life between general elections, and they can utilize the services of a well-established national headquarters to assist them in elections as well as in the processes of party policy-making.

The contrast with the United States, whose party system has become increasingly candidate-based, whose parties find their activities regulated by formal rules and whose central party organizations still enjoy a far more attenuated existence than their British counterparts, could not be greater. Indeed, it might seem that the debates on party finance in the two countries have hardly any point of contact at all. In the United States, the reform of campaign finance has been a response to escalating campaign costs as well as to the Watergate crimes and fears of corrupt influence on the part of special interests. The purpose of campaign reform, therefore, was to contain expenditure, limit large contributions, and guarantee disclosure; and the reforms themselves have led to a spirited debate amongst political scientists (to which the chapters in this volume by David Adamany and Larry Sabato are a contribution) on whether they have been responsible for the alleged "decline of party" in the United States.

In Britain, on the other hand, the concerns of would-be reformers have, until recently, been quite different. For the British political system is such that corrupt influences find it more difficult to gain access to the processes of policy-making, being restrained by strong party organizations and centralized political leadership. When party finance moved to the forefront of political debate in the 1970s, the reason was not corruption or the escalation of campaign costs, but rather runaway inflation, which, so it was claimed, would destroy the financial viability of the parties and undermine parliamentary democracy in Britain. It was this fear that persuaded Harold Wilson's Labour Government to establish, in 1975, an independent Committee chaired by Lord Houghton, "to consider whether, in the interests of Parliamentary democracy, provision should be made from public funds to assist political parties in carrying out their functions outside Parliament". The Committee's report (Cmnd. 6601) appeared in 1976, and it recommended the introduction of a system of state financial aid for the political parties.

This recommendation was not, however, implemented by the Labour Government, and, with the election of the Conservatives in 1979, the proposals of the Houghton Committee seemed moribund, since the Conservatives had always been against state aid. Moreover, fear of financial breakdown proved unfounded as the rate of inflation fell in the 1980s. The parties did not seem to need rescue, and the whole issue of party finance receded from public consciousness.

But, at the same time, reformers have been troubled by a different aspect of political finance—and here there is a point of contact with the American debate: the role of institutions, of companies and trade unions, in the provision of funds for the political parties. The Conservative Government is at present proposing to alter the terms under which trade union money is channelled to the Labour Party, while the Liberal/SDP Alliance has been tentatively groping for a system of party finance in which institutional money will play a less central role. These concerns are, of course, intimately bound up with the debate on the future of the British party system. The Conservatives seek to weaken the financial base of the Labour Party so as to remove the threat to the mixed economy which they believe that Labour poses; while the Alliance seeks to overcome the disadvantage faced by a political grouping unable to rely upon a close connection with companies or unions for its funding. Labour, for its part, is now fully committed to a system of state aid of the kind recommended by Houghton. Moreover, the whole issue of party finance has been reconsidered by a second non-partisan, but, unlike Houghton, unofficial, commission set up by the Hansard Society for Parliamentary Government in 1980. The report of this Commission, *Paying for Politics*, published in 1981, advocated a system of matching state payments to the parties, the level of aid to be dependent upon the number of voluntary contributions which the parties would be able to attract.[1]

Political finance, then, has been a subject of controversy in Britain, as in the United States. In Britain, party finance becomes a matter for debate when the party system finds itself under challenge. The rise of Labour before World War I persuaded the Liberal government of the day to pass the Trade Union Act of 1913 to regulate the flow of political funds from the trade unions. In the 1980s, when social changes seem to be undermining traditional class loyalties, the party system is again in flux. It is not accidental that, in Britain as in the United States, party finance is one of the key issues in the debate on the role and significance of political parties in a modern democracy.

For, if there are obvious contrasts between Britain and the United States, there are also points of similarity. There is, in both countries, a concern with the role played by institutions in the provision of political finance and the danger of undue influence on the part of special interests. But, above all, there is a fundamental issue that the debate can help to clarify: What is the proper role of political parties in a democracy, and how can they be made more responsive to the wishes of the electorate? To what extent do the parties, as currently organized in the two countries, assist rather than undermine the processes of democratic government? These are vital questions, and although they cannot be answered through a consideration of political finance alone, such an analysis may be able to cast light on the preconditions for a responsive and genuinely representative system of party government.

THE PARTIES IN PARLIAMENT

In Britain, "party" comprises three elements: a parliamentary grouping operating together under the discipline of a leader and party Whips, the voluntary organization of the rank-and-file membership consisting of local constituency associations whose purpose is to secure the election of the party's candidates, and a professional party machine—Central Office for the Conservatives and Walworth Road (formerly Transport House) for the Labour Party—whose purpose is to service, advise and generally co-ordinate the work of the party. A complete analysis of party finance must take account of these elements.

In Britain, it has come to be an accepted principle that Members of Parliament and Opposition parties are entitled to financial aid from the Exchequer in respect of their parliamentary work. MPs were first paid salaries in 1911, and since then, apart from regular increases, they have become entitled to various financial allowances and benefits, such as free travel between London and their constituencies, and secretarial and research allowances. In 1983, MP's salaries were raised to £15,308, and they were entitled to secretarial and research allowances totalling £11,364.

In 1975, the Commons approved a scheme of financial aid to Opposition parties to assist them in carrying out their parliamentary work, the amount of aid to be based upon a formula that takes account both of the number of votes gained by a party at the preceding general election and the number of seats won. To qualify for aid, a party must either have had at least two MPs elected at the previous general election or, alternatively, one MP and a minimum of 150,000 votes. In August 1983, the annual payments to the Opposition parties were as follows:

Labour	£317,000
Liberal	£ 63,800
Social Democratic Party	£ 45,000
Scottish National Party	£ 5,700
Plaid Cymru (Welsh Nationalists)	£ 3,500
Official Unionist Party (Northern Ireland)	£ 14,600
Democratic Unionist Party (Northern Ireland)	£ 4,900

No other parties received enough votes in the 1983 general election to qualify for assistance.

The main purpose of financial aid to Opposition parties in the words of John Biffen, the Leader of the House "is to provide . . . some counter-balancing support to that provided for the Government by the Civil Service",[2] and the bulk of the funds provided under the scheme are spent on research assistance.

It is, therefore, accepted that, at *parliamentary* level, the parties can be aided from public funds if that will help to improve the effectiveness of the House of Commons. But state aid is not provided for the general activities of the party in the country outside Parliament, either to the parties' central organizations or to constituency associations (although parliamentary candidates are given assistance in the form of a free postal delivery and the free hire of halls during an election campaign).

The rationale behind this distinction between the parliamentary work of the parties and their activities in the country at large is reasonably clear. Parliamentary parties and Members of Parliament perform important public functions, and it is in the public interest that the performance of these functions is not handicapped by lack of funds. Assistance to parliamentary candidates can also be defended as aiding the effective working of the democratic process. The central organizations of the parties and their constituency associations are, on the other hand, conceived of as voluntary associations, and, as such, their financing is, it is suggested, no concern of the state.

THE PARTIES' CENTRAL FINANCES

The central concern of this chapter is with the financing of the parties outside Parliament—their central organizations and constituency associations. It is not easy, however, to obtain precise figures for the receipts and expenditures of the British political parties. There is, in Britain, no equivalent to the Federal Election Commission, and no requirement on the parties to disclose the finances even of their central organizations, let alone of their constituency associations. Moreover, even where the parties do publish accounts, the form in which they are presented differs so widely that it is difficult, both for the academic inquirer and the interested citizen, to make proper comparisons. Too often the form in which the accounts are published lends itself to comparisons of a crude, careless or unsophisticated kind. There is a strong case for requiring the parties to publish their accounts in standardized form and ending the tradition of secrecy that contrasts so strongly with practices on the other side of the Atlantic.

It is easier to obtain information concerning the central finances of the parties than to secure adequate accounts of constituency finance or reliable estimates of general election expenditures. Between 1968 and 1980, the main political parties all published annual accounts covering the receipts and expenditure of their central organizations. But in 1980, Conservative Central Office, which had begun to publish accounts in 1968, ceased to do so. Unfortunately, the last year for which Conservative accounts were published was 1979–80, an election year, and therefore untypical for our present purposes. Fortunately, there are reasonably reliable estimates of Conservative central income and expenditure for 1980/1981; and 1981 is, at the time of writing, the last year for which direct comparisons between the Conservative, Labour and Liberal Parties can be made. The SDP was not formed until March 1981, and its first set of accounts cover the financial year March 1981 to March 1982.

Table 6.1 lists the central income and expenditure of the parties, together with an estimate of the size of the institutional support that they enjoy.

Perhaps the most obvious conclusion which can be derived from Table 6.1 is that, contrary to what might have been expected, Conservative central income is no higher than Labour's; and the real disparity in financial resources lies between the Conservative and Labour Parties on the one hand, and the Liberals and SDP on the other.

Admittedly, the figures in Table 6.1 may under-state the financial strength of the Conservatives to some extent. For the Conservative Party's central income tends to decline in the year immediately after a general election, as individuals and companies cut down on their contributions. The Conservatives, however, were more willing to incur a deficit, as they had been during the 1979 general election. Labour, on the other hand, budgeted cautiously: "Labour finance", Richard Rose has argued, "reflects a particular state of mind more than a lack of cash in the bank", a state of mind inherited perhaps from the Noncomformist ethos which produced the Labour Party.[3]

Even if Table 6.1 understates Conservative strength, there can be no doubt that the gap between the Conservatives and Labour is much smaller than it was in the 1950s, when the central income of the Conservatives was nearly three times that of Labour. The main reason for this narrowing of the gap is that, while trade union affiliation fees have increased in real terms over the last 30 years, company donations to the Conservatives have declined. Between 1952 and 1981, the cost of living increased around 700%: trade union affiliation fees to the Labour Party, however, increased from £126,000 in 1952 to £2.5 million in 1981, an increase of nearly 2,000%; while

Table 6.1

The parties' central finances (in £ sterling)

	Conservatives 1980–81	Labour 1981	Liberals 1981	SDP 1981–82
Central income	3.2m	3.2m	208,000	855,000
Central expenditure	4.7m	3.1m	191,000	852,000
Surplus	-1.5m	.1m	17,000	3,000
Company contributions	(1980) ~2.7m	—	negligible	negligible
Union contributions	—	2.5m	—	—

Note: All figures are rounded for purposes of simplification.

Sources:

Conservative Party: Conservative and Unionist Central Office Annual Report 1980/81, unpublished, but cited in Michael Pinto-Duschinsky: "Why Big Money is a Mixed Blessing," *The Times:* February 26, 1982.

Labour Party: Labour Party Annual Conference Report 1982. The figure quoted is the total of the NEC General *and* Special Funds (pp. 73, 75–76); this does not include regional accounts.

Liberal Party: Annual Report and Accounts 1982, but these figures *exclude* the accounts of the Scottish and Welsh Liberal Parties—the Liberal Party Organization (LPO) is responsible for England alone—and the English regional parties. They therefore *understate* Liberal income by—in the author's estimate—at least £130,000. (Compare Hansard Society, *Paying for Politics*, p. 31).

SDP: Council for Social Democracy: Agenda for 1982 Conference.

company contributions to the Conservatives are estimated as having increased by around 550%, from £494,000 in 1952 to £2.7 million in 1980.[4]

Nevertheless, it would be mistaken to draw the conclusion that the Conservatives are no better provided for financially than Labour, since the Conservatives can command larger resources than Labour for general election campaigns—although here also, as will be shown, the discrepancy is not as wide as is usually imagined; and the Conservatives, being richer than Labour at constituency level—a consequence, as will be demonstrated, of their higher membership—are largely relieved of the need to sustain ailing constituency organizations, while Labour is compelled to disburse some of its central funds to support them.

The only conclusion that can reasonably be drawn, therefore, from a comparison of the central accounts of the Conservative and Labour Parties is that the Conservatives, although the wealthier party, do not enjoy any vast superiority of the kind alleged in popular mythology.

The real gap in party incomes is not, however, that between Labour and the Conservatives, but between the two "major" parties— the Conservatives and Labour—and the two parties of the Alliance— the Liberals and SDP. The Liberals were estimated in 1981 to have a membership of 200,000, as compared with the Labour Party's individual membership of 250,000. Yet, with 80% of Labour's membership, the Liberals enjoyed an income only one-fifteenth the size of Labour's. The SDP, which had 78,000 members in 1981–82, the first year of its existence, was able to attract over four times the income of the Liberals, despite a membership only 40% as large. Being a new party, the SDP was, perhaps, more fashionable than the Liberals in 1981; but, when the attraction of novelty wears off, the SDP is likely to face the same difficulties as the Liberals have done in securing adequate finance.

The central finances of the Conservative and Labour Parties benefit enormously from their institutional connections. It is this which largely accounts for the fact that they enjoy a higher central income than the parties of the Alliance. These institutional contributions, so it can be argued, help to buttress the status of the Conservative and Labour Parties as "major" parties, so entrenching the two-party system against the incursions of competitors.

THE PARTIES' CONSTITUENCY FINANCES

The analysis of central party finances must now be supplemented with a description of constituency party income. Unfortunately, however, it is even more difficult to ascertain constituency income than it is to obtain an accurate picture of the parties' central finances. For constituency parties in Britain are separate and autonomous associations, although affiliated to their central party organizations and perhaps contributing income to the central finances of their respective parties. Because each constituency party is responsible for its own finances, the Houghton Committee found that the national headquarters of the parties could only "guess at the total income of their constituency organizations, and they could give us estimates of probable membership, and the proportion of income spent on salaries and wages. But they could not give us any firm figures, much less any detailed breakdown of sources of income or items of expenditure."[5] Constituency accounts are generally audited, but there is no common method of presentation of accounts, so that it is not easy to obtain comprehensive information about the state of constituency party finances. The best that can be done is to rely upon two estimates. The first is that of the Houghton Committee, which commissioned a survey of 184, i.e., around 30%, of the constituency parties in Great Britain. The second source consists of estimates given by party officials to the Hansard Society and used in its Commission's Report, *Paying for Politics.* The estimates from these two sources turn out to be fairly similar, bearing in mind that the cost of living increased almost threefold between 1973 and 1980.

The Houghton Committee's Survey

The findings of the Houghton Committee's survey are shown in Table 6.2.

Table 6.2

Houghton Committee estimates of constituency income (in £ sterling)

Average income	*Labour*		*Conservative*		*Liberal*
	Total	*with full-time paid agent*	*Total*	*with full-time paid agent*	*Total*
1973	1,804	4,632	4,713	6,595	964
1974	3,486	6,722	7,421	10,003	2,189

Note: 1974 was, of course, a year of two general elections.

Source: Houghton Report, Annex E, Para. 3.2.6.

Hansard Society estimates[6]

Labour: The Labour Party made available to the Hansard Society Commission the conclusions of the Finance Panel established by the Party's Commission of Enquiry. The Panel had received the annual accounts for the year 1978 of 40 constituency Labour Parties out of 50 selected by the Panel for a sample survey.

Average total income per constituency Labour Party was £4,577, but the Finance Panel indicated that this figure was "probably somewhat high," since the sample included four constituency Labour Parties with incomes of over £16,000 per annum. When these four were excluded, average income fell to £2,985.

Conservative: Central Office indicated that in 1980, the average current income of a local Conservative Association with an agent would be about £20,000 and of one without an agent between £8,000 and £10,000.

Liberal: Estimates provided by the Liberal Party Organisation indicated that the average income of a Liberal constituency party in 1980 would be around £1,444, but the LPO indicated that this estimate was "very rough", and "probably on the high side".

These figures, unlike those for central income, show the Conservative Party enjoying a clear financial advantage. But this advantage does not result from institutional donations. On the contrary, company donations to Conservative constituency associations seem far smaller than aid from the trade unions to constituency Labour Parties. The Houghton Committee concluded from its constituency survey that whereas company donations in 1973 constituted 5% of the Conservative Party's constituency income, trade union donations and grants from the trade unions and the Co-Operative Party in respect of sponsored candidates constituted 11% of the finance of constituency Labour Parties. These figures rose to 6% and 19%, respectively, in the election year of 1974.[7] Pinto-Duschinsky's study of election campaign finance in Oxford City, a marginal constituency, in 1979 indicates that 23% of the total of £5,216 raised by the Conservative constituency association was derived from company donations, but no less than 52% of the constituency Labour Party's income for the general election was derived from trade union payments.[8]

The Conservative advantage over Labour in constituency income cannot, then, be explained as deriving from institutional donations, nor can it be explained by the presumed greater affluence of Conservative supporters. In fact, there is no evidence that the average Conservative supporter contributes much more than the average Labour supporter. Indeed, the bulk of Conservative constituency funds derive from voluntary local activities such as bazaars, jumble sales and coffee mornings.

The estimates in Table 6.3 of the average size of constituency contributions show that Conservative superiority in constituency finance derives less from the affluence of Conservative supporters than from the higher membership of Conservative constituency associations. If Labour could succeed in attracting the same membership as the Conservatives, and each member continued to pay an average of £7.50, then the average income of a constituency Labour Party would be of the order of £15,000.

What must be borne in mind, however, is that Conservative supporters may have more self-confidence and a greater inclination to join voluntary bodies than their Labour counterparts. In Britain, even more than in the United States, giving active support to a political party is a middle-class habit; and, indeed, many of those who support the Conservatives are natural "joiners" and form the

Table 6.3

An estimate of the average size of constituency contributions, 1980 (in £ sterling)

	Labour	Conservative
Average income of constituency associations	2,985	8,000–20,000
Total membership	250,000	1,250,000
Average constituency membership	401	2,006
Average contribution per member	7.50	4–10

Sources:

Average income of constituency associations: Derived from figures given to Hansard Society, *Paying for Politics*, para. 3.6.

Membership figures: Labour Party membership figures are published in the Annual Conference Reports. The figure for the Conservative Party is derived from Michael Pinto-Duschinsky, "Why Big Money is a Mixed Blessing," *The Times*, February 26, 1982. Average constituency membership is derived by dividing the total membership figures by the 623 constituencies in Great Britain in 1980. (Neither the Conservative nor Labour Parties compete in Northern Ireland.)

back-bone of other voluntary organizations in the community. The Conservatives, therefore, like the Republicans in the United States, benefit from cultural factors such as are likely to yield an advantage to any party that can attract the predominant support of the middle class.

The ability of the Conservatives to raise more money at local level than the Labour Party has one important consequence: It means that Conservative constituency associations are more likely to be able to rely upon their own resources and less likely to need help from Central Office. Instead, Conservative associations are able to make sizeable contributions to central funds. Whereas nearly 16% of Conservative central income is derived from constituency contributions, the equivalent figure for Labour is less than 10%. Moreover, the financial weakness of many Labour and Liberal constituency organizations means that they require more help from the centre than their Conservative counterparts. In the general election of 1979, for example, only 2% of the central expenditure of the Conservative Party was used in grants to constituency parties, the equivalent figures for the Labour and Liberal Parties being 23% and 39%, respectively.[9]

THE PARTIES' ELECTION EXPENDITURES

The Conservatives, therefore, have a clear financial advantage over Labour when both central party income and constituency income are taken into account. They are thus able to spend more than the other parties during general election campaigns. This advantage is not, however, as great as would at first sight appear.

At constituency level, the election spending that candidates can incur is restricted by law. The legal limit varies with the size of the constituency, and it is higher for rural than for urban seats. For the general election of 1983, the spending limit was around £4,500 for an average-sized constituency.

No such restrictions, however, apply to central party spending, which is legally unlimited; and the best available estimates show that the Conservative advantage in general election expenditure is quite marked. (See Table 6.4).

It will be seen that in 1979, the Conservatives spent one and a half times as much as Labour, and over ten times as much as the Liberals; while in 1983, the Conservatives spent one and two thirds as much as Labour, and two and two thirds as much as the Liberal/

Table 6.4

The parties' general election expenditure (in £ sterling)

	Conservative	*Labour*	*1979 Liberal* *1983 Alliance*
1979	2,333	1,566	213
1983 (estimates)	4,000	2,250	1,500

Note: All figures are in thousands of pounds.

Sources:

1979: Michael Pinto-Duschinsky: "Financing the British General Election of 1979," in Howard R. Penniman (Ed.), *Britain at the Polls, 1979: A Study of the General Election* (Washington, D. C.: American Enterprise Institute, 1981), pp. 216, 220, 225.

1983: Michael Pinto-Duschinsky, "Party Funds: No Clear Tory Lead," in *The Times*, May 19, 1983 (an article whose contents belie its title!).

SDP Alliance. However, the advantages that a party can derive from extra campaign spending are far less than they would be in the United States. For there are a number of functions which in the United States have to be undertaken by the parties, but which in Britain are the responsibility of the Exchequer or of other public organizations. The cost of voter registration is the most important of these responsibilities. In Britain, this is borne by the Exchequer at a cost that, according to Home Office sources, amounted to around £18 million by the end of the 1970s.[10] This means that, by contrast with the United States, the parties do not have to spend money on expensive voter registration drives.

Even more important is the fact that British law prohibits the purchase by the political parties of advertising time on radio and television; such advertising, of course, constitutes a major campaign expense in the United States. In place of political advertising, the broadcasting authorities—both the BBC and the Independent Broadcasting Authority—make available to the parties free broadcasting time for party political and party election broadcasts. The allocation of time is decided informally by a committee containing representatives of the main parties and of the broadcasting authorities; the general pattern is that the Conservatives and Labour are given an equal number of broadcasts, while the Liberals are allotted a slightly smaller number, although more than they would be entitled to if allocation were based upon the number of votes received at the previous general election. In 1979, the Conservatives and Labour were each given five free television broadcasts, while the Liberals were given three; in 1983, the Conservatives and Labour were again given five broadcasts each, and the Liberal/SDP Alliance was allotted four. This pattern of allocation of party election broadcasts has helped to minimize the importance of the Conservatives' greater financial strength. Indeed, it becomes quite difficult to discover ways of spending large sums of money during the three weeks or so of the general election campaign. During the 1983 campaign, the Conservatives decided to withdraw some of their poster advertising near the end of the campaign; their estimated expenditure of £4 million was more than enough for their purposes. Speculation in the press that the Conservatives were proposing to spend between £15 and £20 million was quite wide of the mark. The Party would not have known what to do with such a sum, even if it had been able to raise it.

Of course, the increasing volatility of voting behaviour has made the campaign period more important as a time when votes can be won than it was, say, in the 1950s; and, to this extent, the financial strength of the Conservatives during the campaign period may offer them greater advantages than it has done in the past. Even so, it has yet to be proved that campaign expenditures by a party can improve its prospects in the absence of a potentially well-disposed electorate. It would, therefore, be quite wrong to explain the Conservative victories of 1979 and 1983—or, for that matter, any previous Conservative victories—by pointing to the financial strength of the party. Neither in Britain nor in the United States are elections decided by this kind of factor.

INSTITUTIONAL CONTRIBUTIONS: COMPANIES

As we have seen, the advantage enjoyed by the Conservative and Labour Parties in raising money as compared with the Liberals and the SDP is to be explained, in large part, by the fact that they have privileged access to institutional contributions from companies and trade unions. It is necessary, therefore, to analyse the nature of these contributions in further detail. This is, however, easier in the case of the Labour Party, which publishes full details of trade union affiliation fees, than it is for the Conservatives, who, even when they published Central Office accounts, did not reveal details of company donations nor the proportion of the Party's income derived from companies. However, the provisions of the 1967 Companies Act, as amended, require companies giving money for political purposes to declare contributions of more than £200, and this enables some estimate of the scale and significance of company contributions to be made.

Company donations to the Conservative Party are transmitted through two main routes: by direct donations and, indirectly, through various free enterprise "money laundries" such as British United Industrialists and Industrialists' Councils. These bodies, unlike companies, are not required to publish their accounts, but it is believed that the vast bulk of their funds is used to aid the Conservatives.

In September 1980, the Labour Party's Research Department published the results of one of its periodic surveys of over 1,600 major companies and revealed that 46 companies made donations to British United Industrialists between August 1979 and August 1980, contributing a total of £444,254, while 59 companies made donations to the Industrialists' Councils, contributing a total of £185,330. This compares with the Labour Party's Research Department's estimate of £1,936,660 contributed directly to the Conservative Party by 370 companies.[11]

It seems, according to Wyn Grant, who has made a study of the role of business interests in the Conservative Party, that it is, in fact, only a minority of companies who make political donations in Britain; and that "only a dozen of the top hundred companies give financial assistance" to the Party.[12] Nor does there seem to be any particular pattern of company donations in terms of size of firm or sector of industry, although in the past building and construction firms threatened with nationalization have been generous contributors. Some large firms such as ICI do not, as a matter of policy, make political donations; nor do such international firms as IBM (UK) and Massey-Ferguson; while foreign-owned multinationals are, in general, extremely cautious in making political contributions. Most companies regard the Confederation of British Industries or their individual industry associations as their main channel of political activity, and they give more to these bodies than to the Conservative Party. Indeed, as we have seen, one reason why the gap between the central income of the Conservatives and Labour is so much smaller than it was in the 1950s is that corporate support for the Conservatives has declined over the last 30 years. Few companies have stopped contributing, but many have failed to increase their contributions in line with inflation. Glaxo, for example, contributed £25,000 in 1981, the same sum as in 1977; Consolidated Gold Fields raised their contribution in 1981 by only £3,000, from £22,000 in 1977 to £25,000.[13]

In the 1979 general election, the proportion of Conservative funds deriving from companies has been estimated as around 80%; while, in a non-election year, the proportion of total Central Office income deriving from company donations is probably in the region of 55-60%; and, overall, company donations probably account for around 30% of the Party's total income in a non-election year.[14]

In Britain, company contributions are made less to secure specific benefits than to defend private industry against the threat of nationalization, to obtain lower rates of taxation for industry as a whole; and, in general, to secure a climate of stability and confidence favourable to industry. That the Conservative Party's industrial policies have been influenced by company contributions has frequently been alleged, but rarely proved. The Conservative Party is, of course, committed to the defence of free enterprise; but this commitment is derived from the Party's values and beliefs, and not from the money it receives from industry. Moreover, the Party has been making strenuous efforts to lessen the proportion of its income which derives from industry. In the 1983 general election, it experimented with a direct mail program, and it is seeking to turn itself into a genuinely mass party after the fashion of the Republicans.

INSTITUTIONAL CONTRIBUTIONS: TRADE UNIONS

The relationship between the trade unions and the Labour Party is quite different from that between companies and the Conservatives, since those trade unions that are affiliated to the Labour Party form an integral part of the Party and play a major role in its policy-making machinery. The Labour Party was, indeed, formed in 1900 to give effect to the demand for working-class representation; and today, nearly 90% of the Party's membership consists of trade-union-affiliated members, as opposed to individual members. (The TUC itself, however, has no organizational connection with the Labour Party). Affiliated trade unions contribute nearly 80% of the Party's central income (see Table 6.1) and probably around 50% of the Party's overall income.

The law regulates trade union political contributions more strictly than those of companies. The principal statute regulating the financial links between the unions and the Labour Party is the Trade

Union Act of 1913.[15] Under section 3 of this Act, as amended, trade unions wishing to contribute money for political purposes must obtain the approval of the majority of those voting in a ballot to establish a separate political fund. In addition, the union must give every member the right to "contract out" of contributing to this fund if he or she does not wish to pay it.

In 1981, 54 out of the 108 trade unions affiliated to the TUC were also affiliated to the Labour Party. Unions affiliated to the Labour Party had a total membership of around 8,000,000, out of the total TUC-affiliated membership of around 11,600,000. 81% of the members of trade unions with political funds contributed to their unions' political funds. Those who contribute to unions affiliated to the Labour Party become trade union members of the Party. Each trade union member of the Labour Party pays a political levy, which varies from union to union, but which in 1983 averaged about 70 pence per member.

Unions affiliated to the Labour Party use the bulk, but not the whole, of their political funds on affiliation payments to the Party. There is a standard affiliation rate which in 1981 was 45 pence per member, but unions do not necessarily affiliate the number of members actually paying the levy to the Party. The main reason for this is that the voting power of affiliated unions at Labour's Annual Conference depends upon the number of members actually affiliated and not upon the number who pay the levy. A number of the larger unions decide to affiliate on fewer members than actually pay the levy so as not to overwhelm the Conference with their voting power. The best-known example of such a practice is the Transport and General Workers Union, Britain's largest union, which in the late 1970s had a total membership of just over two million (although its membership is now around 1,600,000), $98\frac{1}{2}$% of which paid the political levy. Until 1980, however, it affiliated just over one million members, a figure that was then raised to a million and a quarter. If the TGWU had affiliated all of its members who paid the political levy, it would have been able to command nearly one-third of the total votes at the Labour Party Conference. Some unions, however, are accustomed to affiliate all of their levy-paying members, and a few, more members than actually pay the levy: for a period in the 1970s, the National Union of Railwaymen affiliated on more than 100%. In 1977, for example, it affiliated on 110% of its levy-paying members. It is entirely a matter for the union to decide what proportion of its levy-paying members it will affiliate.

But where a union decides to affiliate less than 100% of its levy-paying members, this does not mean that the Labour Party loses money. For all of the cash in the political fund must be spent for political purposes, and the remainder of the political fund is usually spent upon regional and constituency Labour Party affiliations, grants, donations and the sponsoring of candidates. Thus, the percentage of levy-paying members on which a union affiliates is *not* a decision about how much money the union concerned wishes to contribute to the Labour Party, but a decision about the balance between the union's contribution to the Labour Party at national level and money spent elsewhere. As we have seen, affiliated unions paid £2.5 million on national affiliation fees in 1981 (Table 6.1); this came out of a total income of those unions that maintained political funds of £6 million—i.e., around two-fifths of the total income of political funds was paid in national affiliation fees.[17]

The trade unions, then, form an important part of the Labour Party. The complex financial relationship between affiliated unions and the Party reflects a constitutional relationship that is itself a product of the Party's history and, indeed, of its origins. Since trade union members of the Party so outnumber individual members, they enjoy a dominating role at the Party's Annual Conference, in theory the ultimate policy-making body of the Party. Even though many large unions do not, as we have seen, affiliate all of their levy-paying members to the Party, the unions still have a voting power over nine times as great as that of the constituency parties; the trade unions can also determine the composition of the Party's National Executive Committee, the custodian of Conference decisions. In addition, affiliated trade unions sponsor over half of Labour's MPs by paying the bulk of sponsored candidates' election expenses and the salaries of their election agents and by making other contributions to constituency party funds. Since 1981, moreover, affiliated unions have been given a prominent role in the selection of the leader and deputy leader of the Party: for, in the electoral college, which chooses the leader and deputy leader, affiliated unions have 40% of the votes as compared with 30% for the constituency parties and 30% for the Parliamentary Labour Party.

The constitutional influence of the unions within the Labour Party has increased as the individual membership of the Party has fallen. In 1951, when individual membership was 876,000, the ratio of union members to individual members was less than $4\frac{1}{2}$:1, but it has been steadily increasing since the 1950s. As a result, the unions can easily dominate Labour's Annual Conference. Indeed, five major trade unions control a majority of Conference votes, while three unions *each* have more votes than the whole constituency section of the Party. Furthermore, the unions by convention each employ the block vote at Annual Conference, and this increases the influence of the larger unions.

Nevertheless, union dominance is not as stark as the above account would suggest, since the major unions are rarely agreed on the matters that come before Conference. In the past—and especially in the 1930s and 1950s—the unions constituted a fairly solid block of right-wing or moderate opinion, enabling the parliamentary leadership to defeat the constituency activists of the Left. But affiliated unions do not display so united a front today; they tend to operate in a series of shifting alliances rather than as a concerted bloc. Moreover, at a time when union membership is falling as a result of unemployment and the electoral prospects of the Labour Party appear bleak, many union leaders are coming to question the wisdom of taking an open and decisive role in the political affairs of the Labour Party. Yet, even when these reservations have been made, there can be no doubt of the substantial degree of identity between the policies of the major unions and those adopted by the Labour Party; nor of the fact that the leader and deputy leader of the Party now owe their position primarily to the decisions of the major union leaders.

THE REFORM OF POLITICAL FINANCE

The system of political finance in Britain has been profoundly influenced by historical determinants and, in particular, by the special relationship between the trade unions and the Labour Party. It is highly doubtful if anyone constructing *de novo* a system of political finance would regard current arrangements in Britain as being very desirable. But it is these very historical determinants that make it so difficult to reform the system, for the interests that would be affected by reform are very powerful. The problem for reformers is perhaps less to agree upon desirable changes than actually to effect them. In such areas of policy that are so sensitive to the interests of the political parties, the British tradition generally suggests letting sleeping dogs lie. For as long as the system seems to work, there are, it is said, no compelling reasons to change it.

In the 1970s, however, party finance became a matter of contention, because it was believed, probably mistakenly, that the system would be unable to generate sufficient funds for the parties to continue to fulfil their basic public functions. More recently, the formation of the Liberal/SDP Alliance has led many to question a system in which institutional finance plays so dominant a role; and the Conservative government has proposed amending the 1913 Trade Union Act to ensure that the principles animating that Act are better safeguarded. This proposal is, as will be seen, quite limited in substance but far-reaching in its implications.

The Trade Union Act of 1913 requires any union wishing to contribute money for political purposes to hold a ballot of its members before establishing a separate political fund. By the spring of 1914, 63 unions had held such ballots. In a number of cases—e.g., the railwaymen, engineers, gasworkers and dock labourers—although a majority of those voting agreed to the establishment of a political fund, only a minority of the members actually voted. In the case of the dock labourers, only 7.9% of the total membership supported the establishment of a political fund, while in the case of the engineers the figure was 14.3%. In the small minority of cases where those voting opposed the establishment of a political fund, repeated ballots were held until the requisite authority was forthcoming. But once the fund had actually been established, no further ballots were held to ask whether union members wished it to continue. The vast majority of unions have not tested their members' opinions on this question for many years; some have not done so since 1913, the year when the Trade Union Act was passed.[18]

Furthermore, the statutory provisions allowing union members to "contract out" of paying the political levy do not seem to be protecting the conscience of the dissenter very effectively. First, the very high proportions of levy-payers in some unions contradict psephological evidence indicating that only a minority of trade unionists now actively support the Labour Party. In 1980, for example, 100% of the members of the North Wales National Union of Mineworkers and 98.4% of the members of the Transport and General Workers Union paid the levy. Yet, it is highly implausible to suppose that 1,688,713 out of the 1,695,818 TGWU members support the Labour Party.

Further, it is difficult to explain the wide disparities between the percentage of levy-payers in different unions. In 1981, for example, 37% of the members of the National Union of Mineworkers (Durham Area) paid the levy, 69% of the NUM (Kent Area), and 100% in the North Wales Area.[19] Moreover, there is some evidence to suggest ignorance amongst trade unionists of their right to claim exemption from the levy. In their study of the "affluent worker" in Luton in the years between 1962 and 1964, Goldthorpe and his colleagues found that a large number of trade unionists were making a political contribution

> without realising this; that is to say, either they do not think that they pay the levy but have not contracted out or they admit to having no knowledge of the levy at all . . . it is in fact only amongst the craftsmen that a majority of the unionists pay the political levy and know that they do it; in other groups this proportion averages out . . . in the region of only two fifths.[20]

In a more recent study by Moran of a Union of Post Office Workers (now the Union of Communication Workers) branch in Colchester, Essex, members of the branch were asked whether they paid the political levy; 51% claimed that they did, 39% said that they did not, and 10% did not know one way or the other. However, the author was able to establish that all of those in the sample were in fact paying the levy. He commented:

> The most common immediate response to the question was bafflement. Members were often simply unaware of what the question was about, and many of the 'correct' answers came in the form of statements like "I suppose I must" which almost constituted straightforward confessions of ignorance.

Moran's conclusion was that

> The answers to this question clearly show the important role played by ignorance in allowing the UPW to pursue without difficulty a policy which is supported by only a small minority of members.[21]

In the past, these anomalies could perhaps be defended by arguing that the interests of working-class representatives required some special protection if they were to be able to compete satisfactorily with the interests of wealth. The assumption was that it is natural for the individual trade unionist to support the Labour Party, as representative of the organized working class. But this approach has become less and less plausible as class ties have gradually weakened, and fewer and fewer trade unionists come to regard Labour as their "natural" party. Survey evidence suggests that in 1979, just over half—51%—of trade unionists voted Labour, while in 1983 the figure seems to be 39%—the first time since the war that Labour has been unable to attract the support of a majority of trade unionists.[22]

Further, it could be argued that the dominant role played by the unions in the Labour Party actually harms the Party's electoral prospects by tying the Party to an extremely unpopular pressure group, while the easy availability of trade union money can inhibit the drive to increase individual membership. If the unions can always be relied upon to rescue the Party from its financial difficulties, what is the point of engaging in the laborious task of recruiting new members? It is partly for this reason that many constituency Labour Parties now consist only of a small number of unrepresentative activists whose approach to politics is very far from that of the traditional Labour supporter.

Mrs. Thatcher's Conservative government has, as one of its main aims in industrial relations, a weakening of the tie between the unions and the Labour Party. The unions, according to this view, ought not to play so direct a political role, but concentrate their energies on improving the conditions of their members. It is for this reason that the government has proposed that the continued operation of a union's political fund be dependent upon an affirmative ballot of the whole membership of a union (in accordance with the procedure laid down in the 1913 Act) every 10 years.[23] This seemingly minor reform could radically alter the British political system.

Since it seems likely that a number of unions might fail to gain majorities for continuing a political fund, the most obvious consequence could be a weakening of the Labour Party. The Party will only be able to preserve its financial strength if affiliated unions can convince their members that continued affiliation is in their interests; or, alternatively, if the Party can make up for the loss in union revenue by a massive drive for new members, so that more money is raised from individual contributions. But a more likely result, perhaps, is that the new legislation further weakens the links between the trade unions and the Labour Party, making the Party's electoral decline irreversible.

In attempting to revise the historic relationship between the unions and the Labour Party, however, the Conservative Government faces the dilemma that, if trade union contributions to the Labour Party can hardly be said to be entirely voluntary, the same is also true of company donations to the Conservatives. Indeed, company shareholders are, from this point of view, in a worse position than trade union members. For the law does not require companies, as it does trade unions, to hold a ballot before making political contributions; nor is a company required to establish a separate political fund to make such contributions, nor allow "contracting out". The shareholder, unlike the trade union member, has no rights in law if he disagrees with the political contributions made by his company. He can, admittedly, sell his shares, but this would involve him in making a commercial decision on political grounds; while the option of selling is hardly open to a member of a pension fund that purchases shares in companies making political contributions. The shareholder's only option is to raise the question of political contributions at his company's Annual General Meeting, and this has been likened to "a right to slide the stable door across after the animal has galloped into the Conservative Party's coffers".[24] Unless they wish to be accused of vindictiveness, therefore, and a one-sided attempt to weaken their political opponents, the Conservative government would have to reform the law regulating company contributions at the same time as it amends the 1913 Trade Union Act. Such a reform might take the shape of requiring companies to hold a ballot of their shareholders before making political contributions, and making these contributions from a separate fund. There would, however, be serious practical difficulties involved in establishing contracting out provisions for shareholders parallel to those for trade unionists.

There are some indications that a reform of company law along these lines, which has been proposed by the Liberals and the SDP, was seriously considered by the government; and, indeed, some ministers are said to believe that such a reform would serve to *increase*, rather than diminish, company contributions to the Conservatives, since it would alert politically conscious shareholders to the fact that, as we have seen, the majority of companies do not at present contribute.[25] But in October 1983 the government presented its Trade Union Bill, making no mention of reforms in company law.

If company law were, however, reformed *pari passu* with the law regulating trade union contributions, then, short of a vast increase in membership contributions, there would be a shortfall in the finances of the Labour and Conservative Parties: for the bulk of the central income, as we have seen, derives from companies and trade unions. Ideally, no doubt, all political parties should be financed entirely from the voluntary subscriptions of members; but in no large Western democracy does such a situation obtain.[26] It is for this reason that the question of state aid to the political parties is likely to move to the forefront of discussion. Labour is already formally committed to state aid, while the Liberals and SDP are sympathetic to a form of aid whereby the disbursement of public money to the parties is triggered through the decisions of individual citizens to contribute to the parties—a system of the kind suggested by the Hansard Society's Commission in *Paying for Politics.* Some Conservatives might not be averse to state aid if by that means they could secure a lessening of union influence in the Labour Party. Indeed, Timothy Renton MP, president of the Conservative Trade Unionists, indicated in a speech at Southwark in November 1982 that reforms in the political levy "will lead us on to further consideration of state financing for the political parties".[27] But, of course, state aid to the parties, in whatever form, would also run counter to the whole spirit and ethos of Mrs. Thatcher's government.[28]

CONCLUSION

It is easy to see British political finance as a success story. Corruption is almost entirely absent, and, despite the absence of statutory restrictions on the amount that political parties can spend at national level during elections, campaign costs are not excessive by international standards. Whatever theoretical anomalies could be found in the arrangements, they seemed, until recently, to be operating effectively in sustaining a working two-party system in which the financial gap between the major parties, although real, was not such as to impose an insuperable handicap upon the financially weaker party—Labour.

The structure of political finance is now under challenge because the preconditions for its effective working no longer exist. The decline of class feeling has made the conception of a natural tie between the organized working class and the Labour Party something of an anachronism, while the development of a multi-party system has caused many to question the fairness of a structure which offers such great advantages to parties who can command institutional finance. Critics would argue that the pattern of party finance helps to entrench artificially the two-party system and the politics of class associated with it. It is for this reason that the pattern of party finance in Britain is in a state of flux. What the final result of the questioning of current orthodoxies will be, no one can foretell. But what *can* be predicted with some reasonable degree of confidence is that there will not again be consensus upon the appropriate structure of party finance for Britain until the contours of her party system are delineated with rather sharper clarity than they are the present time. In Britain, at least, if not in other democracies also, the pattern of party finance is a product of the constellation of political forces; and the prime element in that constellation is the structure of the party system.

NOTES

1. The Author was Secretary to the Hansard Society's Commission.
2. House of Commons, 8 March 1983, Col. 810.
3. Richard Rose, *The Problem of Party Government* (Penguin Edition, 1976), p. 237. This book contains one of the earliest authoritative accounts of party finance and is still of great value.
4. Figures for Labour's central finances are derived from the Party's annual Conference Reports. Figures for the Conservatives' central income are unpublished, but provided by Central Office to Michael Pinto-Duschinsky for use in his book, *British Political Finance, 1830–1980* (American Enterprise Institute, 1981), p. 18. Estimates for company donations to the Conservatives in 1952 are from *British Political Finance*, p. 231. Estimates for 1980 are from Pinto-Duschinsky, Why big money is a mixed blessing, *The Times*, February 26, 1982.

    British Political Finance is the most complete and reliable account of the subject that has yet been published. Its conclusions, however, are, in my view, questionable.
5. Committee on Financial Aid to Political Parties (Houghton Committee) *Report* (Cmnd. 6601), 1976. para. 5.6.
6. Source: Hansard Society Commission, *Paying for Politics*, para. 3.6 and p. 31.
7. Houghton Report, para. 5.32.
8. Michael Pinto-Duschinsky: Financing the British General Election. In Howard R. Penniman (Ed.), *Britain at the Polls, 1979* (American Enterprise Institute, 1981), p. 108.
9. The figures for constituency contributions to Conservative central funds are derived from the Central Office income and expenditure accounts for 1978/79 and 1979/80. Figures for Labour are derived from the Party's Annual Conference Reports. Figures for the 1979 general election are derived from Pinto-Duschinsky, Financing the British General Election, p. 107.
10. *British Political Finance*, p. 262 fn.
11. Labour Party Information Paper: Company Donations to the Tory Party and Other Political Organisations (Information Paper No. II, Labour Party Research Department, September 1980).

12. Wyn Grant, Business Interests and the British Conservative Party. In *Government and Opposition*, 1979, p. 155. Most of the information in this paragraph is derived from Grant.

13. Michael Pinto-Duschinsky: How Tory Cash Is Dwindling, *The Times*, February 26, 1982.

14. Financing the British General Election, p. 103; *Paying for Politics* (Hansard Society, 1981), p. 18.

15. The most comprehensive analysis of this Act is by K. D. Ewing, *Trade Unions, The Labour Party and the Law* (Edinburgh University Press, 1982).

16. The Annual Report of the Certification Officer for Trade Unions and Employers Associations gives details of the political funds of trade unions, and the percentage of each union's total membership contributing to the political fund. TUC Annual Reports gives details of unions affiliated to the TUC. Labour Party Annual Conference Reports provide details of unions affiliated to the Labour Party. The figure for the average size of the political levy is the author's estimate derived from an interview with an official of the organization, Trade Unions for a Labour Victory, in September 1983.

17. The figure of £6 million is derived from the Annual Report of the Certification Officer for 1982, para. 6.8.

18. *British Political Finance*, p. 69.

19. Annual Report of the Certification Officer for 1982, Appendix 5.

20. John Goldthorpe et al., *The Affluent Worker: Industrial Attitudes and Behaviour* (Cambridge University Press, 1968), p. III.

21. Michael Moran, *The Union of Post Office Workers* (Macmillan, 1974), p. 91.

22. Ivor Crewe, The Disturbing Truth Behind Labour's Rout, *Guardian*, June 13, 1983.

23. See the comments by Mrs. Thatcher in the Queen's Speech, House of Commons, June 22, 1983, together with the proposals in clauses 8–15 of the 1983 Trade Union Bill. Earlier in its consultative Green Paper, *Democracy in Trade Unions* (Cmdn. 8778), January, 1983, the government had floated the idea of replacing contracting out by contracting in, the system in force between 1927 and 1946. This proposal, however, now seems to have been dropped.

24. Peter Archer MP, House of Commons, March 3, 1980, Col. 103.

25. Law Reform Could Help Tory Funds, *The Times*, August 18, 1983.

26. Khayyam Zev Paltiel, Campaign Finance: Contrasting Practices and Reforms. In David Butler, Howard R. Penniman and Austin Ranney (eds.), *Democracy at the Polls* (American Enterprise Institute, 1981), p. 143.

27. Green Paper Threatens 'Labour Levy', *The Times*, November 10, 1982.

28. I have given my own views of the direction in which British political finance should be reformed in Reflections on British Political Finance, *Parliamentary Affairs*, 1982.

7

FINANCING POLITICAL PARTIES IN THE UNITED STATES

David Adamany

"No America without democracy, no democracy without politics, no politics without parties . . ."[1] So opens Clinton Rossiter's influential book, first published in 1960, on the American party system. Less than a decade later came Walter Dean Burnham's widely-cited article entitled "The End of American Party Politics."[2] The debate about the health and prospects of American parties has continued unabated since the revival of scholarship about political parties four decades ago.[3]

Those who currently pronounce the demise of political parties[4] argue that voters are increasingly reluctant to characterize themselves as strongly committed Democrats or Republicans and that in larger and larger numbers they portray themselves as independents. Party organizations are so weakened that they cannot deliver political resources or the vote. And in Congress, party-line voting and party organization, already weak, have continued to atrophy. The spread of presidential primaries has deprived party activists of important rules in nominating candidates and has therefore weakened the link between party organizations and officeholders. Indeed, in recent years officeholders themselves have been largely excluded from the Democratic National Convention.

There are voices of dissent, however.[5] Pronouncements of the death of political parties overlook important trends toward party revival, it is argued. State and local party organizations show roughly the same levels of activity that they did two decades ago, and there is a noticeable increase in their strength as continuing bureaucracies.

153

The national Democratic party has asserted sweeping authority over the process of selecting national convention delegates. And this broad assertion of power has been sustained by the Supreme Court.[6] Moreover, exercising this authority, the Democratic party has adopted new rules ensuring party officials and elected officeholders an important place in the 1984 convention, thus reestablishing the connection between party activists and the presidential nominee.

No arguments and rejoinders about the health of political parties have been so numerous or heated as those about party finance. The new era in American political finance is, in the election of 1982, only a decade old, scarcely enough time for political parties to have adapted, either in weakened or stronger condition, to the new environment. Moreover, throughout the decade, there have been repeated and substantial revisions in the campaign finance laws, which have unsettled their impact on political parties. Many commentators, including this one, believe that many recent amendments have heightened opportunities for party influence.

More problematic is whether political parties—especially the national Democratic party and the local organizations of both parties—will be able to master the new technologies of politics to take advantage of their legal opportunities to play a substantial role in financing politics. The events of 1980 and 1982 do not conclusively point the direction of political parties. The preliminary evidence is, in my view, a cause for optimism that American parties will continue to be about as influential as in the earlier years of the postwar era. But parties will not regain the prominence of their nineteenth-century periods of peak strength. Nor will they become important enough to fulfill the high aspirations of their advocates and supporters in academe, in the press, and in the party organizations themselves.

PARTY FINANCING AT LAW

The law regulating political finance in America before 1972 is now largely irrelevant. Under the state and federal statutory schemes then in force, political parties had virtually an unlimited license to participate in the political process. Numerous restrictions on the law books were unenforced, unenforceable, or so loosely drawn as to make avoidance quite simple.

The Federal Election Campaign Act (FECA) of 1971 and its amendments in 1974, 1976, 1977, and 1979, a modest body of other statutes, and the Presidential Election Campaign Fund Act now govern federal election financing.[7] These laws provide, in general terms, for the following political financing arrangements: (1) limits on expenditures, where constitutionally permitted, (2) limits on the amounts and sources of contributions, (3) full disclosure of campaign contributions and expenditures, (4) public financing of national political party conventions, of presidential general election campaigns, and, in part, of presidential nominating campaigns, (5) independent enforcement, including the issuance of regulations and advisory opinions and the bringing of civil actions in the courts, by an independent Federal Election Commission (FEC). These same arrangements, in various combinations, are now found in virtually all of the American states.

The authority of Congress and the state legislatures to regulate political finance is limited by the Constitution as interpreted by the Supreme Court. This has been an area of vigorous judicial review and intervention, largely because the justices have regarded campaign finance regulations as restricting the First Amendment guarantees of free expression and association that have been accorded special attention by the Supreme Court in the modern era. Judicial doctrine need only be understood in gross to assay the impact on political party finance.[8]

First, the Supreme Court has held that expenditure limits are violations of the First Amendment, thus permitting unlimited expenditures by candidates, other individuals, parties, and nonparty committees. Second, the Court has found protected speech and association elements in political contributions. Consequently it has permitted contributions to be limited only to avoid the actuality or appearance of corruption. Hence, contributions to candidates and to organizations, including political party committees, may be restricted. Expenditures made in collaboration with candidates—so-called "coordinated expenditures"—are treated as contributions at law and are also subject to restriction. On the other hand, contributions from candidates to their own campaigns may not be limited, since a candidate presumably is not corrupted by the expenditure of his own funds. Third, the Court has sustained the full disclosure of campaign receipts and expenditures, although it has recognized that disclosure may deter campaign giving. Consequently, the justices have warned that disclosure requirements may not be applied to minor party organizations or candidates able to show "a reasonable probability" that disclosure of contributors' names will lead to threats, harrassment, or reprisals from government officials or private persons.

Fourth, the justices have held that the expenditure of public funds to subsidize political campaigns and party conventions is within the spending authority of Congress. Fifth, however, the Court has also held that those who accept public subsidies may be required to abide by expenditure and contribution limits that could not otherwise be constitutionally applied to them. These rules become conditions attached to the voluntary acceptance of public funds. Finally, the Court has largely sustained the authority of the Federal Election Commission, but it has required that members of the commission be presidential appointees if the FEC is to wield executive authority to enforce the FECA.[9]

Presidential candidates who accept public financing of their campaigns are subject to expenditure limits, and those limits also affect political party participation in the presidential race. The statutory limit for general election expenditures in presidential campaigns is set at the public subsidy of $20 million, adjusted for inflation since 1974. In 1980, that amount was $29.4 million. Additional expenditures are allowed for accounting and legal services necessary to comply with the law; and further spending, equal to 20% of the expenditure limit, is permitted for fund raising. National political party committees are permitted to make additional coordinated expenditures on behalf of their presidential candidate of amounts not exceeding two cents per voting-age person. Adjusted for inflation, spending permitted by national party committees in 1980 was $4.6 million.

There are two other avenues of party expenditures in presidential campaigns. First, parties may spend unlimited amounts to develop general campaign themes, to promote issues, or to appeal for support for the party ticket generally. Second, state and local party organizations have been authorized by 1979 amendments to the FECA to make unlimited expenditures for certain grassroots campaign activities. Both of these additional opportunities for party spending were substantially used in 1980 and apparently in 1982.

From one perspective, this special authorization for political party spending on behalf of presidential candidates appears to strengthen the role of party organizations, since no other person or group can make such expenditures. From another perspective, however, the special authorization for party spending is unimpressive. Because the Supreme Court has invalidated limits on spending, persons and groups who are wholly independent of the presidential candidate are not bound by his agreement to limit expenditures as a condition for receiving public money. These groups may, therefore, engage in unlimited "independent expenditures." In 1980, individuals and nonparty committees made $13.7 million in independent expenditures to influence the outcome of the presidential race.[10] Fully $11 million of this amount was spent during the general election and was therefore in direct competition with efforts of the political parties to elect their nominees. The Republicans were the overwhelming beneficiaries of these expenditures, with $12.5 million of the total spent to support Republican candidates and another $737,000 spent to oppose Democrats.

Party expenditures, although restricted to amounts well below the level of independent expenditures, may nonetheless be especially valuable to candidates because they may be spent in collaboration with campaign organizations. In 1980, however, the independent expenditure groups generally developed campaign themes consistent with those emphasized by the presidential candidates. And there is some evidence that the Republican party campaign managers engaged in regular information sharing with the managers of independent expenditure committees, thus promoting unified efforts on behalf of Republican candidates.

Political parties appear to have received favorable treatment in the drafting of the FECA's contribution limits. Individuals may give up to $1,000 to candidates in each primary election and each general election. Nonparty committees can make contributions of $5,000 to candidates. And an individual can give up to $5,000 in any calendar year to a nonparty committee. By contrast, individuals may give up to $20,000 annually to political party committees, and nonparty committees may give up to $15,000 to party organizations.

Party committees are also given preference in the amounts they can contribute and spend to directly assist candidates. In Senate races, the national political party committees can contribute $17,500, which is not subject to inflationary adjustment. Vastly more important is a provision permitting national party committees to make coordinated expenditures in Senate races in the amount of $20,000, or two cents per voting-age person in the state, adjusted for inflation since 1974. In 1982, this permissible expenditure was $655,900 in California, the nation's largest state, and $36,880 in the nation's smallest jurisdictions. In states with only a single member of the House of Representatives, the limit in House campaigns is the same as for the United States Senate, generally $36,800. In other states, the limit is $10,000, adjusted for inflation. In 1982, this amount was $18,400.

The FECA also permits state and local party committees together to make coordinated expenditures of two cents per voting-age person in Senate races and to expend an amount equal to the national party committee outlays in races for the House of Representatives. In theory this should open the way for substantial state and local party financial involvement in congressional campaigns. In fact, however, state and local party committees have been only modestly involved in making coordinated expenditures. The Republican state party committees have designated the national party organization as their "agent" for coordinated expenditure purposes, thus effectively doubling national party coordinated expenditures on behalf of candidates. This practice was challenged by the FEC and the Democratic Senate Campaign Committee but was upheld by the Supreme Court as within the meaning of the FECA.[11]

As in presidential contests, independent expenditure committees can spend unlimited sums to support or oppose candidates for Congress. In 1980, these expenditures totaled $2.3 million in congressional races. Republicans were the primary beneficiaries, with $622,000 spent to advocate election of their candidates and $1.3 million spent to urge the defeat of their Democratic opponents. Independent expenditures in 1982 rose more than 150% from 1980 levels, to $5.8 million. Republicans were again the major beneficiaries, with $876,000 spent to support their candidates and $3.9 million spent to oppose their Democratic competitors. In 1982, 80% of independent expenditures were for "negative campaigning" compared to 59% of 1980 congressional spending.

The two largest groups—the Congressional Club and the National Conservative Political Action Committee—recorded total expenditures of $3.6 million to support or oppose candidates. In Maryland, NCPAC spent almost $700,000 to oppose the reelection bid of Democratic Senator Paul Sarbanes. The permissible national and state Democratic party spending limit for coordinated expenditures in Maryland was $230,200. On the other hand, the usefulness of coordinated expenditures may vastly exceed the worth of independent expenditures. In Maryland, the Republican candidate for the United States Senate was so frustrated by the prominence of NCPAC expenditures as a campaign issue that in a television appearance he disavowed the organization and its efforts.

In 1979, Congress greatly expanded the opportunity for local and state political party organizations to participate in the financing of campaigns of their federal office candidates. Limits on coordinated expenditures by state and local party committees were wholly eliminated for three types of activity: slate cards or sample ballots listing three or more candidates recommended by the party organization; registration and get-out-the-vote activities—except mass media advertising—conducted on behalf of presidential and vice presidential candidates; and campaign materials such as handbills, brochures, posters, stickers, signs, and so forth, but excluding mass media advertising, on behalf of any federal office candidate.

The magnitude of these grassroots expenditures in 1980 is not known. The 1979 amendments to the FECA also exempted state and local party committees from reporting these activities if they did not receive contributions or make expenditures in excess of $5,000 and did not make contributions in excess of $1,000. The vast majority of local party committees would not exceed these limits in the ordinary course of campaigning. Reportable Republican state and local party expenditures on behalf of federal office candidates in 1980 were $837,300, according to the FEC, and Democratic party outlays were $375,000. Comparable expenditures in 1982 were $400,000 by Republican committees and $1.1 million by the Democrats. But Herbert E. Alexander has estimated actual outlays by state and local party committees in 1980 at $15 million on the Republican side and $4 million in the Democratic camp.[12] Estimates of state and local party committee activity in 1982 are not yet available.

It is apparent, however, that state and local party expenditures for grassroots campaigning and for mobilizing voters will increase as party officials gain understanding of the opportunity offered by the 1979 amendments. Indeed, because of the limits imposed on national party committee spending in both presidential and congressional campaigns, the 1979 amendments are a powerful incentive for candidates and national party activists to assist local and state party organizations to raise funds. Finally, the 1979 amendments create a very special opportunity for party involvement when taken together with a provision of the FECA that permits unlimited transfers of funds between national, state, and local party committees. Under these combined provisions, national party committees can transfer unlimited funds, beyond their permissible coordinated expenditures, to state and local party committees for grassroots campaigning on behalf of federal office candidates and for mobilizing voters.

Independent expenditure committees can, of course, spend money in unlimited amounts for all of these same purposes. In addition, the FECA specifically permits labor unions and other membership organizations to communicate with their members and corporations to communicate with stockholders and executive/ administrative personnel for the purpose of advocating the election or defeat of candidates. And nonpartisan registration and get-out-the-vote activities are exempt from FECA expenditure rules.

Public financing of campaigns is the newest element in American national policy for regulating politics. It has also been the most controversial. Its bearing on political parties is not at all clear, however. At the national level, subsidies of $3 million are provided to the major political parties to pay the costs of national presidential nominating conventions. Adjusted for inflation, this subsidy amounted to $4.7 million in 1980. A complaint sometimes heard about the public financing of conventions is that the subsidy by law also constitutes an expenditure limit, except under extraordinary circumstances in which case the FEC can permit additional expenditures. Public financing of national conventions greatly relieves the parties of costs they formerly bore, allowing them to use their funds to support candidates or engage in party-building activities.

A candidate for the presidential nomination of a major party is also eligible for public support of his campaign. In summary, the statutory scheme requires a candidate to qualify for public financing by raising $5,000 in each of 20 states in contributions from individuals in amounts not exceeding $250. Candidates who qualify are then eligible to have contributions in the amount of $250 or less matched by federal funds. An overall spending limit of $10 million is imposed as a condition for receiving public funds. Adjusted for inflation, this amount was $14.7 million in 1980. An additional amount, equal to 20% of this limit, may be spent for fund-raising activities, and in 1980 this was an additional $2.9 million. Compliance costs—such as accounting, bookkeeping, legal services—are not subject to the limits. State-by-state expenditure limits are prescribed within the national spending ceiling. Finally, the law provides that a candidate's eligibility for public subsidies terminates 30 days after a primary election in which he receives less than 10% of the vote, and this eligibility may be renewed if he receives 20% or more of the vote in a subsequent primary.

Opponents of this public subsidy scheme argue that it reduces the reliance of presidential candidates on traditional party activists. They are still important, however, in the broad-based fund raising necessary to trigger matching grants. Moreover, the American party organizations have not historically been involved in prenomination contests. The new public financing arrangement does not therefore weaken the party organizations as entities, whatever may be its impact on the influence of individual party activists.

Other aspects of the public financing of prenomination campaigns for the presidency are also controversial. The state-by-state expenditure limits that are attached to the subsidy are generally regarded as unnecessary restrictions upon candidate strategy, and the total expenditure limit is widely viewed as too low. Another complaint is that the availability of public campaign subsidies has encouraged states to adopt the primary system, thus diminishing the role of state and local party caucuses and conventions in selecting the nominees. But the trend toward primaries was already strong before the public financing of nomination campaigns entered the nation's politics.

The general election candidates of major parties are eligible for public grants of $20 million, adjusted for inflation. In 1980 this amount was $29.4 million. As previously noted, this subsidy also constitutes an expenditure limit, with exceptions for compliance expenses, outlays by national party committees of two cents per voting-age person, and spending of an additional 20% to meet fund-raising costs. From the perspective of political parties, this funding of general election campaigns may weaken the link between candidates and party organizations by relieving office-seekers from virtually all dependence on national party committees. This complaint is substantially ameliorated, however, by the authorization for parties to make coordinated expenditures of up to two cents per voting-age person and by their remaining authority to engage in general political advertising stressing issues or partisan affiliation. Moreover, the 1979 amendments give state and local parties wide scope to support presidential candidates directly and the provisions of law allowing unlimited interparty transfers invite the national party organizations to be substantially involved in financing these grassroots campaign activities.

Indeed, it has been argued that the absolute prohibition on private contributions to presidential campaigns creates an opportunity for parties to win financial support from interested citizens who would otherwise have given to presidential candidates. There is evidence, however, that independent expenditure committees have been quicker and more adroit in exploiting this possibility. They can legally claim that they are permitted to campaign directly for the candidate, since they are not restricted by the limit on coordinated expenditures. And they can therefore capture the financial support of persons seeking to support a particular presidential aspirant but barred from contributing directly to his campaign. A number of commentators have urged that presidential candidates be authorized to receive small individual contributions, in order to encourage public participation, but this would not aid the parties. Indeed, it might further attenuate the party's role in presidential campaigns by allowing greater concentration of financial resources in the presidential candidate's own apparatus.

Eligibility for public financing depends on the status of a candidate's political party, thus heightening the importance of party affiliation in American politics. Major parties receive the full statutory subsidy. Minor parties receive a proportional subsidy, and new parties may receive a postelection grant if they gain enough votes.[13] These provisions for new parties had significance for the party system for the first time in 1980. John Anderson, a Republican member of Congress, and Patrick J. Lucey, a former Democratic governor of Wisconsin, ran for president and vice president on a National Unity Ticket. Although avowedly "independent candidates," the Anderson–Lucey ticket was given status as a political party by the FEC. Consequently, John Anderson received a subsidy of $4.2 million after the election, because he had won 6.5 percent of the popular vote.

More importantly, Anderson will apparently be eligible for a similar amount as a "minor party" candidate in 1984, in a presidential year when the underlying public concerns that fostered his independent candidacy may have disappeared. The law's provision for "minor party" eligibility may, therefore, have the effect of denying funding to newly emerging parties during the campaign in which they reflect public opinion and of sustaining funding for them in subsequent elections. This might fragment party politics in those later campaigns when there is no longer significant public support for the minor party candidate.

Experiments with public financing in the American states give considerably more encouragement to political parties than does the national subsidy scheme. Twelve states have adopted some form of public financing of politics.[14] All of them use a tax check-off system to set the level of total funds available. Four other states have adopted an "add on" or surcharge system in which a taxpayer may add $1 or $2 to his tax liability for the support of candidates or parties. These surcharge systems have failed to attract even a modicum of support.

What is surprising is that eight of the twelve states with public financing allocate the subsidies to political parties rather than to candidates. In Utah and Oregon, the subsidies to parties are shared by state and local organizations. In 1980, public subsidies to political parties in these eight states totaled $1.5 million. This amount is quite likely to increase in the future as public subsidy programs become better established and as the parties themselves see an advantage in promoting taxpayer interest in the check-off system.

Although the $1.5 million in total subsidies in 1980 is quite modest in the context of American state and national political expenditures, even this sum represents a commitment to the vitality of parties by lawmakers and permits parties a somewhat more stable funding base for organizational and campaign activities than they have had previously. Indeed, the studies of these subsidy plans are generally optimistic about their effect on political parties. Apparently party organizations have used some of these funds to recruit candidates and to finance campaigns in some districts where party challenges would not otherwise be possible. Most of the funds have been used to build up party bureaucracies, adding staff, technical support, and fund-raising capacity to state political organizations.

THE SCOPE OF PARTY FINANCE

From two different perspectives, political parties play a very limited role in financing American politics. First, their total funds have been only a modest share of all political money raised and spent in elections. Second, their direct financial support to candidates has been a very small percentage of candidates' total funds.

Fewer than 600 of perhaps 7300 party committees at the local, state, and national levels come within the campaign reporting provisions of the FECA. These undoubtedly include a preponderance of the committees with substantial financial activity, however. In 1980, all party committees filing with the FEC reported net receipts of $206.7 million and net expenditures of $196.8 million, including receipts of $10.5 million and disbursements of $9.1 million, largely from public subsidies, for the national party conventions. Preliminary calculations for 1980 suggest that expenditures of $740 million were made by FEC-reporting congressional candidates, political action committees, and political parties and by all presidential candidates and their supporters, including spending not federally reported.[15] When fully estimated, campaign costs will be higher because of internal political expenditures by corporations, associations, and unions, which are exempt from FECA reporting requirements. The $196.8 million in net disbursements by political parties therefore represents a maximum of 27% of total political expenditures for federal candidates and by federally-registered committees.

Political parties substantially increased their financial activity in 1982. Major party receipts were $253.9 million, a 23% increase over 1980. Candidate receipts increased to $301.7 million, or 43% during the same period. Hence, political party financial activity in 1982 rose more slowly than did candidate funding. Since there was no presidential race in 1982, party money nonetheless accounted for a substantially greater percentage of total political money. Those who hope for party revival might well find some modest encouragement in these 1982 financing data.

The financial assistance of parties to candidates cannot be fully measured. Omitted from official reports are party expenditures that need not be disclosed under the 1979 FECA amendments, the value of much party technical assistance and grassroots campaign work, and the benefits to candidates of "institutional advertising" campaigns to promote the whole party ticket, criticize the opposition, or make appeals for support on specific issues. Limiting analysis just to contributions directly to major-party candidates and expenditures specifically on their behalf, political parties accounted for $7.4 million (5.1%) of the $145.5 million in net receipts and coordinated expenditures reported by candidates for the House of Representatives, $7.7 million (6.6%) of the $104.3 million in net receipts and coordinated expenditures reported by United States Senate candidates, and $8.5 million (4.9%) of the $173.4 million in candidate-controlled funds in the presidential campaigns.

In all, the political parties in 1980 accounted for $23.6 million of the $421.4 million in candidate controlled or coordinated funds, or less than 6% of these funds. In 1982, total major-party candidate receipts and party-coordinated expenditures in congressional races amounted to $23.8 million. Party contributions and coordinated spending were $23.8 million. The parties' financial role in congressional campaigns was therefore 7.8%, only slightly higher than their 6% role in 1980.

The relatively modest party role in financing federal office campaigns is echoed in most of the states, although the diversity among them is great. In a recent compilation of campaign contribution reports in six states, Ruth Jones discovered that parties provided as much as 31% of the funds in statewide campaigns in Wisconsin and as little as 1% in legislative campaigns in Missouri.[16] The Wisconsin report seems idiosyncratic,[17] however, since party contributions in other states reached only 12% and 10% in legislative races in Iowa and California, respectively. In all other statewide and legislative campaigns, including the legislative races in Wisconsin, parties did not provide more than 8% of campaign funds.

The modest percentage of candidate funds derived from parties suggests that parties do not play a prominent role in America's candidate-oriented politics. This assessment has much to commend it. But it must also be taken in context. First, parties provide organizational services and engage in campaigning that is not directly incorporated into the campaign of any single candidate. Second, it is doubtful that parties were ever a major source of funds for candidates, except in a handful of jurisdictions dominated by old-style political machines. Alexander Heard's classic analysis reveals that even a quarter-century ago, party financial support of candidates varied widely among locales and various party organizational levels.[18] Very low levels of party contribution to candidates were common even then. Similarly, studies of state parties in the 1960s and of congressional races in the 1970s showed only modest levels of party contributions to candidates.[19] These reports are reminders that the small role of parties in directly financing candidates' campaigns is not new and does not reflect some current decline in party strength or role.

DISPARITY AND SOURCES
OF PARTY FUNDS

Analysis of the role of party funds in American politics conceals important variations in the political landscape. There is a vast disparity in the financial strength of the two political parties. Net receipts of national Republican party committees in 1980 totaled $169.5 million. Their Democratic rivals had net receipts of $23 million. State and local Republican party committees reporting to the FEC had net receipts of $33.8 million, and their Democratic counterparts registered net receipts of only $9.1 million. Total Republican resources totaled $167.1 million (excluding revenues relating to the national party convention), while Democratic funds reached the sum of $32.1 million—a five-to-one margin of financial advantage for the Republicans.

In 1982, the Republican advantage over their Democratic rivals rose to about 5.5:1. National GOP committees reported receipts of $191 million, while their state and local counterparts reported $23.9 million. Democrats reported $31.5 million at the national level and $7.6 million for state and local committees.

The Republicans' early and effective adaptation of modern technology to party fund raising has been a critical factor in their vast financial superiority. As early as Barry Goldwater's 1964 presidential campaign, it became apparent that mass media and mass mailings could raise large sums in small amounts. Similar patterns were revealed in Eugene McCarthy's 1968 bid for the Democratic presidential nomination and George Wallace's third-party presidential candidacy in the same year. The 1972 nomination and general election campaigns of Democratic George McGovern were also largely funded by small gifts.[20]

The Republican party's special contributions to the evolving system of mass fund raising were technology and stability. Unlike candidates, the party organizations have continuing existence and potential continuing appeal to large numbers of party adherents. The Republicans began in the early 1970s systematically to make repeated party appeals to those individual givers who had made small contributions to their presidential candidates.[21] Information on each contributor was maintained in computer data bases. New prospects were developed both from specialized mailing lists and, increasingly, by mass appeals to certain geographic and regional groups.

By 1980, the Republican National Committee (RNC) claimed a contributor base of 1.2 million persons.[22] About 70% of its funds in 1980 were received in small gifts. The RNC has steadily increased the attractiveness of its appeals, the efficiency of its repeat requests to prior givers, and its skill in identifying new prospective givers; and it has taken advantage of economies of scale in computer technology. It has consequently been able to increase its average gift from about $26 to about $29 and substantially to reduce its cost per gift.

The Republican National Congressional Committee also developed a small contributor base. In 1980, 90% of its funds came from a contributor corps of about 300,000, whose average gifts were $23. The Republican National Senatorial Committee followed a different strategy of emphasizing larger gifts. Nonetheless, its 1980 receipts from direct mass appeals were between $13 and $14 million, and its contributor base was more than 350,000. The overall impact of Republican efforts to broaden their contributor base is clear: of $130.3 million in net receipts by all national-level Republican committees in 1980, only $21.9 million (16.8%) was received from individuals in gifts of $500 or more, and an insignificant $835,000 (.6%) came from Political Action Committees (PACs). The remainder was received primarily in small sums raised through mass appeals, principally by mail.

The Republicans certainly did not eschew large gifts. The longstanding Republican Eagles Program, which seeks $10,000 gifts, increased from 198 persons in 1975 to 865 in 1980. A "Victory '80" program, soliciting contributions of $500, $1,000, or $2,500, raised more than $1 million. A convention gala and a network of 19 fundraising dinners in early September, 1980, brought more than $4 million into party coffers, an amount shared with state and local parties. A PAC 40 Club was established to raise sums of $5,000 from political action committees. In all, large-giver events and solicitations raised at least $14 million. The Republican National Congressional Committee (RNCC) operates a Republican Congressional Leadership Council for contributors of $2,500 or more. In 1980 it had more than 400 members. Similarly, the Republican National Senatorial Committee (RNSC) sought large gifts from its 4000-member Business Advisory Board, whose members contribute between $250 and $750, and from the Senate Republican Trust, a group of about 200 corporate executives who contribute $10,000 annually.

It is apparent that in 1982 the pattern of Republican financial dominance persisted and that the GOP's successful mass fund-raising methods were extended. National, state, and local Republican party committees raised $215.9 million, while their Democratic opponents raised only $39 million, a fund-raising margin exceeding 5.5:1. At least as impressive was the Republican party's gain over its own prior efforts: In 1980, national, state, and local party committees had raised $167.1 million, and their 1982 receipts of $215.9 million therefore represented a 29% revenue improvement. The Democratic revenues of $39.1 million were an increase from $32.1 million two years earlier, but the 22% improvement represented a further loss of ground to the Republicans. One report indicates that the RNC expanded its 1980 base of 1.2 million contributors to 2 million by the summer of 1982, before the campaign had reached its highest pitch.[23] Large contributions of $500 or more were only 14.1% of all 1982 local, state, and national Republican receipts, reflecting the continued success of the party's small-contributor strategy.

The Democrats have had some successful mass funding appeals in the past. Both the McGovern and McCarthy campaigns won support from large numbers of contributors, but those rosters were not properly maintained and were not fully shared with the party organization. The Democratic National Committee (DNC) sponsored four telethons between 1972 and 1975. They raised $17.1 million, and the most successful gained responses from almost 390,000 people.[24] Average gifts for the four telethons ranged between $11 and $15. The telethons were abandoned because the FECA made it difficult to obtain the large loans necessary for initial funding and because President Carter, a party outsider, gave very little emphasis to the development of the party apparatus. In addition, it has been alleged that the contributor lists were incomplete and in disarray when the Carter operatives took over the Democratic National Committee. Only in 1982, under the chairmanship of Charles Manatt, were the Democrats finally able to liquidate a lingering deficit, initially more than $9.3 million, incurred in the 1968 presidential campaign of Hubert Humphrey.

This chronic indebtedness prevented the Democrats from investing in modern fund-raising methods. But there was also a lack of party will and unity. Democratic control of the White House and of large majorities in Congress invited each officeholder to go his own way in fund raising, giving little support to party efforts. In addition, the party's traditional coalition character meant that candidates reached out to political action committees, various ideological constituencies, and other special fund sources that were not party-oriented. The liberal/conservative division in the party made fund-raising efforts difficult, since party leaders were confounded by the problem of selecting appeals that would excite contributors without alienating other members of the party. There is evidence that those who responded to the party's telethons were considerably more liberal than the party's adherents as a whole.

Finally, some Democrats have expressed the belief that mass fund raising is not feasible for the party because their constituency is primarily outside the educated middle class whose understanding of politics, level of political activism, and financial status encourage them to make political contributions. These arguments—that ideological division and the party's demographic base are barriers to mass fund raising—have been rejected by Democratic staffers committed to following the Republican lead. The Republican contributor list of 1.2 million, they argue, is only 1% of the voting-age population and about 1.5% of those who voted in the 1980 presidential election. Since more than 80 million Americans identify themselves in the polls as Democrats, very low levels of participation, in the 1.5 to 2% range of party identifiers, would allow the Democrats to duplicate the size of the Republican contributor base.

In 1980 the Democratic National Committee raised slightly more than $15 million, exceeding its initial fund-raising goal of $14 million. Anout $8 million was raised from events and moderate-to-large gifts; about $3 million was obtained by direct mail; and another $3 million came from the party's Finance Council, composed of persons who gave $5,000 or raised $10,000. The Democratic Senate Campaign Committee (DSCC) raised about $1.7 million, and the Democratic Congressional Campaign Committee (DCCC) raised about $2.1 million. Their fund raising relied even more heavily on traditional strategies and givers than did that of the DNC. In all, the DNC had a base of 25,000 contributors, and the congressional committees added very few to that number. Of $23 million raised by all national Democratic committees, $1.7 million (7.4%) came from political action committees and $9.3 million (40.4%) from individuals who gave $500 or more. The comparable Republican figures were .6% and 16.8%.

In 1981, leaders of the DNC and the Congressional Campaign Committee made commitments to invest modestly in mass mail and to reinvest the revenues to expand their small contributor base. In 1981–82, the DNC raised $2.7 million from mass mail appeals and reinvested $2.1 million in further appeals. It increased its contributor base from 25,000 to 200,000. The party continued its efforts to raise large gifts through the newly formed Lexington Club, directed primarily at young business people who gave $1,000 or more, and its Business Council for givers of $10,000 or more. There is some evidence that the Democrats are gradually broadening their fundraising base, however. Individual givers of $500 or more accounted for 18.5% ($7.2 million) of the $39 million raised by all Democratic party committees during the 1982 election cycle, compared with 40.1% raised from these large givers in 1980. Nonetheless, the Democrats were still more reliant on large givers in 1982 than were the Republicans, who received only 14.1% of their funds from individual contributions of $500 or more.

The Republicans have a massive financing advantage and appear to have had considerable success in using modern technology to build a stable base of small contributors. The Democratic party, on the other hand, has been financially weak. After dissipating a foundation for party-oriented, small-contributor financing that it had developed in the early 1970s, the Democratic National Committee began anew in 1981 to use modern technology to appeal to small contributors and to expand its financial base. For the Democrats, this approach is still problematic. Its success turns on stability in party leadership and on the leadership's commitment to investing start-up funds in mass fund appeals. But it also depends on whether the DNC can devise appeals that do not founder on ideological differences among their adherents and whether they can find a sufficient base of Democrats who have the means and the partisan commitment to make repeated small contributions.

MONEY AND PARTY ORGANIZATIONAL PERFORMANCE

Political parties do not emerge as heroic institutions measured by their proportion of total political expenditures or their contributions to candidates. The specific organizational activities financed by their modest treasuries are, however, more impressive. Party electioneering is canvassed elsewhere in this volume, but a brief assessment of the funding of party campaigning and organizational activities adds an important dimension to an assessment of party finance.[25]

First, we revisit the role of the parties in direct financial aid to candidates. Both parties engage in careful targeting of races in which to make financial commitments, with Republicans becoming especially adroit as they have gained financial strength. In 1980, the Republican national organization contributed and spent in excess of $200,000 against Democratic Senators in each of nine states.[26] The largest efforts were made in New York ($754,497), California ($521,741) and Pennsylvania ($508,701). In each of these states, party financial assistance exceeded the contributions made by political action committees. Republicans also directed funds to critical House races where they challenged Democratic incumbents who were assumed to be secure but who turned out, in many cases, to be vulnerable.

It is now well established that campaign expenditures are much more helpful to challengers than to incumbents.[27] They raise the visibility of challengers and communicate their message. This builds campaign momentum, which then rallies support and attention from volunteers, interest groups, media, and additional contributors. The substantial distribution of Republican funds to challengers in a limited number of strategically important races produces more impressive results than is apparent from a gross analysis of party contributions as a percentage of all candidate financing.

The Republican party's success in building a stable, continuing financial base means that a large percentage of party campaign funds becomes available to candidates very soon after their nomination. This early timing is unusual, since most organizational and individual contributors tend to withhold support until they are able to assess candidate prospects in mid-campaign. But early money is valuable to a challenger, since it allows him to build campaign momentum by establishing staff and organization and by gaining exposure.

In 1982, the Republican party organizations were so well financed that they made the maximum contributions and expenditures permitted by law in virtually all states and districts where their incumbents faced even modest opposition. In addition, the Republicans were able to encourage and fund challengers against incumbent Democratic leaders who did not appear vulnerable. Consequently, Democratic party stalwarts throughout the country found themselves tied down by strong opposition in their home districts and were therefore unable to exert themselves on behalf of fellow Democrats elsewhere or on behalf of the party organization's fund-raising and organizational activities.

Second, in a remarkable development, the Republican National Committee has become deeply involved in state and local races. In addition to extensive training of local candidates, campaign staffers, and party activists, the Republican National Committee in 1978 contributed $535,000 to GOP gubernatorial candidates and spent $1.7 million to aid the party's state legislative candidates.[28] Its purpose was to capture legislative houses or governorships that would be crucial to protecting Republican interests in the reapportionment that followed the 1980 election. It also sought to promote promising young Republican candidates for Congress by positioning them in state legislatures.

In 1980, the RNC expanded its recruitment of state and local candidates, its training of them and their staffers, and its direct financial assistance of their campaigns. In 1982, however, national GOP contributions to state gubernatorial and legislative campaigns dropped from the level of $2.9 million reached in 1980 to about $1.1 million—$600,000 from the RNC and $500,000 from GOPAC, a Republican political action committee organized specifically to raise money for state office campaigns.

Democratic efforts have been substantially more modest because of the party's poor financial condition. In 1980 there was no state or local campaign effort, because the Democratic National Committee was dominated by the President's operatives and devoted itself solely to his campaign. In 1981, the DNC initiated its State Party Works program in which a political consultant was hired to offer state parties basic training on organization, communication, and fund raising. Ten state parties were visited in 1981 and another ten in 1982.[29] In addition, the Democrats invested a small amount—somewhat more than $500,000—in direct advertising on behalf of their gubernatorial candidates in a handful of marginal races in states that would be important in the 1984 presidential campaign.

Third, the Republicans undertook aggressive programs of candidate recruitment in both 1980 and 1982. In the former year, they were more successful in state legislative races than in congressional contests. But in 1982 they were able to combine early enthusiasm for the Reagan economic program with assurances of substantial financial support to persuade a number of strong congressional candidates to make early decisions to run.

There is a body of scholarship that holds that candidate attractiveness is the key factor in congressional races.[30] Campaign experience, prior officeholding, and campaign resources, especially money, have been identified as key factors in a candidate's attractiveness. In addition, the personal or policy weaknesses of an incumbent are regarded as essential factors in his vulnerability to challenge. Some commentators argued in 1982 that the availability of Republican party financial assistance would allow the GOP to recruit strong candidates and wage successful challenges to the Democratic majority in the House. As the economy soured, strong Democratic candidates for Congress were attracted by the perceived likelihood of a voter repudiation of administration economic policies. Nonetheless, the relative strength of the Republican campaign under these adverse circumstances has been attributed, in part, to the strong candidates they recruited, the financial assistance they provided them, and the poverty of the Democratic party, which prevented it from effectively funding its candidates.[31]

Fourth, both parties have begun programs of party-oriented advertising. In 1980, the Republicans spent more than $9 million to run a series of six campaign spots in waves, beginning in February and showing periodically until the November election. One advertisement, which gained wide attention, portrayed Democratic House Speaker Tip O'Neill driving a car until it ran out of gasoline, and argued that Democratic policies were responsible for the nation's stalled economy. All of these television spots attacked Democratic "failures" and all concluded with the slogan "Vote Republican. For a Change."

In 1981, Republicans launched a $500,000 media campaign attacking Democratic tax proposals and urging support for the President's plan. This was quickly followed by a $2.3 million advertising program praising the successful Reagan program and promoting the theme: "Republicans. Leadership That Works For a Change." During the 1982 campaign, the Republicans again ran a series of institutional advertisements urging voters to "stay the course" and claiming that President Reagan had increased social security benefits. The RNC also sponsored a weekly radio address by the President, which reached not only program listeners but a vast audience who heard news broadcasts reporting the substance of the President's messages. In the latter stages of the campaign, the Republicans sought to deflect attacks upon their economic policies by a media campaign assigning responsibility for national conditions to the prior Democratic administration, again using look-alikes of O'Neill and former President Carter. These advertisements were quickly withdrawn, however, because of fierce criticism in Congress and the press. In all, 1982 institutional advertising expenditures by the GOP may have reached $15 million.

Democrats counterattacked in 1982 with a television campaign costing approximately $1 million. One of their advertisements showed a Republican elephant on a rampage in a china shop, trampling social programs including social security. Another featured a Baltimore factory worker who had appeared in 1980 Republican advertisements and who now repudiated his earlier support for the GOP. The whole thrust of this institutional advertising is toward a new role for parties, separate from support for specific candidates, in promoting issues, appealing to party loyalty, and developing party-oriented attacks on the opposition.

Fifth, the parties have engaged in renewed efforts to provide training and technical assistance to candidates. Between 1976 and 1980, the Republicans trained more than 10,000 local, state, and federal candidates, campaign managers, political staffers, and party workers in a series of workshops and seminars in Washington and throughout the country. Budget problems forced the Democrats to reduce an extensive training schedule to only two or three sessions. Both parties repeated their training programs in 1982, with the Democrats funding a much more extensive program than in 1980.

Party technical assistance included issue information, polls, identification of target precincts, fund-raising packages, and media management techniques. The preparation of media spots and radio "actualities" as well as press releases was a popular form of direct technical assistance to candidates. Once again, Republican assistance vastly exceeded Democratic efforts.

Sixth, the financial condition of the parties dictated the extent to which they developed full bureaucracies to carry out their functions. In 1982, the Republican National Committee's 350 staffers overshadowed the DNC's 82. The Republican National Congressional Committee had 84 employees, compared to the Democratic Congressional Campaign Committee's 32; and the Republican Senatorial Campaign Committee had 40 personnel, compared to their Democratic counterpart's six.[33] Consequently, the Republicans have been able to expand their elaborate fund-raising program, provide campaign services to candidates and party units, and maintain a system of regional field operatives.

Finally, with the decline in traditional party organizational structures centered around precincts, wards, and towns, the party role in mobilizing voters, registering them, and getting them to the polls has declined. The prosperity of the national Republican party in 1980 allowed it to finance a voter mobilization drive that was a surrogate for the traditional precinct organization. The RNC and the Reagan–Bush campaign conducted a voter registration, identification, and get-out-the-vote program called "Commitment '80." Eventually about 1 million people were involved in some grassroots activity, according to party estimates. About 100,000 volunteers hosted parties in their homes to get the massive voter drive under-way, and 85,000 volunteers participated in training and leadership meetings to give direction to these efforts. Republican party staffers estimated that 700,000 Republican voters were registered.

Some of the funding came directly from national party committees, under provisions of law permitting unlimited transfers between party committees. National party leaders also persuaded contributors and political action committees to make contributions directly to state and local GOP organizations to fund these and other grassroots programs. Some state Republican parties have been developing their own mass-appeal fund sources, and they had comfortable resources with which to support candidates and under-take voter mobilization activities. In all, Republican state and local party committees spent an estimated $15 million, much of it received directly or indirectly from national party sources.

After the 1980 election, Democratic National Committee staffers claimed that the party had spent about $1.3 million for voter targeting, to register about 1.1 million voters, and to place calls to 5 million persons on behalf of the national ticket and the party. Local party groups and Carter–Mondale supporters were involved in this effort. A number of party leaders have expressed doubts about whether a program of this scope was actually conducted. Even a smaller program reflects the potential for national and state party committees, if adequately funded, to conduct short-term voter mobilization efforts to offset the decline in traditional precinct organizations.

PARTIES AND PACS

Political action committees are not newcomers to the American political scene. But they have enjoyed a lush growth in numbers and in resources since 1972.[34] New legal provisions and advancing campaign technology account for much of this growth, as they do for changes in political party financing. In an important sense, political action committees compete with political parties for influence with candi-dates and in government. In another respect, however, PACs are allies of parties—new entities in the long-standing political coalitions that have constituted the American parties.

In 1972 there were only 520 identifiable PACs in operation. By 1980, that number reached 2,785, of which 2,155 made contributions to federal office candidates. As of June 30, 1982, 3,479 PACs had registered with the FEC, and, by campaign's end, 2,651 had made contributions to candidates. The total financial activity of PACs is not well documented before 1976, but in that year total adjusted receipts were $54.4 million, and by 1980 they had risen to $137.7 million. In 1982 there was further substantial escalation of PAC financial activity: PACs raised $199.3 million, a 45% increase over 1980. In 1980, PACs contributed $55.2 million to federal office candidates and made additional independent expenditures of $14.2 million to aid or oppose candidates. In 1982, they contributed $87.3 million to federal office candidates, an increase of 58% from 1980. Independent expenditures declined, however, to $5.3 million because there was no presidential race in 1982.

The total PAC receipts of $137.7 million in 1980 should be compared with total party receipts of $206.7 million (including $10.5 million in receipts, mainly public subsidies, to fund party conventions). In 1982 PAC receipts of $199.3 million still trailed party revenues of $253.9 million. But the parties' 1980 1.5:1 lead in receipts slipped to 1.27:1 in 1982. The parties' $22.3 million in candidate contributions and coordinated expenditures in 1980 was easily outdistanced by PAC contributions and independent expenditures of $69.4 million. In 1982, PAC contributions and independent expenditures rose to $92.6 million, but party contributions and coordinated expenditures remained virtually constant at $23.8 million. The PAC edge in direct aid to candidates thus lengthened from $47.1 million to $68.8 million.

Parties, of course, engaged in substantial grassroots activity, provided technical assistance, and conducted major institutional advertising campaigns. But PACs also engaged in voter persuasion and mobilization activities. Organized labor's voter mobilization activities were estimated by Herbert Alexander to have reached $15 million in 1980; and corporations and associations were beginning for the first time to use their statutory privilege significantly to communicate with stockholders and administrative employees about candidates and issues.

Like political parties, PACs have tended to allocate their funds differentially among candidates and districts. But while liberal and conservative ideological PACs have long supported candidates in marginal races, trade association, corporate, and other PACs affiliated with economic institutions traditionally have tended to favor incumbents, without special regard to party or the intensity of opposition. Labor unions have strongly supported Democratic incumbents and have aided the party's challengers in close races.

In 1980, however, there was evidence that corporate PACs were shifting their strategy toward Republican candidates, including strong challengers, while continuing to support entrenched Democratic incumbents. This trend, if continued, would align PACs along familiar lines in American politics, with liberal and labor PACs supporting Democrats and conservative and corporate PACs favoring Republicans. (Trade association PACs apparently continue to emphasize support for incumbents, because of the association's need for access to officeholders.) In 1982 there was less support for Republican challengers by corporate PACs. They were involved more heavily in assisting vulnerable first-term Republican incumbents elected in 1982; and there were fewer vulnerable Democratic incumbents whose opponents merited support.

An alignment of PACs and parties along ideological lines would greatly heighten the existing disparity in financial resources between the Democrats and Republicans. Labor PACs raised $37.4 million in 1982, while corporate PACs raised $47.2 million. Trade association, membership, and health-related PACs raised $43.2 million. Trade group giving, modified by a preference for incumbents, nonetheless favored Republicans: they gave $13.1 million to GOP candidates and $9.8 million to the rival Democrats. So-called "no-connected" PACs, largely composed of ideological groups, preferred to contribute to Republicans by a margin of $3.4 million to $1.5 million in 1980. But the emergence of new liberal PACs in 1982 brought the "no-connected" group contributions to Democrats ($5.7 million) abreast of support for Republicans ($5.4 million).

In 1980, these groups made independent expenditures of $11.2 million on behalf of Republican candidates and another $1.8 million to oppose Democratic candidates. Liberal groups spent only $44,000 to oppose GOP candidates and another $81,000 to support Democrats. In 1982, independent expenditures against Democrats were $3.9 million and for Republicans $876,000. Opposition to GOP candidates was only $590,000 and support for Democrats $373,000.

PACs have become, in some ways, affiliated with political parties. In 1980, Democratic party committees reported receiving $2.1 million in contributions from PACs; and Republican organizations received $1.1 million. In 1982, PAC gifts to the Democrats rose to $3.1 million, largely because of labor union efforts to assist in party reconstruction. Republican party committees received the same amount of PAC money in 1982 as in 1980: $1.1 million. More importantly, the parties have played a role in directing PAC money to candidates. In 1980, the Republican National Senatorial Committee sent staff members to major cities to meet with corporate PAC operatives to suggest marginal races in which PAC money might tip the balance to Republican candidates. A staff person at the RNC devoted full time to advising PACs. In 1982, the Democrats followed this pattern.

Increasingly, however, PACs have other sources of information. Some follow the endorsements of the Business and Industry Political Action Committee in making contribution decisions. In September, 1982 the United States Chamber of Commerce reached 250 PAC operatives at meetings across the country via communications satellite to urge support for about 100 probusiness candidates. Moreover, with the maturing of PACs, their own staffs will be better able to exercise independent judgement in selecting candidates to support. In short, party organizations do not have the field to themselves in directing or cajoling PACs to use their funds for candidate support.

The prospects for still greater financial activity by PACs are very high. The ideological PACs are using the same mass-mail techniques as political parties. More impressive, however, are the opportunities for corporate PACs. The FECA permits corporations and labor unions to use treasury funds to administer PACs, including solicitation of contributions from shareholders, employees, members, and so forth. Edwin Epstein has shown that at least two-thirds of the nation's largest firms have PACs.[35] But among substantial firms not in the top several hundred on standard business lists, only about one-third have PACs. The potential for future PAC activity in the business sector is therefore very great. As corporate PACs gain experience and flourish financially, they are likely to engage in more direct political activity, especially by urging shareholders to support specific candidates.

Over the long run, PACs will tend increasingly to align along party lines and to collaborate with parties and their candidates. They will engage in a wide range of traditional political activities, such as contributions to candidates, voter persuasion, and voter registration and get-out-the-vote drives. Their alignment with parties will be based on strategic calculations, however, and will not, in any way, make PACs adjuncts to party organizations. Frank Sorauf may have characterized the effect of PACs very well when he observed that they may constitute "a group of intermediate electoral organizations clustering around each of the major parties and trying to influence and mediate its building of majorities. In electoral politics, at least, it is a picture that suggests a shift in American practice to some point between two-party and multi-party electoral politics."[36]

CONCLUSION

Political finance in the United States has been significantly altered by changes in laws regulating political money. But have these changes weakened political parties? That seems doubtful. The FECA treats parties more favorably than individuals or nonparty committees in the size of contributions that can be received and in the amounts that can be given to candidates. It also permits substantial coordinated expenditures on behalf of party candidates for Congress and the presidency. It lifts the burden of convention costs from the parties, and it does not substantially alter the party organization's role in prenomination campaigns for the presidency. It does fundamentally change the manner in which presidential election campaigns are financed; but even here the party may play a significant role through coordinated expenditures by national committees, unlimited grassroots activity by local and state committees, and unlimited transfer of funds between these committees. And there is no limit on party expenditures to develop issues or make partisan appeals.

In recent years, despite the complexities of the FECA, the Republican party has shown the greatest capacity in American party history to establish stable and mass-based party financing. It has effectively used modern technology to appeal to millions of persons for financial support, while at the same time retaining its traditional support among those who made moderate-to-large gifts in the $250 to $10,000 range. The Democrats have had much less success in fund raising. But very few commentators attribute this to the FECA. Rather, the cause is rooted in the coalition character of the Democratic party and has been heightened by Democratic incumbency. The party's inability to raise the start-up money necessary for modern fund-raising techniques and their reluctance to adopt modern technology have also been factors. There is, however, a lurking concern that modern financing methods may be outside the bounds of possibility for the Democrats: their adherents may be too ideologically divided, and their supporters may include too few who possess the characteristics—high level of education and income, political interest, and political activism—that spur political giving.

One scenario, therefore, is that American party finance is rapidly becoming the story of one party that is able successfully to raise the money in the modern era and another that is not. There is little doubt that party organizations in the modern era are heavily dependent on financial capability to carry out their campaign and organizational functions. This distinguishes the contemporary period from most of American political history. And if only one of the party organizations is able to develop a strong financial capability, the role of parties in the modern period will be fundamentally different: one party organization functioning effectively, the other largely a shell.

It has been said, also, that modern political finance is the story of parties that have become more centralized and more bureaucratic. Centralization in campaigns has been caused by the FECA, which requires central accounting and financing in order to comply with contribution and expenditure limits and disclosure requirements. These regulations have not been the sole cause of centralized party finance, however. The impetus for centralization has two other important causes: first, the technology necessary to raise vast sums in small amounts encourages centralization for reasons of both expertise and cost; second, the Republican party has spent money generously on local campaigns and has transferred additional money to local party units, thus knitting those candidates and party committees more closely to the national party organization.

Both parties are spending money to offset the decline in activities traditionally conducted by grassroots activists and local party organizations. The RNC is not only recruiting and training candidates and providing technical assistance, but it is also mobilizing grassroots workers to canvas, register voters, and get voters to the polls. The Democrats are attempting similar activities, although their financial base is dramatically smaller. In addition, both parties are continuing their longstanding efforts to provide direct financial support to their candidates. Under the FECA, this combines their contributions and coordinated expenditures. And, in a departure from the past, both parties are engaging in large-scale "institutional advertising" which promotes the party, attacks the opposition, and emphasizes issues or personalities, but which does not advocate the election or defeat of specific candidates.

Nonetheless, the American political parties are not a dominating presence in political finance or in campaigns. They account for no more than a quarter of all political money, and their direct contributions to candidates are modest. Moreover, the parties are faced with formidable competition from PACs, which raise substantial funds because of FECA authorization and the skillful use of technology. In total, PACs spend almost as much as parties and have a vast potential for further fund-raising. While each PAC is more restricted than the parties in giving direct aid to candidates, the aggregate effect of contributions from many PACs with related interests overshadows party efforts. Finally, PACs can make unlimited independent expenditures to aid or oppose candidates; and they can finance all the same grassroots activities as parties, but these PAC outlays may not be coordinated with candidates.

To be preeminent electoral organizations in American society, parties will need vastly greater sums than they have been able to raise, despite notable Republican financial successes. Indeed, to attain in the modern era the importance they had in a period of more traditional political techniques, the parties will probably need more money than they can raise, even by using the highly successful techniques employed by the Republicans. But commentators should come very slowly to the conclusion that this represents an adverse turn in the financial fortunes of parties. For, as Frank Sorauf has observed: "political parties have historically dealt largely in nonfinancial resources and have never successfully made the transition to the cash economy of the new campaign politics."[37]

The current condition of parties and their relatively modest role in political finance is not, therefore, substantially due to some "decline" in parties or revisions in law. Rather it is caused by changes in the nature of American politics, which make the traditional resources of parties less available to them and vastly less important. By contrast, money, which has not generally been a significant resource of parties, is now much more important. From this perspective, the political parties—especially the Republicans—have made an effort to adapt to a new political era in which funding is a major requirement for effective political action. There are no insurmountable legal barriers to the parties' efforts to adapt to the changing conditions of politics. Only their efforts and time will determine whether they can successfully do so. And whether there is some significant "decline" in the overall role that parties play in the American polity will depend on that success, or failure.

NOTES

1. Clinton Rossiter, *Parties and Politics in America* (Ithaca, N.Y.: Cornell University Press, 1960), p. 1.

2. Walter Dean Burnham, "The End of American Party Politics," *Transaction*, Vol. 7 (December 1969), pp. 12-22.

3. I mark the revival of the debate over the role of political parties as the publication of E. E. Schattschneider's *Party Government* (New York: Rinehart & Co., 1942).

4. See, for example, William J. Crotty and Gary C. Jacobson, *American Parties in Decline* (Boston: Little, Brown, and Co., 1980); Jeane J. Kirkpatrick, *Dismantling the Parties* (Washington, D.C.: American Enterprise Institute, 1979); Austin Ranney, "Political Parties: Reform and Decline," in *The New American Political System*, ed. Anthony King (Washington: American Enterprise Institute, 1979), pp. 213-48; Edward C. Banfield, "Party 'Reform' in Retrospect," in *Political Parties in the Eighties*, ed. Robert Goldwin (Washington, D.C.: American Enterprise Institute, 1980), pp. 20-33.

5. See, for example, Cornelius P. Cotter and John F. Bibby, "Institutional Development of Parties and the Thesis of Party Decline," *Political Science Quarterly*, Vol. 95 (Spring, 1980), pp. 1-27; Gerald Pomper, ed., *Party Renewal in America* (New York: Praeger Publishers, 1980); Xandra Kayden, "The Nationalizing of the Party System," in *Parties, Interest Groups, and Campaign Finance Laws*, ed. Michael Malbin (Washington, D.C.: American Enterprise Institute, 1980), pp. 257-82. See also James L. Gibson, Cornelius P. Cotter, John F. Bibby, and Robert J. Huckshorn, "Assessing Institutional Party Strength," a paper presented to the 1981 annual meeting of the Midwest Political Science Association.

6. *Cousins* v. *Wigoda*, 419 U.S. 477 (1975); *Democratic Party of the United States* v. *Wisconsin*, 450 U.S. 107 (1981).

7. The Federal Election Campaign Act of 1971, Public Law 92-225, 86 Stat. 3 (1972); the Revenue Act of 1971, Public Law 92-178, 85 Stat. 51, as amended 87 Stat. 138; the Federal Election Campaign Act Amendments of 1974, Public Law 93-443, 88 Stat. 1263; the Federal Election Campaign Act Amendments of 1976, Public Law 94-283, 90 Stat. 475; and the Federal Election Campaign Act Amendments of 1979, Public Law 96-187, 93 Stat. 1339.

8. The principal judical doctrines have been laid down in *Buckley* v. *Valeo*, 424 U.S. 1 (1976).

9. It has been suggested that the FECA and the enforcement powers of the FEC have encouraged vast litigation over every aspect of campaign finance and its regulation, with some of this litigation being driven by considerations of political strategy rather than law. On the whole, however, little litigation has actually produced political advantage for those who initiate it. See David M. Ifshin and Roger E. Warin, "Litigating the 1980 Presidential Election," *American University Law Review*, Vol. 31 (Spring, 1982), pp. 485-550.

10. All references in this essay to receipts and expenditures in the 1980 election refer to the two-year election cycle from January 1979 through the final campaign reports filed after the 1980 election itself. Receipt and expenditure reports throughout this essay are based on Federal Election

Commission final reports for 1980 and 1982, unless another citation is provided.

11. *Federal Election Commission* v. *Democratic Senatorial Campaign Committee*, 454 U.S. 27 (1981).

12. Estimates of campaign finance activity in the 1980 election attributed to Herbert E. Alexander are drawn from "Making Sense About Dollars in the 1980 Presidential Campaigns," forthcoming in *Parties, Interest Groups and Money in the 1980s*, ed. Michael Malbin (Washington, D.C.: American Enterprise Institute, 1983).

13. Under the FECA, major parties are those whose candidate for president received 25% or more of the popular vote in the prior presidential election. A minor party is defined as one whose candidate received between 5% and 25% of the popular vote. A new party is one whose candidate received 5% or more of the popular vote in the current presidential election.

14. See Ruth S. Jones, "State Public Financing and the State Parties," in *Parties, Interest Groups, and Campaign Finance Laws*, ed. Michael Malbin (Washington, D.C.: American Enterprise Institute, 1980), pp. 283–303; Jack Noragon, "Political Finance and Political Reform: The Experience with State Income Tax Checkoffs," *American Political Science Review*, Vol. 75 (September, 1981), pp. 667–87; Ruth S. Jones, "State Public Campaign Finance: Implications for Partisan Politics," *American Journal of Political Science*, Vol. 25 (May, 1981), pp. 342–61; and Ruth S. Jones, "Patterns of Campaign Finance in the Public Funding States," a paper presented to the 1982 annual meeting of the Midwest Political Science Association.

15. This estimate includes approximately $275 million spent in the presidential race. See Alexander, "Making Sense about Dollars." Also, FEC reports detail expenditures of $250 million by and for congressional candidates, $70 million by political action committees beyond their contributions to candidates, and $145 million by parties other than candidate contributions. For an earlier estimate that expenditures would reach $650 million, excluding political action committee and party direct expenditures other than contributions, see David Adamany, "Political Finance in Transition," *Polity*, Vol. 14 (Winter, 1981), pp. 314–31.

16. Ruth S. Jones, "State Election Campaign Financing: 1980," a draft paper.

17. It appears that the extraordinary percentage of party spending in Wisconsin's 1978 statewise races is due to large debts undertaken by the Democrats and especially the Republicans on behalf of their gubernatorial candidates, whose resources were exhausted after bitter primary contests in both parties. Other evidence suggests that the role of parties in financing legislative campaigns has steadily declined in Wisconsin. See Elizabeth G. King and David G. Wegge, "The impact of Public Funding in State Legislative Elections: The Wisconsin Experience," a paper presented to the 1982 annual meeting of the Midwest Political Science Association.

18. Alexander Heard, *The Costs of Democracy* (Chapel Hill, N.C.: University of North Carolina Press, 1960), chap. 11.

19. David Adamany *Financing Politics* (Madison, Wis.: University of Wisconsin Press, 1961), pp. 221–29; David Adamany, *Campaign Funds as an Intraparty Political Resource: Connecticut, 1966–1968* (Princeton, N.J.: Citizens' Research Foundation, 1972), pp. 22–25; Roland McDevitt, "The Changing Dynamics of Fund Raising in House Campaigns," in *Political Finance: Sage Electoral Studies Yearbook, Vol. 5*, ed. Herbert E. Alexander (Beverly Hills, Ca.: Sage Publishing Co., 1979), p. 144.

20. For a brief review of the financing of these campaigns, see David Adamany and George Agree, *Political Money* (Baltimore, Md.: The Johns Hopkins University Press, 1975), p. 30.

21. For a brief history of the Republican National Sustaining Fund, see Herbert E. Alexander, *Financing the 1976 Election* (Washington, D.C.: Congressional Quarterly Press, 1980), pp. 711–12.

22. Ensuing descriptions of the fund-raising methods and contributor bases of the political parties are based on party documents, newspaper reports, and interviews by the author and are drawn from a more complete narrative in David Adamany, "Political Parties in the '80s," forthcoming in *Parties, Interest Groups and Money in the 1980s.*

23. Rhodes Cook, "Democrats Develop Tactics; Laying Groundwork for 1984," *Congressional Quarterly Weekly Report*, Vol. 40, No. 27, July 3, 1982, p. 1595.

24. For a description of the Democratic telethons, see Alexander, *Financing the 1976 Election*, pp. 395–97; and John W. Ellwood and Robert J. Spitzer, "The Democratic National Telethons: Their Strengths and Failures," *Journal of Politics*, Vol. 41 (August, 1979), pp. 328–64.

25. More comprehensive assessments of party organization activities in 1980 can be found in Adamany, "Political Parties in the '80s"; F. Christopher Arterton, "Political Money and Party Strength," in *The Future of American Parties*, ed. Joel Fleishman (Englewood Cliffs, N.J.: Prentice-Hall, 1982); and Xandra Kayden, "Parties and the 1980 Presidential Election," in *Financing Presidential Campaigns: A Research Report by the Campaign Finance Study Group to the Committee on Rules and Administration of the United States Senate* (Cambridge, Mass.: Harvard University, John F. Kennedy School of Government, 1982).

26. Gary C. Jacobson, "Money in the 1980 Congressional Elections," a paper presented to the 1982 annual meeting of the Midwest Political Science Association.

27. Gary C. Jacobson, *Money in Congressional Elections* (New Haven, Conn.: Yale University Press, 1980); Jacobson, "Money in the 1980 Congressional Elections."

28. John F. Bibby, "Political Parties and Federalism: The Republican National Committee Involvement in Gubernatorial and Legislative Elections," *Publius*, Vol. 9 (Winter, 1979), p. 231.

29. Cook, "Democrats Develop Tactics," p. 1594.

30. Jacobson, "Money in Congressional Elections"; and Gary C. Jacobson and Samuel Kernell, *Strategy and Choice in Congressional Elections* (New

Haven, Conn.: Yale University Press, 1981). See also, Thomas Mann and Raymond Wolfinger, "Candidates and Parties in Congressional Elections," *American Political Science Review*, Vol. 74 (September 1980), pp. 617-32.

31. Fred Barnes, "GOP Hopes Heavy Spending Will Minimize Losses of House Seats," *Baltimore Sun*, April 12, 1982, p. A3, col. 1; Adam Clymer, "Those Who Recruit Candidates Say The Parties Are Running About Even," *New York Times*, March 8, 1982, p. B4, col. 1.

32. On the 1980 Republican advertising campaign, see Adamany, "Political Parties in the 1980 Election." On 1982, see Bill Peterson, "GOP Unveils Part of $10 Million Ad Drive," *Washington Post*, May 18, 1982, p. A4, col. 1; and Howell Raines, "A Preview of the Democrats' New Commercials," *New York Times*, September 22, 1982, p. A24, col. 3.

33. Martin Schram, "GOP Meets Reality—on the Button," *Washington Post*, May 16, 1982, p. A1 col. 1.

34. The literature on PACs has grown almost as rapidly as the PACs themselves. For two overview essays by one of the nation's leading scholars, see Edwin M. Epstein, "The PAC Phenomenon: An Overview," *Arizona Law Review*, Vol. 22 (1980), pp. 355-72; and Epstein, "Business and Labor Under the Federal Election Campaign Act of 1971," in *Parties, Interest Groups, and Campaign Finance Laws*, pp. 107-51.

35. Edwin Epstein, "PACs and the Modern Political Process," a paper presented to the Conference on the Impact of the Modern Corporation, Columbia School of Law, November 12 and 13, 1982.

36. Frank Sorauf, "Political Parties and Political Action Committees: Two Life Cycles," *Arizona Law Review*, Vol. 22 (1980), p. 469.

37. Ibid., p. 451.

8

NEW CAMPAIGN TECHNIQUES AND THE AMERICAN PARTY SYSTEM

Larry Sabato

Not many years ago, an American president was likely to reward one of his party's organizational kingpins from the Irish-American community with the coveted post of U.S. ambassador to Dublin. However, in 1982 President Ronald Reagan chose his campaign media consultant, Peter Dailey, to be the U.S. representative in Ireland—and the choice symbolized recent changes that have occurred in American politics.

The political parties have been weakened by a multitude of circumstances, and in many respects the influence party leaders once wielded in election campaigns now is exercised by independent political consultants, just as the vital electoral roles once performed almost exclusively by parties are now available to anyone who masters the new campaign technologies such as polling, media advertising, and direct mail. The growth of political consultancy and the development of advanced campaign techniques were combined with the new election finance laws that hurt the parties, favored the prospering consultants, and encouraged the mushrooming of party-rivaling political action committees. In this chapter each of these developments will be examined in turn, and their effects on the American party system will be assessed.

Parts of this article are drawn from the author's *The Rise of Political Consultants: New Ways of Winning Elections* (New York: Basic Books, 1981) by Larry Sabato. The author wishes to thank Lewis Shepherd for his valuable assistance in preparing this chapter.

FROM PARTY POLS
TO POLITICAL CONSULTANTS

It is easy to exaggerate the changes that have occurred in the American system in recent decades, and it is especially dangerous to exaggerate the damage sustained by the political parties. Certainly the parties have declined. But that must be tempered by the knowledge that they have survived all the tumult and remain flexible enough to adapt to new political realities. As this chapter will show, the Republican party, in particular, has become a showcase of new vitality, and it has learned to use to its own benefit the campaign techniques that had threatened to make it obsolete. Slowly but surely, the Democrats are beginning to make similar adjustments.

To understand the transformation of the parties within the American electoral system, it is important first to understand how the perception that the electorate has of them has changed over the years. Martin P. Wattenberg has recently argued[1] that American voters have *not* grown more alienated from the parties (contrary to journalistic myth). Rather, voters have become more neutral in their evaluations of the parties. Why has this happened? As Wattenberg explains it:

> The reason for party decline has not been that people no longer see any important differences between the parties. . . . Rather the problem which the parties must face is that they are considered less relevant in solving the most important domestic and foreign policy issues of the day. *In the voters' minds, the parties are losing their association with the candidates and the issues which the candidates claim to stand for.* [Emphasis added.]

That association between parties and candidates is weakening partly because the parties have ceased to be very important in the process of electing their candidates. Since candidates are not beholden to the party for their elections, they are not responsive to the party's needs or platform once in office.

As the parties have moved to the sidelines, independent political consultants have rushed forward to replace them.[2] Pollster Patrick Caddell clearly identified the alternate nonparty route that consultants have provided to willing politicians:

> Parties traditionally provided the avenue by which candidates reached voters. What we've done with media, what we've done with polling, and what we've done with direct organizational techniques

is that we have provided candidates who have the resources (and that's the important thing, the resources), the ability to reach the voters and have a direct contact with the electorate without regard to party or party organization.[3]

The value of consultants to candidates is perhaps best described by the technologies at the consultants' command. The design and production of media advertising is among the essential skills that consultants offer political aspirants. It is difficult to find a contested race for major office in the United States today which does not feature television and radio commercials, and even campaigns for minor posts such as city councilor and state legislator often employ professional advertising. Quite simply, the paid media advertisements (together with the "free" media of press coverage) have replaced the political party as the middleman between candidate and voter. The candidate no longer depends so heavily on party workers to present his case to voters in his constituency; television can do it more directly and efficiently. The media consultant who can design effective[4] and pleasing advertisements is thus worth his weight in gold to the modern candidate.[5]

Equally prominent in modern campaigns is another kind of political consultant, the pollster. At every stage of the campaign the pollster, his survey data in hand and his role as *vox populi* foremost in mind, aids the candidate and staff in crucial decisions— whether to run at all, how to run, what issues to emphasize and which ones to avoid, which aspects of his opponent's platform and personality are vulnerable, and so on. In doing so, the pollster substitutes for party leaders, since it was exactly this kind of advice that the party kingpins used to dispense and their candidates used to follow. Once again, the new technology replaces the political party as the middleman between candidate and voter. Office seekers formerly depended on party workers to convey to them grassroots sentiment and the opinions of average voters in the constituency. Now random-sample surveys can perform the same chore, but with relative certainty and with a wealth of semiprecise detail that party wheel-horses could only guess at. For example, it would be difficult even for a modern-day George Washington Plunkitt to know which television shows are watched by a population sub-group targeted by the campaign. Simple crosstabulations of standard survey questions used by the political pollsters reveal this, and more, today. While the process of polling has many weaknesses[6] and is rarely as error-free as the unwittingly arrogant disclaimer accompanying most surveys suggests—"this poll is accurate to within a margin of error of plus or minus 4 percent"—survey sampling is usually more accurate and normally more directly useful than the surmises of party leaders. Candidates know it, and that is why polling consultants like Jimmy Carter's Patrick Caddell and Ronald Reagan's Richard Wirthlin have had far more influence on the course of their client's campaigns than have party chiefs. It should be noted, too, that the pollster's dominance has recently been extended to governance as well as campaigning. Caddell, for instance, clearly had major influence on a number of President Carter's decisions (including his crucial 1979 Camp David domestic summit and subsequent "crisis of confidence" speech[7]). Wirthlin's frequent polling studies on a wide range of subjects are reportedly closely studied by President Reagan and his key aides; Wirthlin himself is a frequent White House visitor.

Clever polling analysis and creative media can help a candidate to win, but nothing is more fundamental to a successful campaign than money. Only presidential elections are funded even partially from the public treasury at the federal level, and just a handful of states have substantial public financing of statewide campaigns. So, most candidates must themselves raise the tremendous sums necessary to seek major office in the United States. While campaign finance has always been primarily the candidate's responsibility, the political parties used to bear a reasonable share of the load, directly contributing in many states perhaps as much as a fifth of their standard-bearer's kitty. As in so many other respects, the parties were in financial decline for much of the 1970s, and observers charted the fall in the percentage of funds provided to congressional candidates by the parties.[8] Once more, a group of political consultants has filled the vacuum, using the technology of direct mail.[9] By carefully selecting mailing lists and finding those who are committed to a cause or a candidate, the direct mailers raise campaign cash with thousands of under-$100 contributions, and also cumulatively amass invaluable information about the contributory habits of millions of political donors. The letters they send are often complex stylized packages, highly personalized and intensely emotional and negative. The techniques of direct mail have been refined considerably over the years, and, given the right candidate and circumstances, direct mail can provide a substantial portion of a candidate's warchest—far more, certainly, than the party is likely to ante up.

Even the political party's greatest remaining strength, its precinct organization and network of volunteers, is being duplicated by independent consultants.[10] Some consultants use a technique called

"Instant Organization" (IO), which utilizes paid callers to ring up voters from centralized banks of telephones. Using various tested scripts, block captains are recruited and office volunteers solicited. Subsequent mail and telephone contracts, as well as get-togethers with the candidate and his surrogate, keep the "instant" volunteers motivated.

THE RELATIONSHIP OF CONSULTANTS TO THE POLITICAL PARTIES

The consultants and their new campaign technologies have, then, increasingly been replacing the parties as the middlemen between candidate and voter. If the relationship between the consultants and the parties is a symbiotic or mutually reinforcing one, little harm—and potentially much good—is done. Unfortunately for the political parties, few consultants are vitally interested in the health of the party system. It is fair to describe most political consultants as businessmen, not party ideologues. There are exceptions, and a few are fierce partisans, having had their political baptism as party functionaries and occasionally having had years of direct party employment. One of these, Robert Odell, is inclined to take on just about any Republican in his direct-mail firm because, "Democrats do little or nothing that I respect and Republicans do nearly everything I respect." Striking a rare pose for a private consultant, Odell declares, "The most important goal for me is to make the Republican party effective." Matt Reese holds the Democratic party in similar esteem, observing only half in jest that he is "a partisan without apology. I don't even *like* Republicans, except for Abraham Lincoln." And few professionals have shown as long and abiding a concern for a political party as Stuart Spencer and his partner, Bill Roberts, who both began their political careers as volunteers for the Republican party in California. Their consulting shop actually developed around the GOP and was encouraged by the party. Spencer explained that he and Roberts "wanted to be an extension of the party, a management tool that the party could use," and they viewed each of their early consultant outings as "an opportunity for the Republican party."

The greatest number of consultants, though, are simply not committed in any real sense to a political party. Michael Kaye, for instance, proclaims himself to be an Independent and the parties to be "bull." Revealingly, however, he still sensed that it was a mistake to work both sides of the street, comparing it to his practice while a product advertiser:

> People in political office, most of them are paranoid anyway. And I think it would make someone uncomfortable to think that I was working for a Republican at the same time I was working for a Democrat. That is why I work only for Democrats. I don't work for just Democrats because I think they are the only good pure people on this planet. It is the same reason that in the [product] advertising business I didn't work for two clients in the same business.

Yet, for all of the danger supposedly involved in crossing party lines, consultants seem to yield frequently to the temptation. Democrat Peter Hart conducted Republican U.S. Senate nominee John Heinz's surveys in Pennsylvania in 1976 (and claimed he was told he could not take polls for Jimmy Carter as a consequence). Media consultant David Garth has been "all over the lot," as one of his detractors termed his tendency to take moderate-to-liberal Democrats and Republicans indiscriminately, and it was a surprise to no one in the profession when GOP Congressman John Anderson tapped Garth to help with his 1980 Independent presidential bid. Another Democratic-leaning liberal firm, Craver, Matthews, Smith, and Company, took on Anderson's direct-mail program. The now-defunct firm of Baus and Ross in California secured the accounts of Richard Nixon, Barry Goldwater, and Edmund G. "Pat" Brown, Sr., within a few years of one another. The survey firm of D.M.I. not only worked for both Democrats and Republicans, it actually polled both sides of the same congressional election district in 1966. Vincent Breglio, the D.M.I. vice president, took one side, and President Richard Wirthlin took the other. They ran the research independent of one another and provided consulting services to each side without crossing communications. Apparently the candidates were rather trusting souls who reportedly agreed to this outrageous arrangement (although it was quite a useful one for the firm's "win ratio"). D.M.I. converted permanently to Republicanism in 1967 when Michigan Governor George Romney asked the firm to join his presidential effort on condition that it work only for the GOP. Convinced that the move was good for business, Wirthlin and Breglio made the switch over the objections of the Democratic members of the firm, who nevertheless stayed.

A few consultants work closely with party committees as well as party candidates, helping to strengthen the organization. A third to a half of all Market Opinion Research's political polling work is done for the Republican National Committee or state and local GOP groups, and MOR's president, Robert Teeter, wishes the proportion were even higher: "If I have a preference between working for the party or for individual candidates, it would be for the party because it's more stable—an ongoing, operating entity where our work continues after each campaign." Robert Odell is fully in agreement with his fellow Republican, and perhaps even more dedicated to and enthusiastic about the party. His direct-mail firm has contracts with 13 state party organizations, one-third of his business, and he has taken great pride in building up their fund-raising capacities.

Even though virtually all consultants identify with one of the parties (primarily for business purposes, as Michael Kaye suggested), most of them are at least passively hostile to the parties, some of them openly contemptuous. At times consultants can sound like the evangelical populists they often portray their candidates to be, railing against the evils of boss rule. "Really the only major function of the political party structure these days is to nominate the candidates for president, and my personal feeling is that we'd all be better off if this responsibility also were placed in the hands of the people," consultant Joe Napolitan has written.[11] Media consultant Bob Goodman, in tones echoed time and again by his fellow independent professionals, lauds consultants for unshackling candidates, putting them beyond the reach of the petty party barons:

> We have enabled people to come into a party or call themselves independent Democrats or Republicans and run for office without having to pay the dues of being a party member in a feudal way. Meaning kiss the ass of certain people and maybe down the line they'll give you a shot at public office.

Parties are usually viewed as one more obstacle in the way of the client's election. "In most places the party operation does not do a great deal to help a candidate get elected the first time, and [it] is more of a hassle than it's worth," concludes GOP media consultant Douglas Bailey. Many party-consultant relationships are marked by sharp conflict, explained by Napolitan as the result of party workers' jealousy of consultants, who "have replaced organization regulars in making important campaign decisions" and who are possible usurpers of "what they [party workers] consider their rights to patronage."[12]

A natural consequence of the consultant's antagonism toward the party is his willingness to run his candidates apart from, or even against, their party label. It was difficult to know whether GOP nominee John Heinz was a Democrat or Republican in his 1976 Pennsylvania Senate race, since media consultant David Garth fashioned his advertising campaign around an antiparty theme: "If you think Pennsylvania needs an *Independent* senator, elect John Heinz." One of Garth's spots actually featured a glowing "endorsement" of Heinz's character by Jimmy Carter (delivered in March of 1975), to further confuse the voter. Scrambling labels may seem unfortunate to those concerned about the role of party in elections, but at least the party is not under direct attack, a common tactic in party primaries. Milton Shapp, for instance, won the Democratic nomination for the Pennsylvania governorship in 1966 in a major upset, thanks to Joe Napolitan's "Man Against the Machine" theme.[13]

When they are not running against it, most consultants simply ignore the party, in campaigns and in the way they run their business. Sanford L. Weiner, a former president of the American Association of Political Consultants, who began by representing conservative Republicans and whose clientele is now increasingly Democratic and liberal, dismissed his party contradictions by noting that "no one in California cares that any firm represents both Democrats and Republicans. . . . Strict partisanship just isn't that important anymore."[14] Another pace-setting California firm, the Butcher-Forde direct-mail agency, is positively proud of the agency's and directors' utter lack of personal professional adherence to any party or political philosophy. One of the firm's senior associated described himself and his fellows as "pure advocates," declaring, "We're businessmen first, and politics is our business. . . . It's whoever gets to us first." Their list of recent clients is a grab bag of politicians on right and left, from liberal Democratic U.S. Senator Alan Cranston to Howard Jarvis and State Senator John Schmitz (former presidential candidate of George Wallace's American Independent Party). In addition to toying with the idea of an independent candidacy of his own and aiding George Wallace's direct-mail efforts, rightwing fund-raiser Richard Viguerie has at times been quoted as favoring the dissolution of the Republican party and enjoys working against either party's moderate or liberal candidates.[15] Viguerie's hostility to the organized party and his designs against it are only slightly more grandiose than those of many consultants and leaders of ideological political action committees. As Viguerie's right-wing associate, Paul Weyrich of the Committee for the Survival of a Free Congress, put it, "The parties— they water down, water down, water down until they get something that everybody agrees on, which means nothing to anybody. The political parties have helped to destroy the political parties." With a little help from political consultants, he might have added.

EFFECTS OF NEW CAMPAIGN FINANCE LAWS
ON POLITICAL PARTIES AND CONSULTANTS

The parties' slide and the rise of political consultants has been aided in some respects by the passage of the Federal Election Campaign Act of 1971 (FECA) and the major amendments of 1974 and 1976.[16] FECA is discussed in more detail in another chapter of this volume, but it is worth noting here that the law, originally described as a measure to strengthen the political parties, has not always had the desired effect.

It should be noted at the outset that a number of FECA provisions take reasonable account of the parties' interests. Each national party committee is permitted to make a special general election expenditure on behalf of its presidential nominee (2 cents for each person of voting age, plus a cost of living increase, amounting to $4.6 million in 1980). The Democratic and Republican senatorial campaign committees are also given the right to donate up to $17,500 to each of their Senate nominees. And the parties can make very substantial "coordinated expenditures" on behalf of both their Senate and House candidates. FECA is also broadly supportive of the two-party system in its restriction of access to public funds by third parties. A new third party or Independent presidential nominee can only receive public funds retroactively, once the election is concluded, and only if the party or candidate received more than 5% of the national popular vote. Any monies so received will be in proportion to the third party's percentage of the vote.

But in other important ways FECA has proved to be *harmful* to the major parties. It simply does not create a party-centered system of campaign finance. The stringent reporting requirements and the intricate specifications for the splitting of costs when an expenditure benefiting all of a party's candidates is made have discouraged party umbrella spending, for example, and have encouraged candidates to stay clear of the party and its other nominees. The finance law also restricts the direct contributions of a political party to each of its own candidates to just $5,000 per election—putting the political parties on exactly the same footing as nonparty political action committees.

The campaign laws also cause the national party committees to compete with their own candidates for limited fund-raising dollars to a greater degree than ever before, through a combination of contribution limits and a single small income tax credit covering both candidate and party gifts.[17] It is little wonder that the national party committees guard so jealously their direct-mail lists and generally refuse to share them with party candidates. Moreover, FECA dealt a severe blow to local party organizational and volunteer activity because the limited campaign dollars that were permitted to be spent had to be carefully managed, controlled, and disclosed, resulting in a centralization of most campaign tasks and an elimination of grass-roots programs. The intimidation of the new rules, the threat of prosecution, and the bulky expenditure reporting requirements also have taken their toll. One Republican country chairman in 1976 was actually photographed on a ladder, painting out the name of Gerald Ford from a campaign sign, since the local party committee had discovered it had exceeded the tiny $1,000 maximum it was permitted to spend on behalf of the national ticket. In reflecting on the 1976 presidential campaign, David Broder remembered that "In many big-city neighborhoods and in most small towns, there was nothing to suggest that America was choosing a president—no local headquarters, no bumper stickers, no buttons, and almost no volunteer activity.[18]

FECA's $1,000 contribution limit on individual gifts has also been a godsend for the parties' vibrant rivals, political action committees. PACs, with a $5,000 contribution limit, can offer a greater reward for a more efficient expenditure of a candidate's time and efforts, since individual donations are usually solicited in high-overhead dinners and parties, while PACs are organized and centralized. As a consequence, the proportion of money raised by congressional candidates from PACs doubled between 1972 and 1978, to fully a quarter of congressional campaign expenditures. Because of the role of public funding in presidential campaigns (and the matching funds available for individual but not PAC gifts), political action committees have generally played a lesser role in presidential politics, however.

Not only have the new campaign finance laws weakened parties by strengthening PACs, they have also boosted the role and influence of another group of party competitors, political consultants. Many consultants viewed FECA with concern at first, primarily because the 1974 amendments mandated overall spending limits on congressional campaigns that the professionals feared would drastically reduce the amount of money expended on their services. But after the Supreme Court struck down the spending ceiling sections of FECA in the 1976 case *Buckley* v. *Valeo*,[19] consultants saw FECA in a new light, and for good reason. Since the disclosure requirements naturally tend to direct campaign money to easily disclosable activities such as media advertising and polling, media and polling consultants' roles in a centralized campaign structure are probably increased. Certainly the power and profits of direct mailers and other campaign fund raisers have been enhanced by FECA. The contribution limitations and matching funds for $250-and-under individual gifts fit direct mail like a glove, and contemporary candidates rely on direct mailers and professional money raisers the way their predecessors did on "fat cats" and "financial angels." "Blessed are the gatherers," President Ford's finance chairman in 1976, Robert Mosbacher, was quoted as saying. "No $1,000 contributor is of tremendous value. It's the guy who'll go out and raise $100,000."[20] Consultants also gain from FECA's stimulus to centralized planning. Because of limits, campaigns are forced to plan better and map out their budgets earlier and more precisely—exactly the skills that generalist consultants are touted to possess. There is little doubt that FECA makes the management of cash flow and an early start in fund raising at least as critical to a candidate's success as any issue proposal he might make in the course of his campaign. Almost 60% of the GOP House winners in 1978, for instance, began their fund-raising efforts in the first quarter of 1978, while losers started much later and sought over half their money in the last months of the campaign.[21]

Enough of FECA's shortcomings had become evident by 1979 to prod Congress into making some minor and a few moderately significant reforms in the law. The Congress passed HR $_{5010}$ in December 1979 after bipartisan agreement was reached within the House and Senate Administration Committees.[22] While it avoided the more controversial and serious reforms needed in the areas of PACs and public funding and only went a little way toward redressing the unhealthy tilt of the present system against political parties, HR $_{5010}$ did achieve some useful objectives. The paperwork requirements were reduced in several respects, with fewer reports and less detail being asked for from most candidates. More important, the law permitted state and local party groups to revive grass-roots participation and make unlimited purchases of campaign materials for volunteer activities (buttons, bumper stickers, yard signs, brochures, and the like). Certain kinds of voter registration and get-out-the-vote drives on behalf of presidential tickets were also permitted without financial limit at the state and local levels, and financial reports to the Federal Election Commission (FEC) were waived if annual expenditures for volunteer programs did not exceed $5,000 or nonvolunteer projects more than $1,000. (Previously, if total spending went above $1,000—a ridiculously low threshold—a party committee was forced to fulfill all the FEC's reporting stipulations.[23]) Volunteer political activity itself was encouraged by an increase from $500 to $1,000 in the amount of money an individual could spend in providing his home, food, or personal travel to a candidate without having to file a contributor's report. And, in yet another small step in the right direction, a volunteer was permitted to spend up to $2,000 on behalf of a party before the amount was treated as a contribution.

THE GROWTH
OF POLITICAL ACTION COMMITTEES

Possibly the most far-reaching change wrought by FECA was in its legitimizing the use of corporate funds to establish and administer Political Action Committees (PACs). Labor unions already had that right, and the PAC had long been an essential political tool for organized labor. Now business and trade interests could benefit as well.

Once the floodgates were opened, the growth of corporate and trade PACs was nothing short of phenomenal.

Just between 1976 and 1978, the number of PACs rose from 1,242 to 1,938 and by 1982 PACs totaled 3,371. Their total spending increased from $30.1 million in 1976 to $127.7 million in 1980 and on to $190.4 million in 1982.[24] New business PACs comprised by far the largest share of the growth. In 1978, for instance, when all PACs accounted for $34.1 million of the $199 million in contributions received by congressional candidates, one researcher estimated that business and business-related groups outspent labor by better than two to one.[25] Between 1976 and 1978, corporate PAC gifts to candidates more than doubled, while labor's PAC donations showed only a 25% gain.* Business and trade PACs, which at first favored incumbents (and thus gave more to Democratic candidates), have gradually moved to the GOP's banner.

Of far greater concern to the political parties is another increasingly prominent form of political action committee: the ideological PAC. The National Committee for an Effective Congress (NCEC) on the left and the Committee for the Survival of a Free Congress (CSFC) on the right are typical examples. Both provide organizational assistance to ideologically compatible candidates, irrespective of party. The NCEC is much the elder of the two and was founded in

---

*Labor's figures do not, however, include separate spending for registration, get-out-the-vote, and other activities, which may amount to as much as $20 million in an election year.

1948. It describes itself as a "bipartisan progressive" group dedicated to civil rights, civil liberties, and internationalism. Rather than giving money, the NCEC provides specific services, such as the hiring and paying of the campaign manager, polling, targeting, and organizing. In a normal election year the NCEC will assist in some way up to 60 House candidates and a dozen Senate contenders. Russell Hemenway, executive director of the NCEC, sees his organization as a substitute for the Democratic National Committee, which "provides almost no services to candidates," and for political consultants who "are looking for campaigns that can pay hefty bills."

Many of the same goals are shared by the CSFC, which has sought to imitate somewhat the NCEC and the AFL–CIO's Committee on Political Education (COPE). "I make no secret of the fact that I admire their [COPE's] operations and have to some extent modeled our committee on the labor groups" says CSFC director Paul Weyrich.[26] Founded in 1974 with financial support from Joseph Coors, the conservative Colorado brewer, the CSFC plays a central role in the so-called "New Right," along with Richard Viguerie's direct-mail outfit and other political committees, such as Sen. Jesse Helms' Congressional Club and the National Conservative PAC.[27] Like the NCEC, the CSFC helps candidates assemble a skilled campaign team, usually contributing about $500 a month to pay the salary of a field organizer. The CSFC acts almost like a political party, recruiting candidates, refining candidates' political abilities, performing electoral organizational chores, devising strategy, and constructing campaign staffs. An extensive five-day "candidate school" is held by the CSFC four to six times every two years, and it is attended by prospective congressional contenders and campaign managers from the conservative wings of both parties, who pay a registration fee of $500 per person. The schools enlist incumbent congressmen and consultants as instructors and are organized around problem-solving groups that enable the CSFC directors to evaluate each political candidate's performance. At the end of the course, a simulated election is held, which sometimes serves as an informal primary of sorts since more than one candidate from the same district attends. In 1978, three Republican House contenders from the same Wisconsin constituency attended the CSFC school, and the PAC decided that one of them, Toby Roth, was clearly superior (and the most conservative). After the school's adjournment, Roth received the group's blessing, and he went on to win his party's nomination and to defeat an incumbent Democratic congressman in November.

Ideological PACs are proliferating and strengthening. In 1981–82, the six largest conservative PACs raised a combined total of $29.4

million, up by 25% from the previous election cycle.[28] Liberal PACs did less well, raising about $9.4 million, but five of the six top groups were new-formed in reaction to the conservative PACs' 1980 election successes—and the comparable liberal total was a scant $400,000.[29]

In explaining the explosive growth of all forms of PACs, most (but not all) roads lead to FECA. The 1974 lifting of the ban on corporate funding of PACs was crucial, and the tighter public disclosure requirements, by revealing the previously obscured extent of each corporation's involvement in politics, have produced a "keep up with the Joneses" mentality among business and trade association circles. FECA's $1,000 limitation on individual contributions and its more permissive $5,000 PAC limit encourage candidates to rely on PACs as a more generous source of funds. Also having an effect on the extent and pace of PAC expansion is a growing group of political consultants, who specialize in assisting PAC formation and activity. The professionals are finding PAC consulting to be more stable, continuous, and profitable than candidate work, and almost all consultants have advised at least one or a few PACs from time to time.

Even though PACs are clearly party rivals, both parties seem to be resigned to the age of PACs. Like Willie Sutton who robbed banks "because that's where they keep the money," the parties have begun to direct their attentions to the overflowing PAC treasuries and have hired consultants to ensure that they get their fair share of PAC money.[30] The GOP assists its candidates in soliciting PACs, helping its nominees to secure appointments with PAC officials and directing them toward committees that are likely to donate to them.[31] Behind the facade of cooperation, however, lies the inescapable incompatibility and competitiveness between parties and PACs. Many political action committees are slowly but surely developing into rival institutions that raise money, develop memberships, recruit candidates, organize campaigns, and influence officeholders just as the parties do (or are supposed to do). PACs already outfinance the parties, partly because they drain away potential gifts to them, permitting supporters to tell the Democratic or Republican committee that they have already given at the office.[32] PACs also outspend the parties by a large margin. While the two parties were contributing $21.9 million to their congressional nominees in 1982, for instance, PACs mustered $83.1 million in congressional contributions.

PACs are not organized along party lines and are never likely to be. In the words of one PAC official, "We believe you have to be pretty cold-blooded concerning your giving policy. You simply have to support candidates who support you . . . regardless of party or philosophy."[33] The ideological PACs, of course, make no pretense about their aims. Most of them view the parties with undisguised hostility, attacking them for a lack of ideological clarity and working to defeat the more moderate choices of party leaders in primaries. Paul Weyrich of CSFC proudly cites the case of Republican right-wing political novice Gordon Humphrey of New Hampshire, a former airline pilot who upset incumbent Democratic U.S. Senator Thomas McIntyre in 1978. The GOP senatorial campaign committee gave assistance to Humphrey's more moderate primary opponent, but CSFC helped to engineer a primary victory for him. Now, reports Weyrich, "Gordon is less than enthusiastic about the party," which suits CSFC just fine. It is easy to agree with Weyrich's observation that "both political parties would have an all-night celebration if we were to go out of business." The problem for the parties can be succinctly stated: Groups like CSFC are in no danger of going out of business. In fact, they are flourishing.

THE INDEPENDENT EXPENDITURE LOOPHOLE

One particular anomaly of the federal election rules gives PACs a tremendous potential advantage over parties and could play havoc with attempts to limit the influence of large donors. That anomaly, the provision for independent expenditures on behalf of a candidate, was not a part of FECA but a Supreme Court mandate (from *Buckley* v. *Valeo*). The Court held that Congress could not impose spending limitations on PACs and individuals who desire to advocate a candidate's election without consultation with his campaign. The Federal Election Commission, acting after the Court's decision, defined an independent expenditure as one made by a person or committee "expressly advocating the election or defeat" of a candidate that is "not made with the cooperation, or with the prior consent of, or in consultation with, or at the request or suggestion of, a candidate or any agent or authorized committee" of the candidate.[34] The expenditure, in other words, must truly be independent of the candidate and his campaign; otherwise it would come under the regular contribution limitations. There is no ceiling on the amount, nor stipulation regarding frequency of, independent expenditures. While less than 0.2% of all campaign money spent in 1976 was independent in nature, the 1978 figures indicate that the two top independent spenders alone exceeded the entire total of independent expenditures for 1976 House and Senate candidates, and new records were set again in 1980 at both the presidential and congressional levels. Independent expenditures in 1982 totaled $5.3 million, representing 1.4% of all campaign spending.[35] To this point, independent expenditures have almost always involved advertising in some form, where an individual or committee purchases time and space to endorse or attack a candidate or support or oppose a group of candidates based on an issue or set of issues. Henry C. Grover, a former Texas legislator and Ronald Reagan supporter, independently spent more money than any other individual in 1976 ($63,000) for pro-Reagan newspaper advertisements prior to the Texas and Michigan GOP primaries. And in 1980 Reagan was assisted by an independent backer in the South Carolina primary. Having already spent two-thirds of the nationwide spending limit, Reagan's campaign was unwilling to invest a significant amount of money in the Magnolia State, so U.S. Senator Jesse Helms used funds from his own PAC to launch a television promotion on behalf of the eventual Republican nominee. Liberal financier Stewart Mott spent well over $100,000 just a few weeks later to air advertisements for John Anderson's presidential effort while he was still competing in the GOP primaries.[36]

Political action committees have been slower to investigate the independent route, but when they do, the result is often a major investment. PACs are better situated than most individuals to organize an effective independent program, since they have the administrative structure and the experienced staff that individuals lack. PACs also have direct access to the expertise of political consultants, many of whom are on retainer to them. The American Medical Association's AMPAC has been a path breaker in exploring independent action. In 1978 the committee spent over $42,000 on advertisements supporting favored congressional candidates in six popular magazines distributed throughout 16 congressional districts and the state of Georgia.[37] AMPAC's 1982 independent spending topped $210,000.[38] The National Conservative Political Action Committee (NCPAC) has also concentrated on independent expenditures, but of the negative variety. The group spent about $700,000 in 1979 alone primarily for television advertising to attack liberal U.S. senators up for reelection the following year.[38] All told, in 1980 NCPAC's independent spending in the congressional contests and presidential race (where it backed Ronald Reagan) exceeded $2.3 million; in 1982 NCPAC spent almost $3.2 million independently in congressional races alone.[40]

There are notable obstacles in the path of any group or individual attempting to undertake an independent course of action.

Beyond the reporting burdens imposed by the FEC, which are particularly onerous for individuals, there is the frustrating and difficult prohibition against contact with the candidate or his agents. The AMPAC executive director, for example, felt obliged to require each member of the committee's staff and board of directors to identify any congressional candidate with whom he had had direct or indirect contact for over a full year, so as to eliminate possible violations of the FEC's standards.[41] Additional FEC regulations restrict the flexibility of independent campaigns. Individuals are forbidden to pool their money for an independent effort, thus preventing liberal or conservative persons from combining their resources in order to afford national television time, for instance.[42] Even if the time could be afforded, there is no guarantee advertisements would be run. Many stations refuse to consider the sale of spots or programs for independent campaigns, and the Federal Communications Commission does not require them to do so. The Internal Revenue Service added another inhibiting factor in 1980 by preliminarily ruling that contributions to "negative campaigns" are not eligible for the income tax credit on political donations.[43] Lastly, there is the fear and the danger that an independent campaign would distort or interfere with a candidate's strategy, by perhaps raising an unpleasant issue on a controversial subject or erroneous charges. Candidates, therefore, often try to discourage independent efforts on their behalf.[44] In Idaho, for example, the Anybody But Church Committee, a PAC affiliated with NCPAC, ran independent television commercials against Democratic U.S. Senator Frank Church in 1980. One spot showed empty Titan missile sites in the state and accused Church of opposing a strong national defense. But the advertisement backfired when Church pointed out that the Titans had been replaced by a new generation of more effective missiles under a program he backed. After this incident, Republican U.S. Senate candidates in two other states denounced similar NCPAC media campaigns against their liberal incumbent opponents, openly fearing a sympathy backlash.

Despite all of the real and potential problems involved with independent expenditures, political observers are virtually unanimous in predicting expansion in the field. There is talk among PAC officials of independent polling for a favored candidate to design a better independent media package, of independent telephone banks to identify a candidate's voters and get them to the polls on election day, and of independent persuasive direct-mail programs. One executive of AMPAC was willing to predict that within a decade, half of all the money in the growing treasuries of political action committees would be spent for independent activities—a challenge to the limitation goals of FECA, certainly, but no less a challenge to the influence of political parties.

A PARTY'S REJOINDER:
GOP RENEWAL

One of the two major parties decided to fight back in the mid-1970s and began to acquire the techniques of the political consultant to further its own candidates—and, in the process, nurse itself back to health. The Republican party at the national level has organized exemplary direct-mail and media operations centered around two subsidiaries of the Republican National Committee (RNC), The National Republican Senatorial Committee (NRSC) and the National Republican Congressional Committee (NRCC). The NRSC assists GOP U.S. Senate candidates, while the NRCC aids Republican contenders for the U.S. House of Representatives. It is difficult not to be impressed by the GOP's assemblage of organizational and technological tools. For example, each election year, the NRCC carefully selects 80 to 120 target House districts where Republicans are believed to have a chance to oust incumbent Democrats or fill open seats, and the committee's five full-time field representatives then go to work to recruit outstanding candidates, normally identifying willing participants in 40 to 50 of the districts. If the party feels it has located a particularly strong candidate in a "likely-to-win" district, and other key Republicans in the district and state agree, the NRCC will even back the candidate in a party primary.

The assistance, in both a primary and general election, can be considerable. Both the NRCC and the NRSC have collected voluminous records on House and Senate members' votes and activities. There is also a growing storehouse of postelection research, including studies of voters, nonvoters, campaign managers, and candidates conducted by national polling firms. Key congressional campaigns have instant access to the information by means of portable video display terminals located in their local headquarters and connected to the GOP computer data bank in Washington. The Republican national organizations also help their candidates to solicit PACs and political consultants. An extensive and somewhat evaluative list of consultants is kept current, as is a roster of PACs that have donated to GOP candidates in the past. The party assists candidates in securing appointments with PAC decision makers as well.

Campaign management colleges are yet another regular project of the Republican National Committee. In operation since 1974, the college consists of a week's strenuous training in campaign techniques for twelve-hour-per-day sessions. About 20 "students" are selected to participate in each college, most of them slated to manage GOP House or Senate campaigns. All costs are paid by the Republican party, and the sessions can be held for new groups as often as once a month in an election year. In addition, the special projects division of the RNC sponsors a separate school for campaign press secretaries and more than a dozen three-day "Basic instructional" workshops for all interested campaign staffers at sites scattered throughout the country. (On average, a workshop will draw about 80 participants.) The candidates themselves are not ignored, and the RNC, in cooperation with incumbent Republican congressmen, frequently brings candidates and prospective candidates to Washington long before the advent of the campaign to polish their skills and learn new ones.

The media division of the NRCC is particularly noteworthy, and its evolution is powerful evidence of campaign technology's potential usefulness to a party and its nominees. In 1971 the old broadcast services division of the RNC employed just three people and offered a very limited list of services. The new media division is so active and involved that it is difficult to summarize all of its programs. Audio and videotape "actualities" (i.e., tapes featuring the candidate) are transmitted to every radio and television station in a House member's district and are then used (normally unedited) by the unpaid media on news programs. The taping and transmission can be accomplished within a single working day, so that a congressman's activity in the morning can be highlighted on the six o'clock news. In some respects the NRCC media division has become a part-time Washington correspondent for many stations across the country.

Campaign needs, though, are the major focus of the media division. Commercials for both radio and television are produced for a phenomenally low price (at least compared to what political consultants charge). An entire advertising package, counting salaries, overhead, and all production costs, can be delivered for less than the $5,000 contribution the national party is permitted to make to each of its candidates.[45] The media division is flexible enough to do as much or as little as a campaign needs, sometimes doing the entire advertising package from start to finish, at other times simply working with a candidate's political consultant or local agency to plan Capitol

Hill filming. As of 1980, even the time-buying for many GOP candidates was done by the NRCC, saving campaigns as much as 90% of the normal 15% agency commission fee. Postproduction and editing facilities were also added in 1980, a measure that resulted in even lower media charges for GOP candidates. A major expansion of the division's scope occurred as well. While only 8 media campaigns were taken by the NRCC in 1978, almost 50 were handled in 1980, and 300 individual commercials were produced; in 1982, the number of markets jumped to 90.

The most interesting part of the media divisions's program is the attempt to improve the image of the Republican party with television advertisements. FECA has indirectly encouraged the party to expend funds in this way by limiting its contributions to candidates, and the GOP has made a virtue of necessity, marketing its party label in a way that it hopes will have beneficial side effects for its nominees. After Watergate's devastation, in-house media research indicated that the GOP could not talk about issues effectively until its general image and credibility improved. Out of that finding came the "America Today" series, a group of well-targeted five-minute spots that centered around a "human interest" topic (such as the needs of the disabled or the cardiopulmonary-resuscitation method) and showed what individual members of the Republican congressional delegation were doing about it. "We picked as narrators congressmen who could project what we wanted to say institutionally about the party: that Republicans care about people," reported NRCC media director Ed Blakely. A service element was built into each spot, and viewers were urged to "write REPUBLICANS, Box 1400, Washington, D.C., and we will send you a free brochure telling how you can get involved and what you can do." Each advertisement closed with pictures of all the GOP House members flashed for a third of a second each, as an announcer reminded listeners that "America Today was brought to you as a public service by the Republicans in Congress, 146 men and women working to improve the government and the quality of life of the people of this nation." Each stage of the development and production was accompanied by careful audience testing, and a cyclical schedule of broadcasting (three weeks on the air, then two weeks off, then two weeks on again, and so forth), with different spots shown in each cycle, was designed, similar to an advertising schedule for a commercial product. An extensive study by GOP consultant Robert Teeter's polling firm demonstrates that the advertisements "succeeded in producing changes in the evaluation of the GOP."[46] Viewers thought that Republicans were more caring individuals than they had previously believed and, interestingly, the advertisements concurrently reduced viewers' favourable impressions of Democrats by 3 to 13% on rating scales for nine desirable attributes. The image polishing did not necessarily translate into more votes, but Independent voters, in particular, appeared more receptive to Republicanism afterward.

The same study found that another GOP series of commercials was much more directly useful in corralling voters. The "Issues of the '80s" spots, aired once "America Today"'s image making had run its course, gave standard Republican dogma on a host of topics, such as government spending and rising food prices. After seeing the advertisements (in the absence of countervailing advertisements, of course) a gain of 19% was registered for the GOP side.[47] This package led to an even more strongly partisan advertising campaign first aired early in 1980, a $9.5 million series that attacked the Democratic Congress using themes from a Teeter poll conducted for the RNC. With the tag line "Vote Republican—for a Change," the 30-second, 60-second, and five-minute advertisements attacked the Democratic Congress and lampooned its leaders. One spot had an actor resembling House Speaker Tip O'Neill driving a car until it ran out of gas. Another featured an unemployed factory worker asking pointedly, "If the Democrats are so good for working people, then how come so many people aren't working?" (The inspiration for the series, incidentally, was provided by the advertising package run by the British Conservative party in 1979). The 1980 advertisements were considered so effective that, once in power in 1981, the GOP aired a $2.3 million advertising campaign designed to capitalize on President Reagan's congressional budget successes, on the theme "Republicans: Leadership that works for a change." Yet another $10 million institutional package was run prior to the 1982 midterm congressional elections, claiming "Republicans are beginning to make things better."

Many of the RNC and associated divisions' activities are paid for with profits from a remarkably successful direct-mail operation. Direct mail has brought the Republican party from near-bankruptcy (in 1975 the party raised just $300,000 of its $2.3 million budget) to a financial position unrivaled in its history. The direct-mail packages for all of the national GOP groups collected about $20 million in 1979, at a cost of only about 35 cents per dollar raised; in 1982, those groups raised $130 million in direct mail. The Republican party now has reliable lists containing the names of over 1,000,700 donors, which are maintained by a 25% annual replacement (because of donor mobility, death, etc.) All the GOP's direct-mail programs are coordinated by the Stephen Winchell and

Associates firm. (Winchell, a former employee of Richard Viguerie, was selected after his old boss refused to take the account, demurring because he wanted "to destroy the Republican party by drying up all the contributions to it"—or so charged NRCC finance director Wyatt Stewart.) The GOP has been taking full advantage of a provision passed by Congress in 1978 that gave "qualified political parties" the right to mail letters under the nonprofit rate of 2.7 cents a letter,[48] rather than the usual third-class rate of 8.4 cents.[49] The RNC has even experimented with direct response, combining television advertisements and toll-free numbers with credit card contribution pledging. After some strained negotiation in 1978, for example, the NRCC convinced former President Ford and Ronald Reagan to appear together in a 60-second spot attacking the Democratic Congress and urging credit card contributions to the GOP by means of a toll-free number.

The NRCC plans to stay at its present level of direct-mail solicitation so as to reserve contribution potential for state party committees. In fact, much of the effort in the direct-mail division and in the other RNC subsidiaries is to transfer technology to the state level and strengthen state parties in the process. More than 20 state organizations are already tied into the RNC's "mother computer" via long-distance telephone lines. Access to the computer is made available for a very small fee (about $7 an hour, plus a one-time $300 start-up fee), and each of the subscribers gains entry to a sophisticated data processing network called "REPNET" that contains five major programs for financial mailing list maintenance, donor preservation and information, and correspondence and word processing.[50] In another attempt to help the state parties (and to improve the GOP's congressional redistricting fortunes in the wake of the 1980 census), the RNC formed a political action committee called "GOPAC," headed by Delaware Governor Pierre DuPont, which contributed well over $1 million to state legislative candidates in 1979 and 1980 contests.

There are few Democratic equivalents of the advanced Republican technological programs. In almost every respect, the Democratic operations are pitifully inadequate by comparison with the GOP's; even where there is some visible activity, the effort is a pale shadow of its rival's work. The Democratic National Committee (DNC) and the Democratic Congressional Campaign Committee (DCCC) do schedule several dozen campaign training programs around the country, and they have recently established a Democratic National Training Academy in Des Moines, Iowa, but the workshops held so far do not compare with the more extensive Republican gatherings. The DNC's direct mail program, under contract to Craver, Mathews, Smith, and Company, has only just begun in earnest, and it will take years to reach the GOP's level of sophistication. Thanks mainly to the difference in their direct-mail systems, the Democratic party was able to give less than one-fourth as much as its Republican counterpart to its 1980 House and Senate candidates.[51] During 1979 and 1980, the national Republican party and its allied Senate and House campaign committees raised $122.1 million. The comparable figure for the Democratic party and committees was a paltry $23 million raised. In 1981–82, the ratio actually continued to worsen for the Democrats: the Republican groups raised seven times as much as their Democratic counterparts ($190.9 million compared to $31.4 million).

The technological and organizational gap between the two parties is certainly wider now than it has ever been, but Republicans have generally been more willing and able than Democrats to experiment with new techniques during the entire age of political consultantship. Media consultant Robert Squier, who has worked closely with some officials of the Democratic National Committee, suggested that the Democrats have not matched the GOP in campaign technology "because of a lack of money, a lack of leadership, and a lack of understanding how and why a party has to be involved in modern campaigning."

There are other factors at work as well. The pre-1980 Republican party, as the perennially disappointed underdog, had to try harder and had to be willing to experiment with new ideas, since the old ways were obviously not enough for victory. The Democratic party had been more electorally secure and consequently had less incentive to build the party or change its ways. "The Democratic party as the majority party is simply not frustrated enough," surmised William Sweeney, executive director of the Democratic Congressional Campaign Committee, before his party's 1980 disasters. Many more of the Democratic elite had been in office as well, with the personal staff perquisites that accompany incumbency, making the strengthening of party staff somewhat less important than for office-hungry Republicans. Labor's COPE operations also proved to be a ready substitute for the party's weaknesses, and, until the growth of PACs, COPE's efforts could only be directly challenged with GOP resources. Moreover, it may be that the business and middle-class base of the modern Republican party naturally produced a greater managerial emphasis among its directors, many of whom are drawn from the same sector of society. Whatever the roots of its technological edge, it has proved to be a significant advantage to the GOP in electing its candidates, in strengthening itself, and in competing effectively with rival PACs and political consultants.

The Democrats' jarring defeats in 1980 appear to have shaken the party out of its lethargy and spurred it on to modernization.[52] There is little question that the Democratic party's potential is great if it chooses to exploit its base. RNCC's Wyatt Stewart boasted that he could apply GOP direct-mail techniques to the much broader based Democratic party and "do twice what the Republican party is doing today."

SUMMARY
AND CONCLUDING COMMENTS

While the GOP has made the best of the circumstances, both political parties have been buffeted by a number of forces unleashed by new campaign finance laws and the technologies of political consultants. With a contribution limit five times greater than that of individuals and equal to the parties', a political action committee rivals the party for the affections of candidates, and if the PAC is ideological and organization oriented, it can become a sort of surrogate party. A further expansion of PAC activity and influence is almost guaranteed.

While FECA was strengthening PACs, it was weakening the parties, despite its objectives to the contrary. Political consultants were among the biggest gainers, becoming more necessary than ever for long-range planning and efficient management of larger staffs, and direct-mail fund raising from small donors became one of the most sought-after technologies. Not just FECA but also the weakened parties themselves gave political consultants their modern opening, and they used the opportunity to hawk techniques that replaced the party as the middleman between candidate and voter. A few independent consulting professionals are strongly supportive of the party system, but most are indifferent or even hostile to it, frequently running their client-candidates against or around the party label and also assisting the development of PACs' competitive facilities. Whereas most consultants are nominally loyal to one or the other party for business reasons, a growing number are proud switch-hitters, mercenaries available for hire to the first or top bidder. Others, for ideological reasons, are openly contemptuous of the parties, opposing a flexible party system in toto. However, one of the parties has begun to fight back; the Republicans are showing the way, and their shrewd and sophisticated moves suggest one solution to the dilemmas posed by the rise of political consultants and the new campaign technology.

The GOP's new directions are beneficial not just to its own electoral fortunes but to the political system as a whole. The Republican institutional advertising, media services, candidate schools, and policy briefings are having the effect of drawing candidates closer to the party. The candidates voice similar policy themes, take much the same approach on at least some fundamental issues, and have a stake in the party's present wellbeing and future development. They are beholden to the party, too; sizeable contributions and significant campaign services are not easily forgotten, and there is always the implied threat of their withdrawal in reelection campaigns, should the officeholder prove too much of a maverick. Is it any wonder, then, that House and Senate Republicans were unusually and exceedingly unified on the Reagan budget and tax votes in 1981?[53]

Clearly, the GOP has shown one route of escape from the current candidate-centered and consultant-oriented system of American politics. The Democratic party should follow its rival's lead, and the Republicans can go further. State and local parties, for the most part, have yet to benefit fully from the revolution in campaign techniques. The technology must be transferred there if the parties are to have a vibrant base. Direct mail, party-sponsored telephone banks, and even television solicitation can be used to rebuild and revitalize the atrophied organizational foundations of the American parties. The national parties need to adopt, not just new techniques, but their own version of "New Federalism," if parties are to be the representative and broad-based agencies needed for a healthy democracy.

NOTES

1. Martin P. Wattenberg, "The Decline of Political Partisanship in the United States: Negativity or Neutrality?" *American Political Science Review* 75 (1981): 941-50.

2. Much of the following discussion of consultants and their technologies is derived from Sabato, *The Rise of Political Consultants* (New York: Basic Books, 1981).

3. This quotation, and the others of political consultants that follow, are taken from the author's personal interviews conducted in 1979 and 1980.

4. What makes an advertisement "effective" is still a matter of conjecture. While rigorous audience testing of political commercials is not uncommon, there is no precise formula in designing ads, and political media remains far more an art than a science. See ibid., pp. 121–43.

5. And consultants often charge precisely that. See ibid., pp. 179–82.

6. Ibid., pp. 92–102.

7. Ibid., pp. 74–75.

8. Institute of Politics, JFK School of Government, Harvard University, "An Analysis of the Impact of the Federal Election Campaign Act, 1972–78" (Cambridge, Mass.: JFK School, May 1979).

9. Sabato, op. cit., pp. 221–66. Political action committees (PACs) have also filled the campaign finance vacuum, as will be discussed later.

10. Ibid., pp. 200–4.

11. Joseph Napolitan, *The Election Game and How to Win It* (New York: Doubleday, 1972), pp. 17–18.

12. Ibid.

13. See ibid., pp. 162–208. Shapp lost the general election that year but came back to win the statehouse in 1970.

14. Sanford L. Weiner, "The Role of the Political Consultant," in Robert Agranoff (ed.), *The New Style in Election Campaigns* (2nd ed.) (Boston: Holbrook, 1976), p. 59.

15. See, for example, *National Journal*, January 21, 1978, p. 91; and *Congressional Quarterly Weekly*, October 23, 1976, p. 3028, and December 24, 1977, p. 2650.

16. 86 Stat 3 (1971); 88 Stat 1263 (1974); 90 Stat 475 (1976).

17. Institute of Politics, Harvard University, op. cit., pp. 1–19.

18. *The Washington Post*, September 30, 1979.

19. 96 S.Ct. 612 (1976) or 424 U.S. 1 (1976).

20. *National Journal*, February 9, 1980, pp. 229–31.

21. NRCC, "Campaign Manager's Study: 1978 Post-Election Research" (Washington, D.C., 1979), pp. 2, 5.

22. See *Congressional Quarterly Weekly*, January 5, 1980, pp. 33–34. HR 5010 became Public Law 96–187.

23. As a result of HR 5010, the number of state and local party committees forced to fulfill the FEC's reporting stipulations fell from 744 in 1977–78 to 585 in 1979–80. See *FEC Record* 8 (May 1982): 2.

24. See *National Journal*, February 27, 1982, p. 391, and *Congressional Quarterly Weekly*, April 10, 1982, pp. 814–23; 1982 figures are from FEC press release "1981–82 PAC Giving Up 51%, April 29, 1983.

25. See Edwin M. Epstein, "An Irony of Electoral Reform: The Business PAC Phenomenon," *Regulation* (May/June, 1979): 35–41. Also see FEC release of April 29, 1983 (ibid.).

26. See Paul M. Weyrich, "The New Right: PACs and Coalition Politics," in Michael J. Malbin (ed.), *Parties, Interest Groups, and Campaign Finance Laws* (Washington, D.C.: American Enterprise Institute, 1980), pp. 68-81.

27. *National Journal*, October 23, 1976, p. 1514, and January 5, 1980, p. 20. See also *Congressional Quarterly Weekly*, December 24, 1977, p. 2652.

28. See FEC release of April 29, 1983. See also *National Journal*, January 21, 1978, pp. 88-92, and March 20, 1982, pp. 500-1; *Congressional Quarterly Weekly*, February 27, 1982, p. 482, and March 6, 1982, pp. 499-505. The latter article closely examines the Helms group, which in 1981 became the country's largest PAC.

29. Ibid.

30. The GOP has been more diligent in this, as in most campaign matters.

31. National Republican Congressional Committee. *Financing Republican Congressional Campaigns* (Washington, D.C., 1979), pp. 205-9. See also *Campaigning Reports*, vol. 2, no. 3 (February 7, 1980): 9-10.

32. Institute of Politics, Harvard University, op. cit., pp. 4-8.

33. As quoted in *Campaigning Reports*, vol. 1, no. 6 (August 9, 1979): 10.

34. Federal Election Commission, U.S., "Campaign Guide for Presidential Candidates and Their Committees" (Washington, D.C.: FEC, October 1979), pp. 9, 36-37.

35. See *National Journal*, June 23, 1979, pp. 1044-46, and May 23, 1981, pp. 920-25. For the 1980 elections alone, 112 PACs and individuals spent $16.2 million in independent expenditures; in the 1982 non-presidential campaign, 110 PACs independently spent $5.3 million.

36. See *The Washington Post*, April 9, 1980.

37. See Nathan J. Muller, "Political Advertising in National Magazines," *Practical Politics*, vol. 2, no. 1 (November/December 1978): 16-20, 28.

38. Federal Election Commission, U.S., *FEC Reports on Financial Activity 1981-82, Interim Report No. 4: Party and Non-Party Political Committees* (Washington, D.C.: FEC, May 1983).

39. See *The Washington Post*, August 17, 1979; *Campaigning Practices Reports*, vol. 7, no. 5 (March 17, 1980): 2-4; and *Congressional Quarterly Weekly*, November 22, 1980, pp. 3405-9 and April 10, 1982, pp. 814-23.

40. See *FEC Reports, Interim Report No. 4*.

41. Internal memorandum from AMPAC Executive Director William L. Watson dated June 28, 1978. Also the author's personal correspondence with Donald P. Wilcox, general counsel of the Texas Medical Association, dated December 18, 1979, and with Peter B. Lauer, assistant director of AMPAC, dated December 27, 1979. The staff and members of the board were required to submit a signed certification of noncontact and a promise to refrain from making any contact with any campaign unless specifically authorized by AMPAC.

42. A major court suit was filed in 1979 by liberal and conservative activists challenging this ruling and others: *Mott, et al.* v. *FEC*, U.S. District Court for the District of Columbia, 79-3375, December 17, 1979. See *National Journal*, December 22, 1979, p. 2165. However, the suit was unsuccessful and dismissed in July 1980.

43. *The Washington Post*, April 4, 1980. The ruling was requested by the Democratic party with NCPAC's campaigns in mind.

44. See the *Congressional Quarterly Weekly* Special Report, "The 1980 Elections," Supplement to vol. 38, no. 8 (February 23, 1980): 457, 462, 466.

45. If the total cost exceeds $5,000, or if the NRCC has already made a monetary contribution to a campaign, then the candidate merely reimburses the NRCC for any amount above the $5,000 maximum. A precise, computerized accounting of all work performed by media division personnel is updated daily, and, to avoid illegal extension of credit to candidates, accounts are payable in advance or on delivery of the advertisements.

46. The study consisted of 1200 original interviews and 506 followups, and was conducted between December 1977 and January 1978.

47. NRCC, "Political Advertising on Television," pp. 19, 25.

48. The nonprofit rate was later raised first to 3.1 cents and then (as of July 1980) to 3.5 cents.

49. See *The Washington Post*, April 22, 1979. The 5.7 cents difference is, in effect, a government subsidy to the parties. There has also been controversy as to what constitutes a "qualified party," with all manner of political groups trying to cash in on the provision.

50. The five components of REPNET mentioned here are: CPA (Computerized Political Accounting System); ADONIS (Automated Donor Information System); UNICORN (Universal Correspondence and Word Processing); MAIL CALL (Mailing List Maintenance System); TARGET 20 (Political Targeting and Survey Processing System).

51. See *FEC Record* 8 (May 1982): 1-2. Republican party groups made direct contributions of $10.8 million, compared to the Democrats' $2.4 million; while in the 1982 Congressional races the totals were $4.8 million and $1.2 million, respectively.

52. *Congressional Quarterly Weekly*, April 10, 1982, pp. 814-23.

53. See *National Journal*, May 8, 1982, pp. 800-10.

9

PARTIES AND THE MEDIA IN BRITAIN AND THE UNITED STATES

David Butler

Austin Ranney

In Britain and the United States, as in every modern industrialized nation, the media of mass communications constitute one of the most powerful forces shaping the environments within which political parties must do their work. In both countries newspapers were by far the most powerful medium until the 1920s, when radio broadcasting arrived as an important additional source of entertainment and information for most of the two populations. And in both countries perhaps the greatest change in the political environment since the 1950s has been the advent of television, which, by the 1980s, has become the principal source of both news and entertainment for most British and Americans.[1]

In both countries in the 1980s, admittedly, other mass media, such as radio, magazines, books, and motion pictures, still retain some influence, especially on the small elites of political leaders and politics buffs who regularly consume their political output. But for the vast majority of ordinary people on both sides of the Atlantic television is by far the most important medium of mass communication, with newspapers a distant but still visible second.

In the United States today, for example, television signals can be received in every corner of the country. About 98% of American homes have at least one television receiver, and nearly half have two or more. The average household set is turned on over six hours a day every day of the year. By the time the average American adolescent has reached voting age, he has watched television for more hours than he has spent in school, and the average American adult devotes more hours to watching television than to any other activity except working and sleeping.[2]

Television saturation is as great in Britain. Nearly everyone is within range of a television signal, almost every home has at least one television receiver, and British adults, like Americans, spend more time watching television than doing anything else except working and sleeping.

In both countries the great majority of the people also report that they read some part of a newspaper every day. As we shall note in a moment, however, newspapers are for most people considerably less used—and less trusted—sources of political information than television, and none of the other mass media come close in either regard. Accordingly, in this brief survey we shall focus exclusively on television and newspapers and their role in shaping the environments within which political parties in the two countries must operate.

THE STRUCTURE AND REGULATION OF THE MEDIA

Newspapers

In both Britain and the United States newspapers are almost entirely privately owned and operated as businesses for profit. But their freedom to print what they wish about parties and politicians is greater in America than in Britain. For one thing, the First Amendment to the Constitution of the United States declares that "Congress [and, by judicial interpretation, the states as well] shall make no law abridging ... the freedom of the press," and a series of Supreme Court decisions have interpreted this prohibition so broadly that there is now a powerful legal presumption against the constitutionality of any law, such as the British Official Secrets Act, which might seek to restrict what newspapers can report about government actions. Indeed, in the 1970s Congress enacted the Freedom of Information Act, which guarantees and facilitates the access of reporters, scholars, and other curious citizens to much official information that in Britain is kept secret.

Another noteworthy difference is that the British press is considerably more national than the American. There are no fewer than nine newspapers that are published in London but widely read all over the country: the *Daily Express, Sun, Daily Mail, Daily Mirror, Daily Sketch, Daily Telegraph, Guardian, Daily Star* and *Times*.[3] In the United States, by contrast, only three papers have substantial national circulations and political influence comparable to the British national press: the *New York Times, Washington Post*, and *Wall Street Journal*. The weekly newsmagazines, *Time* and *Newsweek*, also have national circulation and impact, but they fall outside our present purview. The United States also has a number of newspapers of good quality but mainly regional circulation and influence—for example, the *Boston Globe, Baltimore Sun, St. Louis Post-Dispatch, Chicago Tribune, Denver Post*, and *Los Angeles Times*—whereas the British regional and local papers have little influence or circulation outside their particular regions.

Television

1. *Structure.* In both Britain and the United States, television broadcasting is much more centralized than newspaper publishing. In Britain at the present time all noncommercial television broadcasting is produced and controlled by the British Broadcasting Corporation (BBC), which develops and produces its own programs and broadcasts them on two channels on over 100 BBC-owned and operated transmitting stations distributed over the entire country. Since 1954 there has also been commercial television, supervised by the Independent Broadcasting Authority (IBA—formerly the Independent Television Authority), which now also broadcasts programs on two channels over IBA-owned and operated transmitters throughout the country. The programs approved and broadcast by IBA are developed and produced by 20 program companies, such as Granada Television and Thames Television, under contract with IBA.

At first glance, American television broadcasting seems much more decentralized, but the appearance is deceptive. At the present time there are a total of 727 commercial broadcasting stations and 269 noncommercial stations. Most of the commercial stations are owned and operated for (considerable) profit by local owners (some are owned by local newspapers but most by other entrepreneurial groups). The noncommercial stations are owned and operated either by public agencies, such as state universities or state departments of education, or by local not-for-profit corporations supported by contributions from viewers and business corporations. Every broadcasting station, commercial or noncommercial, acquires its legal right to broadcast (and its authorized frequency, power, and hours of broadcasting) from a license issued by a national regulatory agency, the Federal Communications Commission (FCC), and its license must be renewed (and can be revoked) every three years. Since its establishment in 1934, the FCC and the Congress have imposed a number of rules that the local licensees must observe if their licenses are to be renewed, and, as we shall see below, many of these rules deal with how the broadcasters deal with political parties, candidates, and issues.

In fact, however, American television is dominated by the three national networks. Of the 727 commercial stations, a total of 605—or 83%—are affiliated with either the American Broadcasting Corporation (ABC—195 affiliates), the Columbia Broadcasting System (CBS—198 affiliates), or the National Broadcasting Company (NBC—212 affiliates). Network "affiliation" in each case means that the local station signs a contract, usually for two years renewable, with the network. The network produces a variety of entertainment programs, newscasts, and public affairs programs, which it offers to the affiliates, usually paying them to broadcast the programs and keeping the advertising revenues generated for the networks. If the affiliate accepts the payment and the program, as it usually does, it simply transmits over the air the network "feed," which comes over long-distance telephone lines and cables leased by the network.

The upshot is that most of the programs broadcast in peak viewing hours (which, in the United States, are called the "prime time" hours between 8:00 and 11:00 p.m.) are produced by the networks, including all of the national newscasts and most of the public affairs programs that deal with politics.

It should also be noted, however, that about the only programs the local stations produce for themselves are their own local newscasts, covering mainly local news, weather, and sports, with only a dash of national news—and an even smaller dash of national political news—thrown in.

Most of the 269 noncommercial stations are affiliated with the Public Broadcasting System (PBS), but public broadcasting is much more decentralized than commercial broadcasting. Almost all of the programs broadcast by PBS on politics or anything else are developed and produced by local stations (some of the most active are WGBH in Boston, WNET in New York, WETA in Washington, D.C., and WQED in Pittsburgh) and sold to PBS. However, audience surveys show that on average the noncommercial stations draw only about 10% of all viewers, the commercial stations unafilliated with the networks draw another 10% and the network affiliates get the remaining 80%. Accordingly, television broadcasting in the United States is considerably more commercial and somewhat more decentralized than in Britain, but in a brief summary such as this our attention will be focused as much on ABC, CBS, and NBC as it is on BBC and IBA.

In Britain the growing preeminence of television as the prime source of political information has had two effects on the press. Firstly, because television tells the key news and tells it first, the popular newspapers have felt less of an obligation to cover the news comprehensively and have become more like daily entertainment magazines. Secondly, because their readers have access to balanced reporting on television, it becomes impossible to present quite so one-sided a picture as 30 years ago. The political role of the press has been diminished, both by the coming of a dominant rival and by the decline in the lengths to which it has carried partisanship. However, the British press still sways votes and is still an important force in political communication, uncovering stories, analysing trends, and revealing the characters of leaders. Moreover it is a prime source of television reporting. Journalists move between print and camera, and television editors scan the press in their search for material.

2. *Regulation.* As we mentioned above, both in Britain and in the United States television coverage of politics is considerably more closely regulated than is coverage by newspapers. In Britain, for example, both the BBC and IBA operate under a series of formal rules and informal understandings intended to ensure that broadcasting about political parties, leaders, and issues will be "fair" and "balanced"—something no one expects or gets from political reporting in, say, the *Daily Mirror* or the *Daily Express*. For example, in the 1979 general election campaign the Labour party complained about London Weekend Television's plans to show the film *I'm All Right Jack*, which satirized the behaviour of shop stewards and workers, and the IBA finally managed to get the showing postponed until after the election.[4] The Committee on Party Political Broadcasting, a secret, unofficial, but powerful body of broadcasting officials and party leaders, decided to allocate the time given to the political parties for their broadcasts (see below).[5] And all three channels took pains to see that the coverage of the parties in their newscasts was distributed in about the same proportions.[6]

In the United States similar expectations prevail: television's coverage of politics should be "fair" and "balanced" to a degree far beyond what is expected even of the quality papers, to say nothing of the ordinary press. And those expectations are embodied in several sections of the Federal Communications Act of 1934 and a number of administrative rulings by the FCC.

One such rule is the "fairness doctrine," which requires that if a station broadcasts material dealing with a controversial issue of public importance, it must provide reasonable opportunities for the presentation of conflicting viewpoints, whether or not the original broadcast has taken place during a political campaign. A second rule is the "equal time rule," which stipulates that if a broadcaster permits a candidate for public office to campaign on his station, either in free or purchased time, he must offer all the other candidates for the office the same amount of time under the same conditions. A third rule is the "right of rebuttal," which requires that if an attack is broadcast on the honesty, character, or integrity of an identified person or group of persons, the victim or victims of the attack are entitled to reply to the charges against them on time donated by the broadcaster. All three rules have, of course, generated a number of cases and a series of interpretations by the FCC and the courts far too complex and lengthy to be reviewed here. But the net effect has certainly been to set far more stringent limits on how television broadcasters can deal with parties and politics than on how newspapers treat those topics.[7]

3. *Audiences and Trust.* A number of studies done in both countries since the late 1950s have consistently shown that most ordinary people say that they get more of their political information from television than from newspapers or any other source. And most also say that they trust the accuracy and fairness of television newscasts more than they trust newspaper accounts. Typical of such studies is the Roper organization's report summarized in Table 9.1.

By 1964, 65% of people in Britain said that television was their most important source of political information, and its preeminence has greatly increased since then. The British position does differ in many ways from the American, but in both countries the bottom line is clear: most ordinary people get most of their information about parties and politics from television, with newspapers a distant second; and most people trust what they see on television considerably more than they trust what they read in newspapers. Hence in both countries the political "cognitive maps" of most people are shaped mainly by television, and the way politics is covered and portrayed by television is bound to play a major role in shaping the environments in which political parties and party leaders must work.

Table 9.1

Use of and trust in U.S. news sources, 1964–1978 (in percentages)

"I'd like to ask you where you usually get most of your news about what's going on in the world today" (more than one answer permitted)

Source of most news	1964	1968	1972	1976	1978
Television	58	59	64	64	67
Newspapers	56	49	50	49	49
Radio	26	25	21	19	20
Magazines	8	7	6	7	5
Other people	5	5	4	5	5
DK, NA	3	3	1		

"If you got conflicting or different reports on the same news story from radio, television, the magazines, and the newspapers, which of the four versions would you be most inclined to believe?" (only one answer permitted)

Most believable source	1964	1968	1972	1976	1978
Television	41	44	48	51	47
Newspapers	23	21	21	22	23
Radio	8	8	8	7	9
Magazines	10	11	10	9	9
DK, NA	18	16	13	11	12

Source: Surveys by the Roper Organization for the Television Information Office, in *Public Opinion,* August/September 1979, p. 30.

HOW THE MEDIA PORTRAY PARTIES AND POLITICS

Coverage

Both in Britain and in the United States, the national newspapers and the national television programmers pay a good deal of attention to national politics in their daily news stories and newscasts and in special features and "documentaries." But there are several significant differences in the way politics is covered in the two countries.

For one thing, more television time and newspaper space is devoted to national politics in Britain than in the United States. While the *New York Times* and a few other papers will occasionally print the full text of a major presidential speech or congressional bill, no American paper presents a daily summary of the proceedings of Congress comparable to the summaries of action in the House of Commons published by the (London) *Times*, *Guardian*, or *Daily Telegraph*. Moreover, while the American networks broadcast regular interview shows, such as *Meet the Press* and *Face the Nation*, they are broadcast during the low-viewing periods of midday on Sundays, and they are not as lavishly produced or as widely seen as the BBC's *Panorama* or IBA's *Weekend World* and *World in Action*.

To be sure, the U.S. House of Representatives now has gavel-to-gavel live television coverage of its proceedings; but the American chamber strictly controls the broadcasts and prohibits shots of anything but the podium, and the national networks seldom use more than the occasional small snippet of an especially dramatic speech.

In Britain the television cameras have been kept out of Parliament. But, since 1978, broadcasting has been allowed, subject to some limitations. It has not raised the standing of MPs: the hubbub associated with Question Time, particularly questions to the Prime Minister, and the stylised and traditional rudeness of parliamentary rhetoric have made the House of Commons seem frivolous. On television news the disembodied voice over a still photograph or an artist's sketch of the scene appears artificial. Broadcasting has not disciplined the behaviour of MPs, although at rare moments, as in the first Falklands debate on April 3, 1982, a full transmission of the whole of a great parliamentary occasion can have a wide-reaching impact.

In Britain the reporting of politics in the press is carried on by lobby correspondents, a group of 100 or so newspaper reporters who frequent the Palace of Westminster and who are allowed to rub shoulders with MPs in the inner corridors of the House of Commons on the understanding that they conform to certain established rules of discretion. Reporters take in each other's washing. To some extent they write for each other, seeing their competitors as the only people in a position to judge their stories. And political writing is overwhelmingly linked to the Palace of Westminster, where executive and legislature meet together with lobby journalists.

In America, political news comes from the White House and the civil service even more than it comes from Capitol Hill. And it is collected by journalists who see less of each other's output, writing for single-paper cities far away or appearing on more diversified television and radio outlets than exist in Britain. Moreover American politicians have a far greater incentive to make news that will have a special local appeal. British politicians do, of course, like headlines in their constituency newspapers, but it is not essential to their survival as MPs. Political coverage in American newspapers is thus far more pluralist than in British newspapers.

The relations between politicians and the media differ in Britain and America, not just because of the different structure and values of the media in the two countries but also because of the difference in the subject matter being reported. Politics in both countries is a matter of who gets what, when, where, and how. But the prizes of politics can be very different. The contrasts lie partly in national culture—but also in the formal properties of institutions.

The American federal structure means that all national politics has a state basis, a far-flung localized quality that is absent from centralized Britain. Obviously there are Scottish and Welsh, Merseyside and East Anglian dimensions to British politics. But Westminster with its own values is dominant. Winston Churchill represented Dundee and Lancashire and the Home Counties during his parliamentary career: no such carpet-bagging is possible in America. Scant regard is placed in British politics to the local base of a leading politician. In America it must always remain a key factor. The independent complexities of each state's politics widen and diversify the coverage of public affairs in a way that has no parallel in Britain.

The separation of powers also leaves its mark. Executive, legislature, and judiciary each attract their own specialist reporters and their own brand of coverage. There is no equivalent cleavage in Britain to the division between White House and Capitol Hill reporters.

In America the right to know is much more deeply implanted. The First Amendment and the whole tradition of aggressive journalism make it far easier for the investigative American journalist to burrow and bully and publish than it is for his English counterpart. The U.S. law of libel is far weaker; there is no equivalent to British parliamentary privilege; and there is less of the cohesion of a close-knit establishment—a grouping based not just on class but on long-established coexistence at Westminster, living by rules of privacy and nondisclosure. In Britain the solidarity of government, Parliament, and party are entrenched in a way that has little counterpart in Washington, except perhaps in the innerness of the Senate club.

For this reason, the relations between lobby correspondents and MPs are noticeably different from those between the Washington press corps and the various parts of the national government. The lobby correspondents deal mainly with MPs and party leaders rather than civil servants, for the traditions of secrecy and anonymity-to-the-point-of-invisibility among the latter are so strong that they rarely provide publishable news. MPs and party leaders are quite willing to talk rather freely to lobby correspondents, so long as the newspeople observe the conventions. Polemical writing about politicians is constrained by an awareness that they are a prime source of information. There is a trade-off between what a journalist writes today and what he may be able, through continued easy access, to write tomorrow. To say this is not to paint a venal picture of political correspondents refraining from using what they know because writing candidly may cut off next month's sources. Truth cannot be long suppressed. Journalism is competitive. A scoop is a scoop. Nonetheless, there is a certain cosiness between politicians and reporters at Westminster, which any sophisticated consumer of British political coverage needs to know and understand. Political journalism is written in a code, with elaborate pretences that official briefings do not take place and that Cabinet ministers are not constantly engaged in giving informal guidance to see that their case does not go by default.

The atmosphere in Washington is markedly different. For one thing, a good deal of political news is generated not only in the White House and on Capitol Hill but also in many of the presumably subordinate executive departments, bureaus, and agencies and in the "independent regulatory agencies" such as the FCC. For many years, one of the most common types of news events in Washington has been "the leak"—that is, an episode in which a public official secretly reveals to a favored reporter an item of information or a policy under consideration before its release has been officially authorized. "Leakers" have one or more of several motives: they may wish to "float a trial balloon" to see what kind of public reaction a contemplated policy will evoke; they may wish to show themselves off in a favourable light or their bureaucratic antagonists in a poor light; they may wish to block a policy proposal they oppose by making it public before its supporters have had time to generate the necessary support; and, at a minimum, "leaking" gives them a greater control over what the media will print or broadcast than they can get in any other way. Newspaper and television reporters, not surprisingly, are always delighted to receive and publish leaks; they can get information that they could otherwise get only with great difficulty or not at all; and leaks often give them major scoops over their competition. This relationship between leaders and their media outlets in Washington is more of a mutually convenient business arrangement than the member-of-the-same-club cosiness characteristic of politician–lobby correspondent relationships in Westminster. But both kinds of relationships are aspects of the politician–reporter symbiosis we shall consider at greater length toward the end of this chapter.

Another difference worth mentioning is the fact that, up to 1984, a direct debate, discussion, or other confrontation between the leaders of the two major parties had never been televised in Great Britain. Attempts have been made in every election since 1964 by the BBC and the IBA to broadcast such a confrontation, but in every instance one side or other has had good reason to refuse. Usually the leader whose party was perceived to have the lead at the moment has turned down the invitation—the Prime Minister apparently well ahead in each contest from 1966 to October 1974 has not wanted to share his prestige with his challenger. But in 1979 it was the incumbent Mr. Callaghan who challenged the front-running Mrs. Thatcher, and she refused, seeing that she had little to gain and much to lose from such a confrontation.[8]

Perhaps both leaders' changing attitudes were influenced by the experience of the candidates in the three series of "great debates" between presidential candidates held in the United States. Since 1960, the Democratic and Republican presidential candidates have faced each other in live, nationally televised debates: four between Kennedy and Nixon in 1960, three between Carter and Ford in 1976, and one between Carter and Reagan in 1980 (Reagan also participated in a debate with Independent candidate John Anderson in 1980). In all three campaigns the candidate generally thought to be behind challenged the leader. In all three instances the debates attracted the largest audiences of any campaign events in history, the most recent and largest being the estimated 80 million people who watched the Carter–Reagan debate in 1980. In all three instances the challenger was generally thought to have "won" over the incumbent (Nixon was a quasi-incumbent in 1960). In all three instances the incumbent lost the ensuing election, and most observers believed that the imcumbents' "losses" in the debates played a major role—some said a critical role—in their electoral defeat. Thus political leaders on both sides of the Atlantic may feel that the correct strategic rule is simple: if you are behind, challenge the other leader to a debate; if you are ahead, decline the invitation as gracefully as you can.

Nevertheless, it may be that televised presidential debates have now become so well-established a part of the campaigns and so many people look forward to them that no future American president seeking reelection can afford to decline. We shall see.[9] But British party leaders may well wish—and be well advised—to continue resisting being driven into such a corner.

Bias

One of the questions most often raised both in Britain and in the United States about the mass media's presentation of political news is whether that presentation is biased. Many newspapers in both countries, as we have seen, openly champion the cause of particular parties, candidates, and ideologies in their news columns as well as on their editorial pages; but in both countries the national television broadcasters are expected—and claim—to be unbiased. Consequently, most of the argument—and there is a considerable amount of it in both countries—is about whether television's presentation of politics is as unbiased as its producers claim.

In trying to unpack this complicated question, several scholars have found it useful to distinguish between two possible kinds of bias. One is a *partisan* bias, in which the broadcasters would deliberately select and present their political news items and commentaries so as to evoke in their viewers favorable feelings toward a particular party or ideology. The other is a *structural* bias, in which the very nature of the medium and the circumstances in which broadcasters must operate result in a certain view of *all* parties and politicians. Which, if either, kind of bias is evidenced in the treatment of politics by British and American television?

1. Political Bias. In both countries there is no dearth of charges by supporters of particular parties and ideologies that the presentation of political news by the national television broadcasters is systematically biased against them and their ideas. Moreover, such accusations come from all sides: some leaders of the Right charge that television news is slanted in favor of the Left, and some leaders of the Left charge that it is slanted in favor of the Right. In our judgement, however, a close scrutiny of television newscasts and special features in both countries shows no such consistent support of any particular party or ideology. An occasional broadcast may seem to favor one party or view over another, but no consistent support of any particular party can be shown.[10] Indeed, the broadcasters in both countries have at least two excellent reasons for avoiding political bias. One is provided by the need to comply with the many laws and administrative rules that, as we have seen, require "fairness" and "balance" in the presentation of political news, coupled with a fear that any party that feels disadvantaged may, when it gets office, toughen up the regulations. The other stems from the fact that a prime reason why most people in both countries trust television news more than newspaper news lies in the fact that they believe it to be much freer of partisan bias. If the broadcasters were to lose that reputation, they would certainly lose one of their greatest assets, and very few of them seem to be so passionately dedicated to the cause of a particular party or ideology that they are willing to pay so great a price for advancing it on company time and facilities.

   2.   *Structural Bias.* Some observers have concluded that, while there is little or no consistent partisan bias in television's presentation of politics in either country, the structure of the medium in both produces a special kind of bias—a bias against politicians in general as well as an antiestablishment bias. In both countries television broadcasting is highly competitive, and the prize all broadcasters seek is a very large audience—preferably a much larger audience than their competitors draw—for their programs, including their newscasts and public affairs programs. Hence their relative shares of the viewing audience, as shown by various audience-rating surveys, are just as important for the BBC and IBA as they are for ABC, CBS, and NBC—and even PBS is eager for a 14% share over its usual 10% share).

   Yet in Britain there is also an attack on the media as being too proestablishment. The Glasgow Media group has argued that, in its coverage of strikes and of fringe political groups, television, like the press, has a pervasive underlying bias in favor of the powers that be. The contention is that although television may play fair in relation to the conventional party battle in the center, it tends to ignore or underplay or mock those outside the consensus. But many broadcasters would indignantly deny this accusation.

   The first imperative for political programming in both countries is to make it "good television": that is, it must be visually interesting as well as accurate and informative; it must give special attention to the new and the unusual; and, above all, it must be fitted into television's "newsholes," which are so much shorter and less flexible than newspapers' editorial space.[11]

In the United States this imperative leads the networks to portray the world of politics, and politicians in general, in a special way well summarized by Paul Weaver:

[According to television news] politics is essentially a game played by individual politicians for personal advancement, gain, or power. The game is a competitive one, and the players' principal activities are those of calculating and pursuing strategies designed to defeat competitors and to achieve their goals (usually election to public office). Of course, the game takes place against a backdrop of governmental institutions, public problems, policy debates, and the like, but these are noteworthy only insofar as they affect, or are used by, players in pursuit of the game's rewards. The game is played before an audience—the electorate—which controls most of the prizes, and players therefore constantly attempt to make a favorable impression. In consequence, there is an endemic tendency for players to exaggerate their good qualities and to minimize their bad ones, to be deceitful, to engage in hypocrisies, to manipulate appearances; though inevitable, these tendencies are bad tendencies . . . and should be exposed. They reduce the electorate's ability to make its own discriminating choices, and they may hide players' infractions of the game's rules, such as those against corruption and lying.[12]

This structural bias of American television has one other consequence: American political parties are not very good material for television. They are essentially abstractions—aggregations of individuals occasionally associated for limited purposes. Moreover, they are loose aggregations, whose members are often in as much or more conflict with each other as with the numbers of the other party. Consequently, the broadcasters find it hard to present them as anything much more than mobs of delegates milling about (or waving banners or sleeping through boring speeches) at national party conventions. Individual politicials, on the other hand, are great subjects for television. They are easy to interview and dramatize. They are almost as varied in appearance and manner as the actors who play the roles in the dramas and "sit-coms." So American television gives most of its attention to individual politicians, and little is said about the parties as anything more than the labels politicians happen to bear.

The situation in Britain is considerably—but not entirely— different. British national parties, if they can secure half the seats in Parliament, control and are controlled by the government. They have a cohesion that facilitates collective image-building, both by themselves and by their adversaries. It makes far more sense to write and broadcast about "what the Conservatives are up to" than it can ever make to deal with "what the Republicans are up to." British parties are not monolithic, but Mrs. Thatcher does represent a far more unified and cohesive grouping than does Mr. Reagan. Although British politics are more personalized than they once were, Mrs. Thatcher's regime comes far nearer to reflecting a collective Conservative will than Mr. Reagan's administration a collective Republican will.

Each party in Britain has a press officer and a broadcasting specialist. Each knows that it lives or dies by the media. But each recognizes the limitations of any attempt at media manipulation. Journalists resent being used or deceived. During the 1979 election, as a result of a carefully contrived "media event," photographs of Mrs. Thatcher cuddling a newly born calf appeared on the front page of almost every newspaper—but there was also a large amount of satirical coverage about the stage-management of this insubstantial happening. The television reports showed shots of the photographers almost as much as of Mrs. Thatcher.

Broadcast journalists will speak of being guided by news values within the necessary confines of balance. Newspaper journalists will also speak of news values, but there is less talk about balance. The partisan inclinations of almost all newspapers are very clear. The occupants of 10 Downing Street have often courted their proprietors and, with different kinds of flattery and rewards, sought to influence their editorial policies. The Conservative party has always had a great advantage in the number of papers supporting it, although at one time because of the success of the crusading tabloid, the *Daily Mirror*, the balance of circulation was not too disproportionate.

Some observers believe that British politics, especially during general election campaigns, is becoming more and more "Americanized," in that the media focus more and more on each major party's leader and less and less on its whole front bench. If that is the case, then one of the prime reasons for it is the structural need of television in Great Britain no less than in the United States to focus on telegenic individual political leaders rather than on hard-to-picture political collectivities. Such a bias may not be partisan, but it is a bias nevertheless.

HOW THE PARTIES USE THE MEDIA

Party leaders and candidates both in Britain and in the United States are only too well aware that how they and their activities are portrayed by television and the newspapers profoundly affects their chances for success or failure. But they are far from being helpless puppets jerked about solely by the whims of the broadcasters, reporters, and editors. Being practical people facing pressing practical needs, political leaders in both countries typically spend little time or energy on bemoaning the media's political power (though few of them are delighted with it), certainly less of both than many academics spend. Most of their effort is given to finding ways of using the media for their own personal and partisan advantage. So much is true of both countries, but there are a number of differences in the way British and American politicians try to use the media. We shall note a few of the most obvious.

Paid Political Advertising
in the United States

In Britain, as in most but not all modern democratic countries, it is illegal for political parties and candidates to purchase television time for political advertising.[13] In the United States there is no such inhibition, and paid political advertisements are a major feature of most political campaigns, not only for the presidency but for most lesser offices as well. Most of the political advertisements are short "spots," ranging from as little as ten seconds to as long as two minutes, and they average thirty seconds in length. They are broadcast, just as advertisements for commercial products are, in the "commercial breaks" that regularly come during and between entertainment programs, sports events, and the like. Producing such advertisements and purchasing optimum television time for showing them has been taken over almost entirely by specially trained and well paid "media specialists," and their efforts, along with most other campaign events, are coordinated by a new breed of professional "political consultants," such as Joe Napolitan, John Deardourff, and David Garth. This development has had at least two major consequences. One is that the formulation and execution of campaign strategy and tactics has passed almost entirely from the old-style party-based politicians, like Jim Farley and Ray Bliss of ancient memory, and is now controlled by the political consultants, most of whom have emerged from the advertising business, not from party politics.[14] The second consequence is that the cost of electioneering has enormously increased.

    The great majority of these political advertisements are broadcast on behalf of particular candidates and are developed and paid for by their personal organizations rather than by the political parties whose labels they bear. To be sure, in the late 1970s the Republican National Committee under the leadership of chairman Bill Brock became the first national party organization to broadcast advertisements promoting the cause of the whole party, and some national ideological pressure groups—notably the National Conservative Political Action Committee (NCPAC)—broadcast advertisements attacking the records of liberal/Democratic candidates in a number of states. In the early 1980s the Democratic National Committee and some liberal PACs (political action committees) began to broadcast their own advertisements, but most political advertising in America continues to be produced and paid for by individual candidate organizations rather than parties.

Many foreign observers are more horrified than most Americans are by the volume, cost, and tastelessness of American political advertising. Contrary to a widespread impression, the side with the best-financed, most numerous, and best-produced advertisements by no means always wins the election, and, indeed, if the idea gets around that a particular candidate is trying to "buy" an election by swamping his opponent with a flood of slick advertisements, there can often be a backlash against the big spender, sympathy for his opponent, and a consequent "upset" victory for the latter. The most we can say on the basis of many studies of the question is that if, but only if, all other factors influencing the election outcome are equal—such as the candidates' personal attractiveness and public records, the distribution of party loyalties among the voters, the state of the economy, and the like—then the candidate who can outspend his opponent by a large margin will win, more often than not. But the other factors often favor the smaller spenders, and the evidence suggests that the bigger spenders win only about half the time.[15] In short, money is unquestionably more important in American elections than in British elections (though it is hardly negligible in the latter),[16] and paid political advertising accounts for most of the difference.

Publicly Financed, Party-Controlled Broadcasts
in Great Britain

In the United States neither the national networks nor the national government has ever donated any free time on radio or television to political parties to use as they see fit.[17] In Britain, on the other hand, such time is regularly given to all the substantial political parties during general election campaigns. As we noted earlier, the time is allocated among the parties by an informal but powerful committee of broadcasters and party leaders in rough proportion to the parties' relative voting strengths in the previous general election. The committee also sets certain rules about what the parties can and cannot do with their allotted time: For example, each party must use its allotment in a specified number of broadcasts, each of which must be of a specified length. Thus in 1979 the Labour and Conservative parties were each given five ten-minute television broadcasts, the Liberals were given three such broadcasts, the Scottish Nationalists were given three that were broadcast only in Scotland, and Plaid Cymru were given one broadcast beamed only at Wales. With one exception, all the party programs were broadcast at the same prime evening times. Aside from these limits, each party has been free to use its time as it sees fit, and in recent years both Labour and the Conservatives have been turning more and more to professional media experts rather than party officials to design and produce their programs. This has made them more costly, and in 1979 the Conservatives spent a total of £100,000 producing their five broadcasts, while Labour spent £50,000.[18]

These party-controlled broadcasts have evoked mixed responses from British viewers and commentators. Most of them comment on the fact that the broadcasts give the parties a chance to state their cases as they wish without having them filtered through the editing and commentaries of the BBC and IBA news divisions—and some Americans believe that ABC, CBS, and NBC should be required by law to give Democrats and Republicans similar opportunities to achieve similar benefits. On the other hand, some British commentators and many viewers are less than enthusiastic about the party broadcasts' quality or utility for educating the voters. As one major study put it:

> Ten-minute party broadcasts . . . are so little respected that broadcasters sometimes refer to them virtually as sops, thrown to the parties in the hope that thereafter their own hands will be untied to produce the kinds of political programmes that they want to prepare; while some party officials describe them as safety valves, *useful mainly for counteracting unfavourable tendencies developed in media coverage elsewhere*. It is true that, due partly to their brevity and sheltered status, they reach large audiences. But labelled from the start as unopposed propaganda—and standing "solitary" in that respect from the rest of election output, as one person put it— they seem almost tailor-made to put audiences on their guard and to trigger anti-party and antipolitical sentiments.[19]

Favorable Exposure
on Broadcaster-Controlled Television

In both countries, most of what most voters know about the parties and their leaders, candidates, and programs comes, not from party-controlled paid political advertising or party-controlled free time on television, but from the regular newscasts and political programs produced by the broadcasters. Politicians in both countries know this very well, and so perhaps the most important single objective of their election campaigns is to get the greatest possible exposure and the most favorable possible treatment on the broadcaster-controlled newscasts and political programs. Not only is such exposure largely free from the taint of partisanship that inevitably attaches to party-controlled advertisements or broadcasts, but it slips before the viewers in the course of general programming and is therefore less likely to be tuned out by viewers who are bored, bothered, and bewildered by politics—of whom there are many in both countries.

To get the amount and kind of exposure they want, however, the politicians' words and deeds must meet the broadcasters' needs for material that is new and interesting. As one British broadcaster put it:

> When politicians find some way of making a more dramatic splash into the limelight, the news people like to follow that and to make something of it. We don't like the 40-second snippets of hustings extracts with all their yah-booing any more than you do. That is why, when [Harold] Wilson tried a dramatic initiative in the 1970 election period by deciding to go on walkabouts in localities and constituencies, it was news, it looked interesting and exciting at the time, and we were keen to follow him and to take advantage of this element of extra interest and dramatic appeal that he injected.[20]

For the politicians, then, the trick is to do and say things that the broadcasters will find interesting. In both countries, politicians have developed a number of techniques for this purpose—"walk-abouts" in shopping centers and housing estates, marathon walks from one end of a state to the other, sending candidates from one place to another by helicopter, photographing candidates working at a succession of the kinds of jobs their constituents have, regular press conferences with some new development—a new poll result or a new campaign strategy—to announce at each one, and so on.

In both countries at present most campaign activities are designed and staged solely or mainly to get the best exposure for the parties and their leaders. As one British reporter put it:

> The whole point of making the evening speech is to get into the television news bulletin. The Leader on such an occasion is not aiming to address the 600 people in the hall where he is talking. His real aim is to get a message across to the six million viewers watching BBC news and ITN.

And an aide who wrote speeches for one of the major British parties added:

> In writing these speech handouts I learned that it was absolutely essential to take account of the needs of television. The prime thing about drafting a good one was to include within it a two-minute slot that *News at Ten*, say, could use, containing the essence of what the Leader was saying on that particular occasion.[21]

All this may have certain social costs, and even the politicians may grow weary of the "televization" of everything. For example, Malcolm MacDougall, the director of advertising for Gerald Ford's presidential campaign in 1976, reported American television's portrayal of the campaign as he saw it on his own set:

> I saw Carter playing softball in Plains, Georgia. I saw Carter kissing Amy. I saw Carter hugging Lillian, I saw Carter, in dungarees, walking hand in hand through the peanut farm with Rosalynn. I saw Carter going into church, preaching in church, coming out of church. I saw Carter trying to explain his ethnic purity statement. I saw Carter trying to explain his *Playboy* interview. And then I saw two full, wonderful weeks of people commenting about Carter's *Playboy* interview. I saw Ford misstate the problems of Eastern Europe—and a week of people commenting about his misstatement. I saw Ford bump his head again. I saw Ford in Ohio say how glad he was to be back in Iowa. I saw marching bands and hecklers, and I learned about the size of crowds and the significance of the size of crowds. And I saw Carter carrying his own suitcase a lot. But in all the hours of high anxiety that I spent watching the network news, never did I hear what the candidates had to say about the campaign issues. That was not news.[22]

We can all sympathize, but, like it or not, the facts of political life in both Britain and the United States in the television age require party politicians and their advisers in ways that the broadcasters are likely to find attractive for showing their audiences on the programs they control; and those programs provide the great majority of the televised politics that most voters see.

THE IMPACT OF THE MEDIA ON THE PARTIES

It should be clear from the foregoing that both in Great Britain and in the United States the mass communications media play a major role—perhaps *the* major role—in shaping the environment in which political parties must operate. It is equally clear that the increasing dominance of television since the 1950s has greatly altered the political environments in both countries. Of course, British political parties were quite different from American parties before the advent of television in the 1950s, and, as the other chapters in this book detail, the two party systems are still quite different from one another at the height of the television age in the 1980s. Yet the general impact of television on the parties has been quite similar in both countries, particularly with respect to the decline in voters' party loyalties and the transformation of party conferences and conventions. We shall conclude by briefly reviewing each development.

The Decline of Voters' Party Loyalties

Almost all studies of the attitudes and behavior of voters in Great Britain and the United States in recent years agree that in both countries there has been a sharp decline in the voters' party loyalties, which were shown to be so strong and influential in the 1960s. In both countries substantially fewer people in the 1980s feel strongly attached to a particular party and can be counted on to vote for its candidates in election after election. In both countries some of these defectors have transferred their loyalties to other parties, but most of them have become disillusioned with *all* parties—and perhaps even with parties as desirable institutions.[23]

No doubt many factors have contributed to this transatlantic decline in party loyalties, but there is general agreement that television has played a major role. Before the early 1950s, people received almost all of their political news from the press. In Britain over 80% saw at least one of the nine major Fleet Street newspapers every day, and Fleet Street carved up the market not only into quality and popular papers, but also into Conservative and Labour papers. The ordinary British voter reading his newspaper derived a very one-sided view of politics, usually having chosen his paper to suit (and unconsciously to reinforce) his prejudices. When television replaced the press as the prime source of political information, the citizen was suddenly cross-pressured. In contrast to the one-sided diet he had got from the press, he now became exposed to much more balanced fare.

Politicians, as they learned the television game, added to the change. The stridency of Parliament and of the press was quite unsuited to the hearthside style of television. It was necessary to be moderate and reasonable as one intruded through the screens into the intimacy of ordinary homes. The discourse of politics changed. Before the cameras, the parties found it prudent to project a moderate, like-minded image. The adversary situation of television, the two talking heads separated by a chairman, usually transformed itself into a ritual dance between two Oxbridge smoothies. Political encounters on television often demonstrated to the public that there is more in common between two elected persons of different parties than there is between an elected person and a nonelected person of the same party. They also showed that the parties are less at odds than the outsider might have supposed.

In fact, democracy can survive only if the bulk of politicians are agreed on the bulk of the national agenda. Television in the 1960s and 1970s drove this point home to voters in both countries. It became harder for ordinary voters to be profoundly partisan, convinced that their side were angels and the other side devils. The enormous increase in the volatility of both electorates since 1960 has had many causes—for example, the increase in education, the necessary disappointment of rising expectations, and the repeated alternation of governments and administrations that have so conspicuously failed to produce remedies to the nations' ills. But one central force must be the advent of television as the prime source of information about politics, demonstrating in the most forceful way that there is not so much difference between politicians or parties as their traditional rhetoric had suggested.

Add to this the previously discussed tendency of television to focus on individuals instead of parties and to portray all politicians as self-seeking players of a sometimes boring and sometimes disgusting game, and there can be little doubt that television has done a good deal to weaken party loyalties in both countries.

The Transformation
of Party Conferences and Conventions

For many decades, the annual national conferences of British parties and the quadrennial national conventions of American parties have provided the main arenas for bringing all the parties' sections, elements, and constituencies together and giving them the opportunity to get acquainted with each other and thereby strengthen the solidary loyalties of party activists. Many of the activists in both types of party gatherings were designed to promote these ends, and they contributed a good deal to making the parties into truly national aggregations of local organizations and activists. In Britain, however, the party managers have more and more shaped the conference arrangements with an eye to providing the best possible television show; Conservative conferences, always managed and consensual affairs, have become almost wholly sterile; the Labour Party is still far more rumbustious, but at least the timing of the big speeches and the conduct of votes and agenda problems have been greatly modified by the presence of the cameras.

The transformation of the American national party conventions has been even more radical. From the early 1830s to the late 1960s, most of the delegates were chosen by national, state, and local party leaders, and at the conventions those leaders negotiated, bargained, compromised, and finally chose the presidential candidate, to whom their delegates then loyally voted the nomination. In the 1980s, however, nearly three-quarters of the delegates are chosen by direct primaries in the states—in elections in which television plays a role of great significance—and those delegates are bound by law or custom to vote for the candidates preferred by the people who vote in their states' primaries. Consequently, the national conventions have lost almost all of their significance as decision-makers or party-unifiers. As George Comstock sums it up:

> Television has changed the nominating conventions from deliberative, if volatile, bodies to orchestrated showcases. This has come about in several ways. By opening the conventions to the television viewer, politicians have become fearful of offending anyone by what transpires. The function of television as entertainment cannot be ignored, as the parties wish to hold as many viewers as possible for the display of the nominee and his running mate. Inoffensive, contrived excitement is packaged. When that is what the parties offer, television can only conspire in its transmission in as dramatic a manner as possible,

for the medium shares a goal with the party—a large, attentive audience.

The transformation has been hastened by what television has done to the primaries and by the journalistic machinery assembled by television for convention coverage. By focussing attention on the primaries as if each were *High Noon* again and again, the role of negotiation among party leaders in selecting a candidate has been reduced. For delegates and leaders alike less remains to be decided or bargained for at the conventions.[24]

CONCLUSION

Politicians and the mass media are, necessarily, locked together in a never-ending battle. Each depends on the other, and each attempts to exploit the other. Political journalists get most of their information from politicians, and politicians depend upon journalists both for their ammunition and for their prominence. Journalists want to know everything and say everything. Politicians want to feed journalists material that will reflect well on them. Both coexist in a reluctant symbiosis. Neither, if it can be avoided, behaves in a way that will prevent a continued relationship. Politicians try to manipulate journalists; journalists try to manipulate politicians. But neither plays the game to the limit. Both know that they have to live together to fight or cooperate on another day.

In the mid-1950s a great scholar of comparative political parties, Sigmund Neumann, concluded his major work thus:

> Above all, [the revolution of our time] challenges our ingenuity to articulate workable programs, to organize functioning movements and to put them to constructive action—weighty responsibilities which rest primarily with the people's great intermediaries: the political parties.[25]

It seems unlikely that so acute an observer as Neumann looking at British and American parties in the 1980s would still call them "the peoples' great intermediaries." Despite their differences in the many other respects detailed in this book, in both countries the parties' traditional roles of being the chief transmitters of political reality to ordinary voters have been largely taken over by the mass media, particularly by television. In the 1980s they still play noteworthy roles in the governing schemes of both countries, and they are likely to continue doing so. But the great changes in their working environments brought about by the communications revolution, which, after all, is the greatest revolution of our time, have made it unlikely that either the British or the American political parties will ever again carry—or be expected to carry—the great responsibilities that Neumann assigned to them.

NOTES

1. The scholarly literature dealing with this vast change is itself vast, and a comprehensive listing of the major studies would take far too much space here. We have found these works to be especially useful. For the communications revolution in general: Anthony Smith, *Goodbye Gutenberg* (New York: Oxford University Press, 1980); and Sidney Kraus and Dennis Davis, *The Effects of Mass Communication on Political Behavior* (University Park and London: The Pennsylvania State University Press, 1978). For Britain: Jay G. Blumler and Denis McQuail, *Television in Politics* (London: Faber, 1968); Colin Seymour-Ure, *The Political Impact of the Mass Media* (London: Constable, 1974); and Jay G. Blumler, Michael Gurevitch, and Julian Ives, *The Challenge of Election Broadcasting* (Leeds: Center for Television Research, University of Leeds, 1978). For the United States: Edward Jay Epstein, *News from Nowhere* (New York: Random House Vintage Books, 1974); Doris A. Graber, *Mass Media and American Politics* (Washington, D.C.: Congressional Quarterly Press, 1980). We have also drawn from Austin Ranney, *Channels of Power: The Impact of Television on American Politics* (New York: Basic Books, 1983).
2. Graber, *Mass Media and American Politics*, pp. 2-3, 120; George Comstock, *Television in America* (Beverly Hills, Calif.: Sage Publications, 1980), pp. 32-33.
3. David Butler and Anne Sloman, eds., *British Political Facts, 1900-1979*, 5th ed. (London: Macmillan, 1980), p. 449.
4. Michael Pilsworth, "Balanced Broadcasting," in David Butler and Dennis Kavanagh, *The British General Election of 1979* (London: Macmillan, 1980), p. 204.
5. Ibid., p. 201.
6. Ibid., Table 1, p. 209.
7. The case law is well summarized in: Howard Simons and Joseph A. Califano, Jr., eds., *The Media and the Law* (New York: Praeger, 1976); and Fred W. Friendly, *The Good Guys, the Bad Guys, and the First Amendment: Free Speech v. Fairness in Broadcasting* (New York: Random House, 1976).
8. Pilsworth, "Balanced Broadcasting," pp. 201-2.
9. See Austin Ranney, ed., *The Past and Future of Presidential Debates* (Washington, D.C.: American Enterprise Institute, 1979); and Myles

Martel, *Political Campaign Debates* (New York and London: Longmans, 1983).

10. For a detailed argument for this conclusion, see Ranney, *Channels of Power*, Chap. 2.

11. A few years ago, the president of CBS News had the entire script for one of his nightly half-hour newscasts set in the same type as that used by the *New York Times*. He found, reportedly to his chagrin, that his newscast took up less than a quarter of the newspaper's front page.

12. Paul Weaver, "Is Television News Biased?" *Public Interest*, Winter, 1972, pp. 57-74, at p. 69.

13. Anthony Smith's survey of practices in 20 democratic countries finds that only four—Australia, Canada, Japan, and the United States—allow paid political advertising on television: "Mass Communications," in David Butler, Howard R. Penniman, and Austin Ranney, eds., *Democracy at the Polls* (Washington, D.C.: American Enterprise Institute, 1981), pp. 173-95, Table 8-1, pp. 174-75.

14. The best description of the background and activities of the new campaign professionals in the United States is Larry J. Sabato, *The Rise of Political Consultants* (New York: Basic Books, 1981); Robert Agranoff, ed., *The New Style in Election Politics*, 2nd ed. (Boston: Holbrook Press, 1976); and Robert McClure and Thomas Patterson, *The Unseeing Eye* (New York: G. P. Putnam's Sons, 1976).

15. See, for example, Michael J. Malbin, ed., *Parties, Interest Groups, and Campaign Finance Laws* (Washington, D.C.: American Enterprise Institute, 1980); Herbert E. Alexander, *Financing Politics* (Washington, D.C.: Congressional Quarterly Press, 1976); and F. Christopher Arterton, "Political Money and Party Strength," in Joel L. Fleishman, ed., *The Future of American Political Parties* (Englewood Cliffs, N.J.: Prentice-Hall, 1982), pp. 101-39.

16. See Michael Pinto-Duschinsky, *British Political Finance* (Washington, D.C.: American Enterprise Institute, 1980).

17. On occasion local radio and television stations, both commercial and non-commercial, have given free time to local candidates and, more rarely, to local party organizations. Anthony Smith's survey shows that Norway, Sri Lanka, and the United States are the only countries that do not give free party-controlled air time: see Table 8-1 in "Mass Communications," cited earlier.

18. The details are given in Pilsworth, "Balanced Broadcasting," pp. 221-29.

19. Blumler, Gurevitch, and Ives, *The Challenge of Election Broadcasting*, p. 10, emphasis added.

20. Quoted in ibid., p. 15.

21. Both statements are quoted in ibid., p. 16.

22. Quoted in Sabato, *The Rise of Political Consultants*, p. 153.

23. The scholarly literature making this point is voluminous, but the leading studies include, for Great Britain: Ivor Crewe, Bo Särlvik, and James Alt, "Partisan Dealignment in Britain, 1964-1974," *British Journal of Political*

Science, vol. 7 (April 1977); Samuel H. Finer, *The Changing British Party System, 1945–1979* (Washington, D.C.: American Enterprise Institute, 1980), chap. 2; and Samuel H. Beer, *Britain Against Itself* (New York: W. W. Norton, 1982), pp. 80–83. For the United States: Norman H. Nie, Sidney Verba, and John R. Petrocik, *The Changing American Voter* (Cambridge, Mass.: Harvard University Press, 1976); Martin P. Wattenberg, "The Decline of Political Partisanship in the United States," *American Political Science Review*, vol. 75 (December 1981); and Helmut Norpoth and Jerrold Rusk, "Partisan Realignment in the American Electorate," *American Political Science Review*, vol. 76 (September 1982).

24. Comstock, *Television in America*, p. 59.
25. Sigmund Neumann, *Modern Political Parties: Approaches to Comparative Politics* (Chicago: University of Chicago Press, 1956), p. 421.

10

AN ENGLISHMAN'S POSTSCRIPT: THE GENERAL ELECTION OF 1983 AND THE BRITISH PARTY SYSTEM

Vernon Bogdanor

THE RESULT

The 1983 general election resulted in a massive victory for the Conservatives – a landslide in terms of seats, although based on just over 40% of the popular vote (see Table 10.1). This result was a remarkable one for many reasons, and it raises fundamental questions about the future of the British party system, and also about the viability of the first-past-the-post electoral system in a situation in which there are three, rather than two, political groupings competing for power.

The general election of 1983 was the first since Harold Macmillan's victory in 1959 to see the endorsement of a government that had already served a full term. It was the first since *1900* and the days of the great Lord Salisbury to see the reelection of a *Prime Minister* who had already served a full term. The election result, therefore, was a political triumph for the Conservative Party, and a remarkable personal achievement on the part of Mrs. Thatcher, the Conservative leader.

Such a result would scarcely have been predicted eighteen months earlier, when survey data had suggested that the Conservatives enjoyed the support of only 27% of the electorate, and Mrs. Thatcher's Gallup poll rating was the lowest ever recorded for a Prime Minister. The unpopularity of the government was due, primarily, to what was perceived as the failure of its economic policy. Unemployment was just about to reach three million, around 15% of the labour force,

Table 10.1

British general election results, 1979, 1983

	Seats		Percentage of votes	
	1979	1983	1979	1983
Conservatives	339	397	43.9	42.4
Labour	268	209	36.9	27.6
Liberal/SDP Alliance	11	23	13.8	25.4
Others	17	21	5.4	4.6
Total	635	650	100.0	100.0

Note: Neither the Liberal/SDP Alliance nor the SDP were in existence in 1979, and the Liberals fought the election of that year as a separate party without allies. In 1983, by contrast, the Liberals and SDP agreed upon an electoral pact by means of which they would refrain from opposing each other in the constituencies. After somewhat laborious negotiations, the constituencies of Great Britain were divided between the two parties on a 50/50 basis.

while the fall of 20% in industrial production during the Conservatives' period in office was greater than had occurred after the slump of 1929.

It was, of course, events in the South Atlantic which transformed the political situation. Britain's victory in the Falklands seemed the first occasion for many years when a government had actually achieved precisely what it had set out to do. Mrs. Thatcher gained the priceless asset of credibility, and the electorate became more willing to trust her judgment that the recession was a temporary yet essential phase in the restructuring of the economy. Mrs. Thatcher was able to appeal to the virtues of national resolution and self-confidence, generated by the Falklands campaign, as solvents of Britain's economic problems.

Moreover, the government did achieve one important success on the economic front—a reduction in the rate of inflation from 10.4% in 1979 to under 4% by June 1983. Critics could argue, of course, that this improvement was purchased at too high a price in mass unemployment and industrial bankruptcies, but to the electorate the fall in the rate of inflation must have seemed an encouraging sign that Conservative policies would, after all, produce economic revival.

Mrs. Thatcher's critics—Left-wing Conservatives (the so-called "wets"), the Alliance and Labour—all believed that no government could hope to win a general election against a background of three million unemployed. Indeed, the maintenance of full employment had been a central tenet of the post-war consensus, first adumbrated in the White Paper of 1944 and accepted in principle by governments of both Left and Right. The 1983 general election, however, showed that Mrs. Thatcher was correct in her belief that the constraints imposed by this consensus could be ignored without incurring any electoral penalty. This was in part because, as survey evidence indicated, many voters blamed the trade unions rather than government for the rise in unemployment; while a majority remained distinctly sceptical of the claim that alternative policies, whether those of Labour or the Alliance, would be able to secure a genuine reduction in the number out of work. Indeed, one noticeable feature of the election campaign was the degree to which the moralistic language characteristic of Margaret Thatcher's brand of conservatism seemed to reflect the attitudes of the electorate. The rhetoric of responsibility, self-discipline and patriotism struck a real chord with voters and seemed to have replaced belief in the beneficent action of the state as an influence upon electoral behaviour. In Britain, as in the United States, it was the Right and not the Left which benefitted from the breakdown of the post-war consensus; and the 1983 general election showed that high unemployment need not necessarily prove a barrier to the popular endorsement of a government of the Right.

The Conservatives were greatly assisted by the disarray of the official Opposition—the Labour Party. Between 1979 and 1983, Labour had undergone a period of travail, severe even by that Party's standards, and by 1983 the time-honoured struggle between Right and Left seemed to have been resolved to the advantage of the Left. The constitutional reforms discussed in Leon Epstein's chapter shifted the balance of power in the Party to the Left; while the Right was damaged by the defeat of its candidate—Denis Healey—by Michael Foot in the 1980 leadership election, and by the defection in 1981 of many of its leaders to the Social Democrats. This was a clear signal to the electorate that many on the Labour Right believed that the Party could no longer be saved for the kinds of policies associated with previous leaders such as Attlee, Gaitskell, Wilson and Callaghan.

Michael Foot, the Labour leader, saw himself as a unifier, but to the public he seemed weak and ineffective. His poll ratings from the time he assumed the leadership were the lowest ever recorded for any major party leader. Foot had long favoured unilateral nuclear disarmament and Britain's withdrawal from the Common Market.

Labour's election manifesto committed the Party to both of these measures as well as to a vast extension of trade union influence over many areas of national life. These policies were—with the possible exception of withdrawal from the Common Market—bitterly opposed by the majority of the electorate.

Moreover, the Party was clearly not united in support of its central policies, and during the election campaign it became apparent that both Denis Healey, the Deputy Leader and Shadow Foreign Secretary, and James Callaghan, the last Labour Prime Minister, were somewhat sceptical as to the wisdom of a policy of unilateral renunciation of nuclear weapons. One member of Labour's Shadow Cabinet—widely assumed to have been Peter Shore, the Shadow Chancellor—leaked to the press the comment that Labour's manifesto was "the longest suicide note ever penned," and there can be little doubt that fear of Labour was an important factor in Mrs. Thatcher's victory. The election, which Labour hoped would focus upon unemployment and economic policy, was, instead, skilfully turned by the Conservatives into a test of the Opposition's credibility—a test the Opposition was quite unable to meet.

THE ELECTION AND THE PARTY SYSTEM

Despite the government's success in the Falklands and in reducing inflation, the massive Conservative majority was not accompanied by any widespread enthusiasm for the Party amongst the electorate. This is, perhaps, the central paradox of the election. The gap between the Conservatives and Labour—14.8%—was by far the largest between the two major parties since 1935; Labour's majority of 146 in 1945 was based upon a lead of only 8% in the popular vote. But the Conservative share of the vote was the lowest of any of its post-war victories. Indeed, there is only one other example in twentieth-century British politics—apart from 1979—of a party winning a comfortable overall majority on a vote of less than 45%, and that was in 1922, when Bonar Law's Conservatives won 345 out of 615 seats on 38.2% of the vote. But Bonar Law's overall majority was only 75 compared with Mrs. Thatcher's 144, while, by contrast with 1983, there were 42 Conservatives returned unopposed in 1922 thus artificially deflating the Conservative percentage of the vote.

The massive Conservative lead in the popular vote in 1983 reflected not so much enthusiasm for the Conservatives as fear of Labour and a split in the Opposition vote between Labour and the

Alliance. Indeed, the results of a Gallup survey reported by Ivor Crewe suggest that 59% of all voters and 55% of Conservative voters were influenced in casting their vote primarily by negative factors; amongst those who decided how they would vote during the campaign, the figures were 73% and 78%, respectively.[1] The anti-Convervative majority amongst the electorate had, in fact, grown between 1979 and 1983—from 56.1%, or 2.8 million voters, in 1979, to 57.6%, or 3.7 million voters, in 1983; The Conservatives, therefore, are very far from being a predominant party electorally as they were in the inter-war period when, in four out of the seven elections, they won, either alone or with coalition allies, over 48% of the vote.

For Labour, the election was an unmitigated disaster. The Party suffered the greatest loss of votes by any major opposition party this century, forfeiting the support of one in every four of those who had voted for it in 1979, itself the Party's worst electoral performance for nearly 50 years. Labour's share of the vote was, in fact, its lowest since 1922. But, in 1922, Labour had contested only 411 out of 615 constituencies, and its average percentage vote per candidate was 40.0%, over 12% higher than in 1983. Taking the criterion of average percentage vote per candidate rather than the percentage share of the total vote, Labour's performance in 1983 was actually its worst since the Party was founded in 1900. Moreover, the Party failed to secure $12\frac{1}{2}$% of the vote, thereby forfeiting the £150 deposit, in no less than 119 constituencies, the largest number ever lost by a major party since the deposit was introduced in 1918. In the South West, the Party lost its deposit in 56% of the seats it contested, and in the South East in 43% of seats contested.

The Labour Party's catastrophic decline can be appreciated more clearly from Table 10.2, which charts the Labour vote at every general election since 1922. It will be seen that the Labour vote reached its zenith, paradoxically, in 1951, the year in which it lost power to the Conservatives, despite the remarkable achievement of having increased its share of the vote after six years in government. Until 1951, the Labour vote rose steadily, declining only in the crisis year of 1931 and, marginally, in 1950. Since 1951, however, the Labour vote has declined in six out of nine elections, increasing only in 1964, 1966 and October 1974. The Party has not been able to secure 40% of the vote since 1970. This seems a clear indication that the collapse of Labour is not to be explained solely by short-term factors, but is to be understood as the inevitable response of the electorate to a party which, unlike most of its Continental counterparts, has refused to recognise the facts of social change. In retrospect, the immediate post-war period seems to be that in

Table 10.2

Labour vote at general elections since 1922

	Percentage of Labour vote	Change in percentage share of Labour vote from previous elections
1922	29.5	+7.3
1923	30.5	+1.0
1924	33.0	+2.5
1929	37.1	+4.1
1931	30.6	-6.5
1935	37.9	+7.3
1945	47.8	+9.9
1950	46.1	-1.7
1951	48.8	+2.7
1955	46.4	-2.4
1959	43.8	-2.6
1964	44.1	+0.3
1966	47.9	+3.8
1970	43.0	-4.9
1974 (February)	37.1	-5.9
1974 (October)	39.2	+2.1
1979	36.9	-2.3
1983	27.6	-9.3

which social solidarity was at its strongest; and with the decline in social solidarity has come a secular decline in the Labour vote. In 1983, defections from Labour were greatest amongst expanding sections of the population, especially home-owners, while Labour's vote held up best amongst council tenants, blacks and the over-65's. For the first time since the war, Labour failed to gain the support of a majority of trade union members, survey evidence suggesting that only 39% of trade unionists voted for the Party.

Thus, although the Labour Party managed to retain 209 seats in the Commons, its strength has come to be even more severely concentrated in its traditional fiefs—the conurbations of the North of England and Scotland which returned, on 35.1% of the popular vote, 41 Labour MP's, one-fifth of the whole parliamentary Party. In the South of England, outside London, Labour was wiped out.

South of a line from the Wash to the Avon, and excluding Greater London, Labour now retains only three out of 176 seats—Ipswich, Thurrock and Bristol South. There is no Labour seat south of the line from Bristol to Dover.

Moreover, in many of these seats, Labour is not even the main challenger, coming third in 150 out of the 176. It is the Alliance which, in this area, has replaced Labour as the main challenger to the Conservatives and the likely beneficiary of any anti-Conservative swing. In the country as a whole, Labour was third or worse in 292 seats—more than it actually won. Its total vote in the country was less than 680,000 ahead of the Liberal/SDP Alliance, while in 1979 its vote had been over 7 million ahead of the Liberals. To secure even a small overall majority at the next election, Labour needs to win 117 seats. Since it was second in only 132 seats, this means that it will need to gain nearly nine-tenths of the seats in which it came second in 1983. To secure a working majority large enough to last for the lifetime of a Parliament it would need to win seats in which the Party came third. It is little wonder that the general election of 1983 has caused commentators to ask not only whether Labour is still a major opposition party, but whether it can any longer be considered a national party at all, or whether it is in a state of terminal decline.

The Liberal/SDP Alliance was a major beneficiary of Labour's collapse. Indeed, the Alliance was the only one of the three major political groupings to improve upon its performance of 1979, (treating the Alliance vote as the successor to the 1979 Liberal vote). The Alliance did spectacularly well for a third party which in Britain is always handicapped through fear of the "wasted vote." The two-party share of the vote was the lowest, and the Alliance's vote the highest, for any third party since 1923. Whereas in 1951 nearly 80% of the electorate voted for one of the two major parties, only 50% of the electorate could be persuaded to do so in 1983.

The Alliance, however, was cruelly punished by the electoral system which awarded it only 23 seats out of 650 for 25.4% of the vote. Securing only 2.2% less of the vote than Labour, it gained less than one-tenth of Labour's seats. Nevertheless, the Alliance stands second in many more seats than Labour—it is second in 312 seats, as compared with Labour's 132 second places. Moreover, of the 312 seats in which the Alliance is second, 265 are held by the Conservatives. In large areas of the country, therefore, the struggle at the next general election will not be between the Conservative and Labour parties, but between the Conservatives and the Alliance. In fact, the next general election will be the first since the 1920s which will be multi-dimensional in nature rather than a uni-dimensional struggle between the Conservatives and Labour. For there will be two different electoral battles—one between the Conservatives and Labour, and one between the Conservatives and the Alliance. Whatever its result, therefore, the general election of 1987 or 1988 will be a different *kind* of election from any previously seen in the post-war period, a consequence of the fact that Britain now has a three-party system at electoral if not at parliamentary level.

THE ELECTION
AND THE ELECTORAL SYSTEM

The most striking feature of the general election apart from the massive Conservative majority was the glaring discrepancy between seats and votes. For, whereas it took around 33,000 votes to elect a Conservative MP, and 40,000 to elect a Labour MP, it took nearly 340,000 votes to elect an Alliance Member. Indeed, the 30% who chose to vote for a party other than the Conservatives or Labour were rewarded with only 7% of the seats in the Commons. The two-fifths of those voting who supported the Conservatives gained over three-fifths of the seats; while, within the remaining three-fifths of the votes, seats were distributed between Labour and the Alliance in a ratio of approximately 9:1 for a roughly comparable vote. No less than 336 of the 650 seats were won on a minority vote.

The election laid bare a fundamental feature of the "first past the post" system of election, a system that can work effectively when only two major parties command the loyalties of the vast majority of the electorate, as during the 1950s and 1960s, but will produce an unrepresentative, and indeed unpredictable, result when, as in 1983, there is a three-party system. For, under the "first-past-the-post" system, the number of seats a party wins is a function not only of how many votes it receives but of where these votes are cast. In particular, the electoral system tends to reward parties whose vote is relatively concentrated at the expense of parties whose vote is comparatively evenly spread across the country as a whole. It is for this reason that Labour did so much better than the Alliance on only a marginally higher vote. The Labour vote is very much concentrated in the older industrial conurbations of the North, and so the Party was able to win a number of seats in that region, while losing deposits in the South. The Alliance vote, by contrast, was evenly spread across the country. In every region of England and

Wales, Alliance voting gains were within 2% of the national average. The Alliance thus performed relatively well everywhere without being able to make a decisive breakthrough in any particular region of the country. The Labour vote remains predominantly working-class (even though the working class is no longer predominantly Labour); the Alliance vote is evenly spread amongst the social classes, as shown in Table 10.3.[2]

Since social classes are not randomly distributed amongst the population but tend to be segregated through different residence patterns—working-class and middle-class housing being geographically as well as socially separated—parties whose support is predominantly class-based will benefit under the first-past-the-post electoral system because their vote is geographically concentrated. Parties whose support is not predominantly class-based will find their vote evenly distributed, and the electoral system will discriminate against them. It is for this reason that the Alliance wins many fewer seats than Labour on a similar proportion of the national vote.

In 1983, not only did the electoral system yield an unrepresentative House of Commons, it also distorted the result in particular regions of the country, exaggerating the support of the leading party in each region, while discriminating against second (and third) parties. As we have already seen, Labour, which polled around 17% south of a line from the Wash to the Avon, (excluding Greater London), secured only three out of 176 seats. The Alliance gained 29% of the vote in the same area but won only 5 seats, leaving to the Conservatives 168 out of the 176 seats on 54% of the vote. Thus, in most of the counties of Southern England, there is one-party, Conservative representation based upon little more than half of the vote.

In the northern cities, by contrast, it was Labour that benefitted. In Glasgow, the Conservatives failed to win a single one of the eleven seats although gaining 19% of the vote. In Sheffield, Labour won

Table 10.3

Alliance vote by social class (in percentages)

A, B	(professional and managerial)	27
C_1	(office and clerical)	24
C_2	(skilled manual)	27
D	(semi-skilled and unskilled manual)	28
	Unemployed	26
Total percentage of the vote		27

five out of the six seats, leaving the Conservatives with only one seat for 30% of the vote: while, similarly, in the county of Durham, the Conservatives gained only one out of 6 seats for 30% of the vote.

These anomalous results could have important political effects. For, despite their landslide victory, the Conservatives remain almost completely unrepresented in the major conurbations of the North. In the eight major industrial cities of Bradford, Glasgow, Hull, Leeds, Liverpool, Manchester, Newcastle and Sheffield, the Conservatives hold only 6 out of the 43 seats. They may, therefore, find it difficult to represent effectively those in the inner cities suffering most severely from the effects of the recession. Conversely Labour, which holds no seat at all in the rural South, or in the areas of comparative industrial prosperity, could easily become insensitive to the needs of commuter suburbs, agricultural areas or areas of new industry. It is hardly surprising that supporters of proportional representation claim that the British electoral system is an important factor in the exaggeration of regional and class differences, which make Britain appear rather more divided than it is in reality.[3]

As might have been predicted, the result of the 1983 general election led to renewed agitation for a change in the electoral system, and shortly after the election a national petition was launched in an attempt to secure a referendum on the issue. Its chances of success, however, are quite remote. Mrs. Thatcher is resolutely opposed to change, as are the bulk of Conservative MPs who are, after all, beneficiaries of the present system. For proportional representation to return to the political agenda, there would have to be a "hung" parliament, i.e., one in which no single party enjoyed an overall majority; or alternatively, a renewal of the fear, expressed by many in the 1970s, especially members of the business community, of a Left-wing government gaining an overall majority in the Commons on less than 40% of the popular vote. For the present, however, the agitation for a change in the electoral system will meet with no response from those with the power to alter the rules.

THE ELECTION AND THE CONSTITUTION

The 1983 general election may come to be seen as having made fundamental alterations to the British Party system and therefore to have put the adequacy of the electoral system as a method of securing a reflection of popular opinion in the Commons under question. Yet the result poses a fearful dilemma for the Opposition parties.

Labour cannot gain a secure overall majority without a massive swing in its favour—greater than has been achieved by any party since 1945. The Alliance, although enjoying many more second places than Labour, remains imprisoned within the constraints imposed by the electoral system. If it had gained another 10% of the vote, evenly spread across the country, it would still have won only another 29 seats, giving it 52 seats for over 35% of the vote. The Alliance would need to win over 38% of the vote in order to begin picking up a large number of seats.

It would, therefore, require an electoral earthquake for either Labour or the Alliance to win the next election outright. An anti-Conservative swing is much more likely to result in a hung parliament than in an overall majority for one of the opposition parties. Thus it can hardly be said that Britain still possesses a political system in which two alternative governments compete for power.

The opposition parties will, therefore, have to consider what their strategy should be in this novel situation. Neither can hope, in the normal course of events, to win an overall majority on its own. The Alliance cannot hope to "break the mould" because of the electoral system, while Labour cannot hope to win, having been pushed back so far into its traditional heartlands. It might seem, therefore, as if the Conservative hold on government can only be broken through some form of co-operation—an electoral pact or coalition agreement. Yet, many of the members of the Social Democratic Party—and all of its MPs—are defectors from Labour and continue to regard their old party with considerable hostility; while Labour, almost alone amongst the socialist parties of Western Europe, refuses to entertain the possibility of entering into a peace-time agreement with another party, a legacy, of course, of the traumatic events of 1931. Labour and the Alliance, therefore, seek to destroy each other, rather than combining to secure a viable opposition Yet, unless these attitudes can be changed, the Conservatives seem likely, as in the 1920s, to remain in power as a result of the divisions of their opponents.

For this reason, the election result also raises a fundamental question about the British Constitution, which, unlike the American, imposes no formal constraint upon the power of a Commons majority. The Conservative government is therefore able to implement its policies without let or hindrance although rejected by nearly three-fifths of the voters. An American administration, by contrast, even if it has just won a landslide victory, finds that its power is checked by Congress, the States and the courts. In 1978, Lord Hailsham, the Conservative elder statesman and Lord Chancellor between 1970 and

1974 and again since 1979, described the British system of government as one of "elective dictatorship," for it offers no constitutional protection in the form of a powerful Second Chamber, Federal system or Bill of Rights of the kind enjoyed by many other democracies. Instead, Britain relies upon a never consciously formulated belief in a sense of moderation on the part of the government of the day, a respect for the views of those who have not supported it at the polls; and upon the alternation of power. Government can be restrained from excess through fear of the Opposition; the abuse of power can be counteracted through the swing of the pendulum. Flimsy as these methods of protecting rights and liberties may seem, they have not proved entirely insufficient in the past in yielding (at the very least) a comparable degree of constitutional protection to that enjoyed by those democracies with written constitutions.

But in a society whose representatives reflect, and even over-emphasise, social and regional differences, and when the consensus, whose progenitors were Keynes and Beveridge, no longer unites the parties, traditional methods of protecting rights and liberties may no longer be sufficient. The problem is exacerbated if the pendulum ceases to swing and one party comes to enjoy a temporary monopoly of power so that it need no longer fear the reactions of a powerful Opposition. So, if the result of the general election of 1983 causes the political scientist to ask fundamental questions about the nature of the British electoral and party systems, it should also make him turn to the United States to consider whether there are any lessons in the experience of that country whose *leitmotiv* is constitutionalism, which could prove applicable to Britain's condition. For it is the adequacy of Britain's *constitutional arrangements* as well as of her *electoral system* which seem to be placed in question, and such issues as the reform of the House of Lords and introduction of a Bill of Rights are likely to move to the forefront of discussion in the years to come. For this reason, if no other, the Anglo-American dialogue on forms of government and party systems, of which this volume forms a part, is likely to continue well beyond the end of the twentieth century.

NOTES

1. Figures taken from a Gallup survey, commissioned by the BBC, and designed by Professor Ivor Crewe. See Ivor Crewe, The Disturbing Truth Behind Labour's Rout, *Guardian*, June 13, 1983.

2. Ibid.
3. I have discussed the case for proportional representation in *The People and the Party System: The Referendum and Electoral Reform in British Politics* (Cambridge University Press, 1981) and in *What is Proportional Representation? A Guide to the Issues* (Martin Roberton, 1984), and the development of a multi-party system and its likely constitutional consequences in *Multi-Party Politics and the Constitution* (Cambridge University Press, 1983).

11

AN AMERICAN'S EPILOGUE

Gerald M. Pomper

Britain and America, claimed Oscar Wilde, are divided by a common language. In the study of political parties, a similar problem has often created misunderstandings. Because of the many parallels in political culture, observers have found more analogues from one nation to the other than actually existed.

Yet, I will argue, there now is a growing resemblance, and considerable similarity, between the two-party systems. Common social trends, common technologies, and common political problems are facilitating trans-Atlantic travel of party qualities. The evidence for this major proposition is partially found in the foregoing essays and partially in my own speculations. While it will always remain true that Britain and the United States are distinct and different, they are becoming less different than they were in the past.

BASES FOR COMPARISON

Previous comparisons of the party systems set aside institutional contrasts, as I will do. The fundamental constitutional arrangements of the Anglo-American democracies remain distinctive and critical. The differences are obvious between a parliamentary system governing a centralized state without a written fundamental law, in contrast to a system of separated institutions in a federal nation bound by a codified Constitution.

The apparent similarities stressed in previous discussions were political, rather than formal. In both nations, power was dominated by two parties, and this pattern of duopoly had asserted itself for over a century, even against a variety of "third-party" challenges and even with substantial changes in the names, composition, and programs of the two major contestants. To be sure, the two-party systems were quite different. The Liberals could survive in Britain, even as a minor party, while the various American "Progressives" disappeared after 1912, 1924, and 1948. Nationalists in Scotland, Wales and Northern Ireland proved hardy, while regional revolts of southern Dixiecrats quietly subsided. On the critical matter—the holding of power—however, our nations were akin in typically confining competition to only two parties: Conservatives vs. Liberals, or Conservatives vs. Labour, and Republicans vs. Democrats.

In both nations, the dominance of two parties could be attributed to such factors as the plurality, single-member electoral system, and the concentration of national power in the executive branch, even if the form of that power was as different as Britain's Cabinet or America's Presidency. On each side of the Atlantic, one could find the two major parties' mass base rooted in deep, even hereditary allegiances.[1] On each shore, the parties on the elite level typically followed the Downsian logic of imitating one another's moderate programs.[2]

These similarities—or, at least, superficial parallels—in the past have caused as many problems as they have provided insight. The most notable problem was probably that of Americans enshrining Britain as the model of a "responsible party system" and consciously seeking to imitate its alleged features. That effort, most conspicuously made in the famous report of the American Political Science Association,[3] was denounced as both empirically ungrounded and theoretically inappropriate.[4] Nevertheless, the attraction continues to be evident to contemporary writers such as Charles Hardin,[5] just as others find the original model even less apposite.[6]

Parallel problems can be expected when British scholars seek to import American party features. A striking illustration is Samuel Finer's advocacy of primary elections as a means of nominating candidates for Parliament. Among American party specialists there is general agreement that the primaries' effect over the twentieth century has been to cripple the political parties and thereby to impair seriously their ability to aggregate interests and to serve their vital democratic functions. As Ranney[7] summarizes the evidence, "the direct primary is the best way to keep the parties weak without destroying them altogether." Despite this experience and such judgements, Finer concludes his evaluation of British parties by advocating primary elections (albeit more controlled than in the United States). Significantly, his language resembles that of progressive reformers in America: "A party's candidate should be the choice of all its members, not a handful; this entails a statute obliging parties to conduct primary elections. ... The practitioners of politics have become professionals, and to all intents and purposes they are operating a closed shop. It is time to break it open."[8]

As scholars, we may agree that comparisons between the two nations have been inaccurate, or that institutional borrowings are dangerous and inappropriate, that imitation is not flattery but far-fetched. Still, our common language encourages these transfers. The encouragement is evident on the simple verbal level, as in the Labour party's creation of an "Electoral College" to nominate its Leader and Deputy Leader and in the Democratic party's holding of mid-term "conferences" to decide on policy programs. More basically, it is evident politically—as in the "progressive" trends in the Labour party found by Epstein in his essay, and in the organizational centralization of American parties, analyzed by Williams.

Change is occurring on both sides of the Atlantic. Although the product of very different nations, with quite different institutions, I believe the two party systems are coming increasingly to resemble one another. What is occurring is not a linear development, in which one nation serves as the "model" for the other. We are not seeing the political education of American barbarians by the "civilizing" mission of British politicians, nor the inevitable adoption of American practices as forecast in a different context by Tocqueville. Rather, the process is one of convergence toward greater similarity. I do not know how far this process will go. Certainly, it will leave the two systems dissimilar in many respects—to the undoubted relief both of Britons and of Americans. I argue only that the trend is in the direction of more similarities and fewer differences.

SOCIAL TRENDS

The root cause of this convergence is not politics narrowly, but the increased similarities of the social systems of the two nations, to which parties and politicians react.[9] Four general trends are evident.

For one, there is the shift from an economy based on manufacturing to one based on a combination of primary products, high-technology, and service industries. Britain, of course, led the world into the first industrial revolution, while the United States initiated the system of mass production. In both nations today the heavy industrial base is shrinking, with output and employment falling rapidly in such traditional sectors as steel, automobiles, and textiles. Their industrial future lies, if anywhere, in the newer industries of microelectronics, space, and communications. At the same time, the two economies are also developing as sources of primary products—oil for Britain, food in the United States. Ironically, these trends—although of lesser importance than the primary technological shift —may transform these erstwhile industrial giants into "colonial" producers of goods for late-coming industrial powers, such as Japan.

A second fundamental change is the development of the mass media, particularly television, as the major means of societal communication, replacing interpersonal relations. The United States is the pacesetter in this trend, but Britain evidences the same development. Geographical mobility, evident in the United States since the days of the frontier, has grown in the United Kingdom as well, disrupting traditional communities and close family ties. Impersonal communication becomes the dominant mode. McLuhan may have exaggerated the influence of the mass media in creating a "global village," but his comment is closer to the mark in describing television's influence on the Anglo–American nations. The exchange of "Dallas" for "Benny Hill" tends to create a common mass culture in the two nations.

These societies define themselves less by traditional neighborhoods, or by kinship ties to counties and shires. The national events and symbols portrayed on television become the new definitions of community. These trends are not accepted happily by either cultural elites or mass populations, and resistance is evident in such diverse phenomena as the neighborhood movement in the United States[10] and the revival of Celtic languages in Britain. Still, even these local and regional groups must rely on the mass media for effective communication.

The media have also influenced a third common trend, the alterations of life style. Both nations are living, to some degree, in a "postmaterialist" world, in which concerns for self-fulfilment and participation take priority over needs for economic success and personal security.[11] These differing values are most evident in younger generations, and the change in values is the source of more obvious generational differences in musical taste, dress, and mores. Significantly, these newer values remain evident even in the current period of economic recession in the Western world. Postmaterialism has become still more evident in the 1970s, to the point that it is no longer confined to the young. It is a "deep-rooted phenomenon with important political consequences."[12]

The new life styles are also grounded in the profound expansion in educational opportunities that has affected both nations, although in very different ways. Where the United States now makes a university education available to over half of its 18-year olds, the United Kingdom provides financial grants for all of a severely limited student body. There are great differences between America's egalitarian approach to higher education and Britain's meritocratic policy, but they are alike in increasing opportunities and in reducing the social class bias of the academy.

A final trend is the diminished position of the two nations in international affairs. That change occurred in Britain by the end of the Second World War, although it was not acknowledged by most until the Suez invasion of 1956 and, indeed, was still not acknowledged by some at the time of the Falklands campaign. America's postwar history was different, for its triumph in the Second World War, combined with economic strength and atomic weaponry, brought a period of world leadership, if not dominance. That period has now ended. Vietnam eroded American self-confidence, for our history books taught us that we had never lost a war. Nuclear proliferation, the emergence of the EEC and OPEC, and the Soviet arms buildup all contributed to the decline of America's relative international position. To be sure, the United States remains a truly major world power, while Britain inevitably takes a place in the second rank. Nevertheless, the trend is similar for the two nations, from past primacy to present parity.

POLITICAL CONSEQUENCES

If, as I have argued, these two societies are becoming more alike—but not by any means identical—we would then expect their parties and politics to become more alike as well. This greater similarity can occur in very different ways. On some matters, Britain and America are moving along similar paths. The most obvious of these trends is the increasing reliance on mass media campaigning. On other matters, however, the convergence of the two nations is being accomplished by directly opposing trends. In voting behavior, the previously fractured American electorate is evidencing more national orientations, while local variations are disturbing the previous uniformity of British voting. The result of these various trends is a greater similarity between the two countries.

The convergence of the two-party system is evident in four ways. (1) The parties are becoming more ideological. (2) Their electorates are less loyal affectively and more volatile behaviorally. (3) As organizations, the parties are more bureaucratic. (4) They are approaching a common centrist orientation, modified by localist influences. As a result of these trends, British and American parties alike face continuing problems of reconciling the conflicting demands for individual participation and centralized efficiency. Each of these points requires elaboration.

A striking similarity in the two nations' recent politics is the development of ideological extremism. This development was historically surprising, since it followed the long postwar period of policy moderation, expressed politically by Eisenhower in the United States and "Butskell" in Britain and justified intellectually as "the end of ideology." The development was also academically surprising, since it violated the elegant Downsian theory of party moderation and empirical tests of that theory.[13] Surprising as it is, we cannot deny the reality of governments on both sides of the Atlantic that hold to their economic theories, whatever the human or political costs of double-digit unemployment.

This movement to the right is matched in Britain—but not yet in America—by a more dogmatic ideological stance on the left, where the Labour party is now cohesively supportive of such programs as unilateral nuclear disarmament and the wholesale extension of socialist ownership. Such extremism would be expected, by Downsian theory, to provide an easy ride for a new party of the center, such as the SDP. It is significant, however, not only that the SDP has failed to maintain its original momentum, but that it is criticized for its "lack of policies." Since the SDP actually has policies on virtually every subject facing Britain, the criticism should be read as "The SDP doesn't have ideological policies"—a very different and unexpected criticism.

This growth of ideology is related to the social trends previously discussed. Ideology is a likely development of perceived social problems or failures. Successful policies can rely on incrementalism and muddling through; those that fail need larger world views. As Britain and America have seen their economic dominance wane, some citizens have looked to new, even radical, solutions. The common element between Reagan neo-laissez-faire and Benn neo-socialism is their condemnation of the recent past as economic failures. This economic disillusionment is paralleled by anxious attitudes toward their nations' international position, the perceived threat to Britain being Cruise missiles and the I.M.F., the perceived threat to America being the Soviet SS-20 missiles and the U.N. Conference on the Law of the Sea. In their criticism, these leaders are not simply expressing their own peculiar ideas; they are reacting—whether or not appropriately—to the real decline in their nations' standing.

The development of ideological extremism reflects as well changes in the activist base of the parties. In a postmaterialist society, more emphasis is placed on participation and the formulation of party policy by the party membership. This kind of demand is particularly likely to be voiced by the educated, the middle-class, and the young.[14] The expansion of educational opportunities has meant that there are more people to express these demands, and that they are better trained to give voice and effect to their demands.

At the same time, the decline of the manufacturing sector means that there are fewer members of the "pragmatic" working class in a Labour or Democratic party, that they will have less influence in party councils, and that their votes need be given less anticipatory concern when party manifestos are written. The party activists newly recruited are likely to be social workers or polytechnic graduates rather than dockworkers, as the specific constituency of Bermondsey illustrates.[15] Even when unions remain active, the greater influence is likely to be exercised by teachers rather than steelworkers, as shown by the last Democratic party convention.

The influence of ideological activists has already been seen in the United States in such episodes as the success of "purists" in winning Presidential nominations for Barry Goldwater and George McGovern, and more generally in the movements of "amateur" Republicans and Democrats.[16] The British equivalent may be the entrance of middle-class leftists into the Labour parties of working-class constituencies. With generational replacement, party organizations are likely to be increasingly voicing the postmaterialist demands of their new activists. These demands, for participation and self-fulfillment, are inherently less specific and less bounded than previous demands for security and economic improvement and therefore are particularly likely to encourage ideological emphases. One small-scale study of British party activists shows this likely trend.[17]

Ideology provides a stimulant to these campaign workers. They are no longer devoted to the party for the materialistic reasons that once cemented American parties, nor by the generational loyalties that existed in British parties. Purposive incentives can be a substitute. When patronage is unattractive or unavailable, as is essentially the case now in both countries, and when emotional commitment to the party name lessens, as is increasingly true in each nation, men and women can still be induced to ring doorbells by their commitment to "the cause"—whether that cause is "socialism," "liberty," or some other emotive goal.

These incentives have always existed but, as Robertson has shown,[18] their manifestation was impeded by the demands of electoral competition. Today, those impediments are lessened as a result of the changes among the mass electorate. On this level the most striking similarity between Britain and America is the recent volatility of the electorate, as noted above by Crewe. With regard to governments, this volatility is evident in the refusal of either electorate—except the British in 1983—to reelect a full-term incumbent administration since the 1950s. Four of the last six American national elections have seen a change in the party in control of the White House, as four of the last six elections (combining the two 1974 polls) in Britain have changed the occupant of 10 Downing Street. These results have followed from substantial swings of the electorate—a gross change of 25% among voters in the two Carter races of 1976 and 1980 and a 37% shift (including abstainers) in Britain from 1974 to 1979.[19]

The vote for competitors of the two major parties is another indicator. Although we still refer to the Anglo–American democracies as two-party systems, the two factions have been facing significant challenges. Both George Wallace and John Anderson were supported in U.S. opinion polls by one respondent in five and, despite the logic of the "wasted vote" argument, captured millions of ballots. In Britain, in the 1983 general election, one in four voters supported the Liberal/SDP Alliance. This disloyalty to the major parties is the source of the marked instability of opinion polls and of the sharp swings in British by-elections.

Underlying, and reflecting, voter volatility is the weakening of party identification, another point made by Crewe. This concept has been the foundation of psephological research. It is now challenged as a stable or even reliable indicator[20] and is clearly of less explanatory value when fewer people have any party commitment, or when only a fourth of the electorate is strongly identified. Simply as an inheritance from one generation to the next, or simply as an affective loyalty devoid of retrospective judgment or prospective intent, party identification has little effect in today's Anglo–American politics.

The decline in party loyalty is related, in complex ways, to the spread of the mass media in the two countries. Television substitutes an (apparently) direct tie between the voter and the government for the indirect tie of party identification. It allows the contemporary voter, more educated and more familiar with communications technology, to vote independently of party identity. We glimpse this impact when the causal factors of the vote are disaggregated; candidate assessments and issue preferences have become more important over time, while party evaluations have become minor influences.[21]

There is a two-fold effect. First, television personalizes politics, so that the individual leader becomes more significant than the party he or she leads. A Thatcher or a Reagan (perhaps even a Foot or a Mondale?) can be made telegenic, in contrast to the anonymity of a party. Second, television places relatively more emphasis on policy programs than on the party as a sentimental tie. While television has often been criticized as slighting issues, it still provides at least some focus on policy questions and does give them more stress than can be found in appeals to party tradition alone.

The change to a more issue-oriented politics is affecting both Britain and America. For the parties, the principal effect may be to reinforce other trends toward ideological politics. With fewer votes available to a party simply on affective grounds, other reasons must be provided. Ideology is particularly suited to this purpose. By stressing its issue positions, a party provides current grounds for holding old supporters and for gaining converts among the newly-enfranchised and among the oppositions's erstwhile loyalists. In this regard, it may be indicative that the length of party platforms or manifestos has increased noticeably in recent elections.

Another common tendency among the party organizations of Britain and America is the development of bureaucratized central organizations. Bureaucratic characteristics, such as specialization, expertise, and rationalization, have existed for some time in Britain and, as Williams' essay elaborates, they are now evident in America as well. These bureacratized parties show such characteristics as large staffs, specialized training, and central funding. Equivalent developments are occurring in the U.S. state organizations.[22]

At the same time, these two nations' parties show declining mass membership. The latter trend is probably more striking in the United Kingdom, since the United States never had large numbers of organizational activists. Labour's loss of some three-quarters of its previous million enrollees is matched by the Conservatives' loss of almost half of their two million activists since the 1950s. Similarly, the fabled American precinct committeeman can rarely be found canvassing his friends and neighbors. The personnel is simply lacking—in both nations—for campaigns consisting primarily of literature distribution and "knocking-up" voters.

Instead, greater reliance is being placed on mass media campaigning. This stress is in keeping with the basic social trends. A mobile population is more appropriately reached by impersonal advertising than by neighborly contact. Persons who make their own living through verbal manipulation are more open to being manipulated by other persons' words.

The reliance on mass media and indirect campaigning is shown by the parties' financial statements, discussed in previous chapters. Government policy may even have encouraged these tendencies, through public funding of campaigns in the United States and free media time in the United Kingdom, but the basic trend exists independently of government action. The contemporary political campaign is a media campaign. America has shown the way here, but British politics is moving in the same direction. The Social Democratic Party, whatever its specific success in the intermediate future, may best represent this trend. Organized from the beginning as a national party, its leadership has resisted strong constituency associations. It early took on such bureaucratic features as centralized fundraising, and direct mail solicitation, established the first national list of party members, and even outraged some traditionalists by allowing dues to be paid by credit card.

Bureaucratic parties and mass media campaigning are mutually reinforcing. Impersonal organizations devote themselves to impersonal campaigning. At the same time, greater reliance on the mass media requires more bureaucratic parties. These programs involve a considerable degree of technical expertise. While leafletting can be decentralized or amateurish and campaigns may still succeed, the production of good advertising and media appeals requires elaborate skills. The effect therefore is to bolster the party bureaucracy, an expert group of insiders.

Bureaucracy often implies centralization, but these are actually two different concepts. The first concerns the character of work in an organization, the second its degree of hierarchy. A particular group can be both bureaucratic and decentralized (e.g., the conglomerate corporation) or nonbureaucratic and centralized (e.g., absolutist monarchies). While the Anglo–American party systems are increasingly bureaucratic, they do not show similar tendencies toward complete national integration of these bureaucratic structures. Rather, they show convergence—from opposite directions—to high, but not total, centralization.

The existence of a national party system in the United Kingdom is usually taken for granted. I do not dispute that basic orientation of the British organizations, but I also would note some trends toward a less cohesive system, a movement at least in small degree toward the more localistic American party system. The support given nationalist parties in Scotland, Wales, and Ireland is one indication of this movement away from a purely center orientation. The success of the Liberals, both before and since the conclusion of the alliance with the SDP, is in part related to their claims of being more concerned with particular local communities. The SDP itself, although organized on a national basis, has still given some heed to these sentiments by its suggestions for regionalization of government in England.

The incipient movement toward a decentralist politics is also evident in elections. Where electoral swings were once essentially uniform throughout the country (an aid to psephologist predictions on polling day), there has recently been an increase in local variations around the country-wide mean,[23] thus showing the influence of local factors, such as individual candidates and more particularistic concerns.

The new means of nomination in the Labour party will certainly reinforce any trend in this direction. When MPs must court the favor of activists in their constituency associations—as some deselected Members already have learned—they will give more consideration to these localist pressures and somewhat less to parliamentary whips. The increased independence in the Commons and the establishment of more select committees and provision of more staff for MPs will further promote decentralist tendencies. We can never expect these Members to have the autonomy of U.S. Congressmen, but the tendency toward more independence and more localism is evident, bringing the British parties at least a step in the direction of traditional American party decentralization.[24]

The more striking change, however, is on the western shore of the Atlantic, where nationalization of the parties is rapidly developing. Party reforms among both Republicans and Democrats have aided this movement. In the Republican case, now imitated by the Democrats, we see the development of a national party organization, which pursues victory throughout the states in the manner and with much of the efficiency of a manufacturing corporation deciding where its products should be marketed, how they can best be sold, and which advertising and promotional techniques to employ. Republicans do not distribute funds uniformly to all candidates, but choose their targets on the basis of detailed cost/benefit analysis. Public opinion polls, television technology, and management training are not confined only to national contenders, but are employed for candidates for the state legislatures and similar "entry level" positions.

In the Democratic case, the party has established national standards for membership, has enforced national rules to govern state parties—even overriding state law in the process—and has given a national plebiscitary cast to presidential nominations, even if the plebiscite is conducted in different weeks in different states. The latest party reforms of the presidential nominating process do not reverse this nationalizing trend, for they simply give a greater role to national elected officials, particularly Senators and Representatives. They do nothing to restore the erstwhile power of state and local politicians and provide only limited influence for the party's governors. Even where the party's power is challenged, the challenge comes from national interest groups, not local particularistic groups. For example, the AFL/CIO is likely to have a decisive influence on the next presidential nomination, if it can unite behind a single candidate late in 1983. If this occurs, American labor's power will look strikingly like the ability of the TUC to dominate the decisions of the British Labour party.

The new nationalization of American politics was demonstrated in the 1982 Congressional elections. Financially, the dominant role was taken by the national interest groups, operating through PACs and, less importantly but still significantly, by the national parties raising money throughout the country and then distributing it where it would most benefit the total effort.

The campaign itself showed a similar national emphasis. The old cliché described a mid-term election as simply a collection of individual races, although political science scholarship has demonstrated the importance of such factors as Presidential popularity and economic conditions.[25] Whatever the past truth of that cliché, it certainly did not hold true in 1982. Both parties agreed on the central issue of the campaign: the Administration's economic program. Their evaluations and exhortations about that program certainly differed, Republicans urging the voters to "stay the course" and Democrats condemning a vague concept called "Reaganomics." The voters responded to this set of issues, with some 75% citing economic issues as predominant in their decisions.[26] The change from the 1980 results was strikingly uniform among most groups, a general 5% change from Republican to Democrat. When joined with the 1980 results, we have now seen two successive U.S. elections decided by national party swings and based on common economic issues. In other words, we are now seeing the American electorate acting as if it were following past descriptions of the British voting public and the British party system.

As organizations, the party trends are toward British adoption of American techniques, U.S. adoption of U.K. orientations, and the common evolution of bureaucratic, largely national parties. One problem is the inherent conflict between bureaucratization and centralization on the one hand, and local involvement and membership participation on the other. This tension was analyzed early by Michels, who pessimistically saw party oligarchy as the inevitable result of the technical expertise of party leaders and electoral pressures toward party efficiency. At present, the tension may be even greater, for party operatives require even more expert skills than in the first decades of the twentieth century. At the same time, the demand for participation is both better articulated by educated, ideological, postmaterialist activists and voiced by a smaller and possibly less representative membership.

These conflicts are evident in our contemporary parties. We find it, illustratively, in the U.S. Democratic party, where nominating reforms to increase participation are now being altered as the national party tries to imitate the Republicans' success in promoting an efficient national bureaucracy. We find it as well—following Epstein— in the Labour party's left-wing demand for more participation and the right-wing and trade unions' reassertion of centralized control. The SDP, the newest party in our group, shows the same conflict, with the membership mutinying against its original leadership to mandate direct election of the party leader and the establishment of individual constituency associations.

Party trends even raise questions about the legitimacy of the party role in Anglo–American democracy.[27] When parties are mass organizations, with strong roots in local communities, they can be accorded legitimacy as the expressions of a mobilized populace. But parties are losing their members, their roots, and their affective ties to the electorate. They are becoming only Downsian competitors in the electoral marketplace. Nevertheless, parties could still be considered legitimate if they functioned effectively as aggregative bodies, consolidating demands into national programs. Ideological extremism limits their usefulness in this regard. Furthermore, incipient technological developments may further detract from the parties' aggregative function. Cable and regional television, direct mail, and personal computers make it increasingly possible to divide the total electorate into smaller and more particular groupings. Electoral appeals may be more effective through this technology, but electoral meaning will be more difficult to locate.

THE PARTY FUTURE

These trends indicate (at least to me) a convergence in the two nations' party systems. But what of the future? Can we simply extrapolate to some time when American and British politics will be identical? It seems hardly likely. We can, however, note the continuing common influences and some general factors that will shape the future. These may continue the trends toward party convergence.

Tomorrow's parties will be affected by three kinds of influences. In order of importance, they are: the parties' own actions, their nations' laws and institutions, and their social structures, or "customs." Considerable attention is devoted to the first of these factors, deliberate efforts to control their environment. The four "reform" commissions of the Democratic party are paralleled by programs of organizational revival in the Labour party, all of them implicitly based on the premise that the party will be able to revive, if only it can find the "right" structural solution. Certainly rationalization can aid a party, but parties do not really control their own destiny, for organization cannot overcome two greater problems.

The first of these problems is human lack of knowledge and the inability to foretell future consequences. Latent functions, "the unintended consequences of purposive social action," are typically more decisive than the intended effects. The Democrats' reform of the presidential nominating process may come to be recognized as the classic demonstration of this principle. Members of these commissions have agonizingly testified that they had no intention of weakening the political parties, but their well-meant alterations in party rules have had precisely these results. Now, the latest (Hunt) commission seeks to reverse these effects by bolstering the role of elected officials in the national conventions.[28]

Such changes are too little and too late, in my opinion. Reversal could come only through radical actions, such as the elimination of most state primaries—actions inconceivable within the American democratic ethos and likely to be opposed, in any case, by important factions within the party. Therefore, the national nominating conventions are likely soon to be no more important than the Electoral College. They will be reduced to "dignified" rather than "efficient" parts of the American constitution.[29]

The second problem in deliberate party reform is that electorates have their own logic, which is not completely subject to control by the parties, however clearly they operate. For the Labour party, the basic problem is not organization but numbers. The declining industrial base of Britain, the decreased sense of class solidarity, and the geographical movement away from the party's northern and urban heartlands are the basic causes of the party's decline from its postwar peak. Organizational innovations will not reverse these trends.

Convergence between the parties is not likely to be deflected by deliberate party actions, but it can be slowed or hastened. British parties can purposively assume American campaign methods, as American parties can purposively promote nationally integrated structures. The eventual outcome of these efforts will depend greatly on more fundamental features, laws and customs.

In some respects, change in the formal governmental institutions may contribute to convergence. Cabinet unity and responsibility has weakened in Britain, allowing more visible expression of intra-party differences and nudging the United Kingdom somewhat closer to the open factional disputation evident in the U.S. Congress. The creation of permanent substantive committees and of backbencher groupings in the Commons has had similar effects. The institution of primary elections, as already suggested, would be even more significant.

In America, feasible legal change can also promote these trends. Governmental financing of the national parties, or even of Congressional candidates, would accelerate the trend toward the dominance of national parties and of national politics. Imposition of a national presidential primary—a change favored by a large majority of the public—would effectively restrict the party's national leadership to the most prominent national figures and finally extinguish the dying species of the "dark horse" and the state "favorite son."

The more important effect of laws and formal institutions, however, is in the opposite direction, not promoting convergence but sustaining differences between the two party systems. The most fundamental differences between the two nations remain: separation of branches and federalism in the U.S., vs. parliamentary party rule and centralization in the U.K. With all trends and qualifications made, it remains true that America's institutions still work (as they were intended to) by letting "ambition counteract ambition," by having politicians fight across institutional and geographical barriers. In contrast, Britain's institutions work by giving power to an identifiable, relatively cohesive groups of politicians who are then held accountable, in principle. These institutional features are as permanent and immutable as anything can be in a human world. Even forseeable formal modifications such as devolution in Britain or revitalization of the American Congressional caucus would not change the basic character of the systems or their effects.

The most important influence on political life, Tocqueville taught us, is not laws but customs, the social character of a nation.[30] To the extent that the mores of our two nations are becoming similar, we can then expect the party systems to resemble one another. In some respects, we do see such a convergence in these customs. Changes in the economic structure, in communications, in life style, and international posture are making Britain and America more similar.

More generally, the two nations are coming closer in their accepted patterns of authority. Since the time of Tocqueville, it has been commonplace to emphasize the influence of egalitarianism on American life and politics. Its impact was evident already in the Jacksonian period, with the coming of white manhood suffrage and the spoils system. It has continued through many periods of party reform, as exemplified in the spread of primary nominations and the establishment of demographic quotas by Democratic party reform commissions.

Now that same egalitarian trend is evident in British politics. Deferential and traditional politics was maintained for an astonishingly long time, and is still evident today. As late as 1945, it was predominant in the Labour constituences of Staffordshire[31] and reverberates in Conservative party annual conferences. Yet the egalitarian impulse is evident in British party politics as well—in the adoption of the referendum as a means of direct democratic decision-making, in the Labour party's adoption of reselection and other innovations, in the Liberals' and SDP's direct election of the party leaders, and even in the Conservatives' extension of power to the backbenchers. This social convergence can be expected to promote party convergence.

CONCLUSION

Parties are being transformed in similar ways in the two nations. The local, mass-based organizations of the past are declining. In their place, parties are arising which campaign through the mass media, are national rather than local in outlook, are bureaucratic rather than interpersonal, and rely on ideological appeals more than on affective loyalties. These parties then face the problem of reconciling centralized efficiency with demands for greater participation from a smaller and less necessary party membership.

Britain and America are, and will be, different. Yet, most basically, their parties are alike in facing the common problems of contemporary democracy. Political parties have been championed as means by which the citizenry can enforce some degree of retrospective judgment and exert some degree of prospective control over government. Do parties any longer serve these purposes if they are torn from their local roots and transformed into national bureaucratic competitors? Do they offer a meaningful choice if they are increasingly ideological and share no common ground? Are "participatory" parties truly democratic if the participants are few and unrepresentative?

Beyond the specific characteristics of our future politics, these are the most vital questions. As has always been true, the future of political parties is bound up with the future of Anglo-American democracy.

NOTES

1. Angus Campbell et al., *The American Voter* (New York: Wiley, 1960), chap. 7; David Butler and Donald Stokes, *Political Change in Britain*, rev. ed. (London: Macmillan, 1974).
2. Anthony Downs, *An Economic Theory of Democracy* (New York: Harper, 1957), Chap. 8.
3. American Political Science Association, Committee on Political Parties, "Toward a More Responsible Two-Party System," *American Political Science Review*, 44 (Sept., 1950), Supplement.
4. David Butler, "American Myths about British Parties," *Virginia Quarterly Review*, 31 (Winter, 1955) pp. 46–56; Evron Kirkpatrick, "Toward a More Responsible Two-Party System: Political Science, Policy Science or Pseudo-Science?" *American Political Science Association Review*, 65 (Sept., 1971), pp. 965–90.
5. Charles Hardin, *Presidential Power and Accountability* (Chicago: University of Chicago Press, 1974), Chap. 10.
6. Leon Epstein, "What Happened to the British Party Model?" *American Political Science Review*, 74 (March, 1980), pp. 9–22.
7. Austin Ranney, *Curing the Mischiefs of Faction* (Berkeley: University of California Press, 1975), p. 131.
8. S. E. Finer, *The Changing British Party System, 1945–1979* (Washington: American Enterprise Institute, 1980), p. 230f.
9. I adopt these trends, with thanks and without shame, from the forthcoming analysis by Philip Williams and Stephen Reilly, *Social Change and Party Realignment: Trends in Anglo-American Politics*, to be published by

Praeger in 1985. We disagree on the last trend, and they are not at all responsible for my presentation.

10. Harry C. Boyte, *The Backyard Revolution* (Philadelphia: Temple University Press, 1980), Chap. 2.

11. Ronald Inglehart, *The Silent Revolution* (Princeton: Princeton University Press, 1977).

12. Ronald Inglehart, "Post-Materialism in an Environment of Insecurity," *American Political Science Review*, 75 (Dec., 1981), p. 897.

13. David Robertson, *A Theory of Party Competition* (London: John Wiley, 1976).

14. See Everett Ladd and Charles Hadley, *Transformations of the American Party System* (New York: W. W. Norton, 1975), pp. 304-28.

15. Contrast the description of Bermondsey in John Turner's 1962 study, *Labour's Doorstep Politics in London* (London: Macmillan, 1978) to the current situation and the 1983 by-election in the constituency.

16. James Q. Wilson, *The Amateur Democrat* (Chicago: The University of Chicago Press, 1962).

17. Using data gathered in the constituencies, Mr. Fred Solop has found significant age differences among party activists. The original data, re-searched at Nuffield College, are reported in Patricia Sykes and Gerald Pomper, "'Democracy' in British and American Political Parties" (Paper presented to the American Political Science Association, 1982).

18. Robertson, op. cit., Chap. 5.

19. For detailed analysis, see Gerald Pomper, *The Election of 1980*, chap. 3 and p. 87n; Crewe's essay above; and his essay in Howard Penniman, ed., *Britain at the Polls*, 1979 (Washington: American Enterprise Institute, 1981), Chap. 9.

20. Morris Fiorina, *Retrospective Voting in American National Elections* (New Haven: Yale University Press, 1981), esp. chap. 5; David Valentine and John Van Wingen, "Partisanship, Independence and the Partisan Identification Question," *American Politics Quarterly*, 8 (April, 1980), pp. 165-86.

21. Norman Nie et al., *The Changing American Voter* (Cambridge, Mass.: Harvard University Press, 1976), esp. Chap. 10; Richard Trilling, *Party Image and Electoral Behavior* (New York: Wiley, 1976), Chap. 4.

22. A series of papers on this subject have been presented. See, for example, Cornelius Cotter et al., "Party-Government Linkages in the States." (Paper presented to the American Political Science Association, 1982).

23. David Butler and Dennis Kavanagh, *The British General Election of 1979* (London: Macmillan, 1980).

24. See John Schwarz, "Exploring a New Role in Policy-Making: The British House of Commons in the 1970s," *American Political Science Review*, 74 (March, 1980), pp. 23-37.

25. Barbara Hinckley, *Congressional Elections* (Washington: Congressional Quarterly Press, 1981), esp. Chap. 7.

26. CBS News/New York Times Poll (October 23–28, 1982); William Schneider, "Ambiguous Verdict," *National Journal*, 14 (Nov. 6, 1982), p. 1892.

27. See Vernon Bogdanor, *The People and the Party System* (Cambridge: Cambridge University Press, 1981), esp. Part IV.

28. On future reform of American parties, see William Crotty, *Party Reform* (New York: Longman, 1983), and Joel Fleishman (ed.), *The Future of American Political Parties* (Englewood Cliffs, N.J.: Prentice-Hall, 1982.

29. This is an obvious adoption of Walter Bagehot's terms in *The English Constitution* (London: Oxford University Press, 1928; originally published 1867), p. 4.

30. Alexis de Tocqueville, *Democracy in America*, ed. Phillips Bradley (New York: Vintage, 1954), Vol. I, p. 330.

31. Frank Bealey et al., *Constituency Politics* (New York: Free Press, 1965).

Index

and parties, 213–39
structure and regulation of, 214
use of, by parties, 227–33
Michels, R., 267
Midwest Political Science Association, 182
Mill, J. S., x
Miller, A., 123
Miller, W. E., 123–25
Minkin, L., 69
Mitchell, J. N., 24
Mondale, W., 174, 263
Moran. M., 147, 152
Morley, J., xvii
Mosbacher, R., 195
Moss, L., 91, 97
Mott, S., 200
Muller, N. J., 211
Mulley, F., 67

Napolitan, J., 191, 210, 228
National Committee, 32
National Committee for an Effective Congress (NCEC) 196
National Conservative Political Action Committee (NCPAC), 158, 200, 229
National Education Association, 19
National Executive Committee, 62
National Organization of Women, 19
National Republican Congressional Committee (NRCC), 202, 211
National Republican Senatorial Committee (NRSC), 202
National Union of Mineworkers (NUM) (NUM), 146
negativism resulting in antipartisanship, 105–6
Nelson, M., 37
Neumann, S., 239
neutralism associated with antipartisanship, 106–8
newspapers, 214–15
Nie, N. H., 99, 100, 112, 123, 124, 239, 272
Nixon, R., xiv, 7, 21, 23, 25, 26, 81, 190, 223

nominations, presidential, 19–21
Noragon, J., 182
Norpoth, H., 124, 126
North Wales National Union of Mineworkers, 146
Norton, P., 69

Odell, R., 189, 191
O'Neill, T., 172, 205
Oppenheimer, B. I., 34
organizations, party, national, 26–31
Ornstein, N. J., 34, 36
Orren, G., 13, 28
Owen, D., 58, 59, 61, 68

PACs see Political Action Committees
Parliamentary Labour Party (PLP), 47
Parteienstaat, 1
parties
  bypassed by other institutions, 4–6
  central finances of, in Britain, 131–34
  changes in, 11–15
  constituency finances of, in Britain, 134–38
  decline of, 1–6
  and ideology, in Congress, 22
  and media, 213–39
  modernization of, 40–43
  national, 26–31
  and party systems, 7–37
  power and, 7–11
  and political consultants, 186–96
  and public, 71–97
partisan stability, forces producing, 103
party
  elements of, 130–31
  finance
    in Britain, 127–52
      assessment of, 169–74;
      central, 131–34; company
      contributions to, 140–42;
      constituency, 134–38; trade
      union contributions to, 142–45;
      Hansard Society estimate
      of, 136–38; Houghton Committee Survey of, 135

Tribunites in Labour party, 48
Trilling, R., 272
Trotskyites in Labour party, 48
Truman, H. S., 7, 21, 33
Tufte, E. R., 97
Turner, J., 272
Turner, J. E., 69
two-party system, 10–12, 84–85
  in Britain, 72–73
  in U.S., 73–74

Udall, M., 118
Union of Post Office Workers, 147
United States Federal Election Commission, 211
University of Michigan
  Center for Political Studies, 104
  Institute for Social Research, 124

Valentine, D., 272
Van Wingen, J., 272
Verba, S., 99, 100, 112, 123, 124, 239
Viguerie, R., 192, 197, 206
volatility, electoral, 79–82
vote, major-party, 72–74

voting decisions, wavering in, 80–81

Wallace, G., 20, 84, 85, 94, 118, 120,
  122, 165, 192, 262
Warin, R. E., 181
Watson, W. L., 211
Wattenberg, M. P., 105, 106, 107, 108,
  125, 186, 209, 239
Weaver, P., 226, 238
Weber, M., ix, 2, 3
Wegge, D. G., 182
Weiner, S. L., 192, 210
Weyrich, P., 192, 197, 199, 211
Whiteley, P., 66
Wilcox, D. P., 211
Wilde, O., 255
Williams, P. M., xi, 7–37, 257, 263,
  271
Williams, S., 68
Wilson, H., xiii, 74, 128, 231, 243
Wilson, J. Q., 34, 272
Wilson, W., xvii
Winchell, S., 205, 206
Wirthlin, R., 188, 190
Wolfinger, R., 184

About the Contributors

David Adamany is Professor of Law and Political Science and President of Wayne State University. He is the author of *Campaign Finance in America* (1972) and *Financing Politics* (1969) and the coauthor of *Political Money* (1975). He has also published articles on constitutional law, the judicial process, and party politics and financing.

Vernon Bogdanor is a Fellow of Brasenose College, Oxford, and a member of the Council of the Hansard Society for Parliamentary Government. His previous publications include *Devolution* (1979); *The People and the Party System* (1981); and *Multi-Party Politics and the Constitution* (1983).

David Butler is a Fellow of Nuffield College, Oxford, and senior author of the Nuffield studies of British general elections since 1951. He is coauthor (with Donald Stokes) of *Political Change in Britain* and coeditor (with Austin Ranney) of *Referendums: A Comparative Study of Practice and Theory*. His most recent book is *Governing Without Majorities* (1983).

Ivor Crewe is Professor of Government at the University of Essex. He was Director of the SSRC Data Archive from 1974 to 1982 and codirector of the 1974 and 1979 British Election Studies. He has written numerous articles on electoral behavior and public opinion in Britain and is coauthor (with Bo Särlvik) of *Decade of Dealignment*, a study of voting patterns in Britain in the 1970s.

Leon D. Epstein is Hilldale Professor of Political Science at the University of Wisconsin–Madison where he has taught since 1948. He has written on political parties in Britain, Canada, Australia, and the United States. Among his books and journal articles is *Political Parties in Western Democracies* (1967). He was president of the American Political Science Association in 1978–79.

S. E. Finer has been a Fellow of Balliol College, Oxford, Professor of Political Institutions at the University of Keele and Professor of Government at the Victoria University of Manchester. He has recently retired from the Gladstone Chair of Government at Oxford. Among his books are *The Man on Horseback* (1965), a global study of military intervention in politics, *Comparative Government* (1970) and *Five Constitutions* (1979). He has also written *The Changing British Party System* (1979) and edited *Adversary Politics and Electoral Reform* (1974), a comparative study of party systems and electoral systems.

Gerald M. Pomper is Professor of Political Science at Rutgers University, a former Academic Visitor at Nuffield College, Oxford, and Director of the Center on Political Parties at the Eagleton Institute of Politics at Rutgers. He is the senior author of *The Election of 1980* and *The Election of 1976*. He has written *Elections in America, Voters' Choice,* and other works on U.S. politics.

Austin Ranney, a former Professor of Political Science at the University of Wisconsin–Madison and a former President of the American Political Science Association, is codirector of the Program in Political and Social Processes at the American Enterprise Institute. His recent works include *Participation in American Presidential Nominations, The Federalization of Presidential Primaries,* and (coedited with David Butler) *Referendums: A Comparative Study of Practice and Theory.*

Larry Sabato is Professor of Political Science at the University of Virginia. He is the author of *Goodbye to Good-Time Charlie: The American Governor Transformed, 1950–1975* (1978) and *The Rise of Political Consultants: New Ways of Winning Elections* (1981).

William Schneider is a Visiting Fellow at the American Enterprise Institute and a political consultant to *The Los Angeles Times.* He is senior editor of *Opinion Outlook,* a Washington-based newsletter on public opinion. He is coeditor with Seymour Martin Lipset of *The Confidence Gap: How Americans View Their Institutions.* He has taught political science at Harvard University and held an International Affairs Fellowship from the Council of Foreign Relations.

Philip M. Williams has been a Fellow of Nuffield College, Oxford, since 1958 and has also taught at Columbia and Princeton. His publications include *Crisis and Compromise,* a study of the French Fourth Republic, a biography of the British Labour leader Hugh Gaitskell, as well as numerous articles on American electoral politics. His next book, *Social Change and Party Realignment: Trends in Anglo-American Politics,* will be published by Praeger in 1985.